BIBLIOGRAPHY OF JOHNSON

Reissue, Illustrated

A BIBLIOGRAPHY
OF
Samuel Johnson

BY

WILLIAM PRIDEAUX COURTNEY

AND

DAVID NICHOL SMITH

OXFORD

AT THE CLARENDON PRESS

Oxford University Press, Ely House, London W. 1

GLASGOW NEW YORK TORONTO MELBOURNE WELLINGTON
CAPE TOWN SALISBURY IBADAN NAIROBI LUSAKA ADDIS ABABA
BOMBAY CALCUTTA MADRAS KARACHI LAHORE DACCA
KUALA LUMPUR HONG KONG TOKYO

FIRST PUBLISHED 1915
REISSUED WITH ILLUSTRATIONS 1925
REPRINTED LITHOGRAPHICALLY IN GREAT BRITAIN
AT THE UNIVERSITY PRESS, OXFORD
BY VIVIAN RIDLER
PRINTER TO THE UNIVERSITY
1968

LIST OF TITLE-PAGES
and
Other Facsimiles

Miscellaneous Observations on the Tragedy of Macbeth; with Remarks on Sir T. H.'s Edition of Shakespear. To which is affix'd, Proposals for a New Edition of Shakeshear, with a Specimen. 1745. 12°.

(1) Title-page. (2) The leaf of Proposals.

See page 17. (2) is reduced; the type in the original is $10\frac{7}{16}$ inches in height.

Prologue and Epilogue, spoken at the opening of the Theatre in Drury-lane 1747. 1747. 4°.

See page 19. Reduced; the type in the original is $8\frac{1}{2}$ inches in height.

The Plan of a Dictionary of the English Language; Addressed to the Right Honourable Philip Dormer, Earl of Chesterfield.

See page 20. 1747. 4°.

The Vanity of Human Wishes. The Tenth Satire of Juvenal, Imitated By Samuel Johnson. 1749. 4°.

See page 22.

Irene: A Tragedy. As it is Acted at the Theatre Royal in Drury-Lane. By Mr. Samuel Johnson. 1749. 8°.

See page 24.

The Rambler. *Nullius addictus jurare in verba magistri, Quo me cunque rapit tempestas deferor hospes.* Hor. 1751. F°.

The Rambler. Volume First. *Nullius* etc. 1753. F°.

See page 30. The 1753 title-page is slightly reduced; the type in the original is $8\frac{1}{4}$ inches in height.

The Rambler. Volume I. *Nullius* etc.

See page 32. Edinburgh. 1750. Sm. 8°.

The Rambler. Volume the First. *Nullius* etc. 1752. 12°.

See page 33.

A New Prologue spoken by Mr. Garrick, Thursday, April 5, 1750. At the Representation of Comus, for the benefit of Mrs. Elizabeth Foster, Milton's Grand-Daughter, and only surviving Descendant. 1750. F°.

See page 36. Reduced; the type in the original is $9\frac{5}{16}$ inches in height.

An Essay on Milton's Use and Imitation of the Moderns, in his Paradise Lost. *Things unattempted yet in prose or rhime.* Milton.

See page 36. 1750. 8°.

The Adventurer. Volume the First.—*Tentanda via est; quâ me quoque possim Tollere humo, victorque virûm volitare per ora.* Virg.

1753. F°.

See page 39. Reduced; in the original the type is 8¾ inches in height.

A Dictionary of the English Language. . . . By Samuel Johnson, A.M. In Two Volumes. Vol. I. . . . 1755. F°.

See page 54. The facsimile is reduced. The original is in black and red, and the type measures 13¾ × 7⅝ inches.

Christian Morals: by Sir Thomas Browne. . . . The Second Edition. With a life of the author, by Samuel Johnson; and explanatory notes. 1756. Sm. 8°.

See page 73.

Proposals for Printing, by Subscription, the Dramatick Works of William Shakespeare, Corrected and Illustrated by Samuel Johnson. 1756. 8°.

See page 78. From the only known copy, sold at Sotheby's on 10 July 1923.

The Idler. In Two Volumes. Duplex libelli dos est, quod risum movet, Et quod prudenti vitam consilio monet. Phaedrus. Χάρις μικροῖσι. Volume I. 1761. 12°.

See page 83.

The Prince of Abissinia. A Tale. In two volumes. Vol. I.

See page 87. 1759. Sm. 8°.

The Plays of William Shakespeare, in Eight Volumes, with the Corrections and Illustrations of Various Commentators; To which are added Notes by Sam. Johnson. 1765. 8°.

See page 107.

Mr. Johnson's Preface to his Edition of Shakespear's Plays.

See page 107. 1765. 8°.

Miscellaneous and Fugitive Pieces. Volume the First. London, Printed for T. Davies. [1773.] 8°.

See page 116.

A Journey to the Western Islands of Scotland. 1775. 8°.
(1) Title-page. (2) The two lists of errata, which distinguish the true first edition from the second impression of the same year. (3) Original state of the cancelled p. 48.

See pages 122–123.

Taxation no Tyranny; an Answer to the Resolutions and Address of the American Congress. 1775. 8°.

See page 125.

Political Tracts. Containing, The False Alarm. Falkland's Islands. The Patriot; and, Taxation No Tyranny. 1776. 8°.

See page 127.

Prefaces, Biographical and Critical, to the Works of the English Poets. Volume the First. 1779. Sm. 8°.

See page 140.

The Lives of the English Poets; and a Criticism on their Works. By Samuel Johnson. Dublin, 1779. 8°.

See page 141. This volume contains the *Prefaces* published in 1779 (Vols. I–IV); it was followed in 1781 by Volumes II and III, containing those published in that year (Vols. V–X). It is the first edition called *Lives*.

The Lives of the most eminent English Poets; with Critical Observations on their Works. By Samuel Johnson. In Four Volumes. Volume I. 1781. 8°.

See page 142.

The Principal Additions and Corrections in the Third Edition of Dr. Johnson's Lives of the Poets; collected to complete the Second Edition. [1783.] 8°.

See page 142. The collation is Ll–Oo in fours, pp. [505]–534 and one blank leaf. Very few copies of Volume IV of the edition of 1781 contain this supplement.

A
Miſcellany
OF
POEMS
By ſeveral Hands.

Publiſh'd by *J. HUSBANDS*, A. M.
Fellow of *Pembroke-College*, OXON.

———*ſtulta eſt Clementia, cum tot ubique*
Vatibus occurras, periturae parcere Chartae.
Juv.

OXFORD:
Printed by *Leon. Lichfield*, near the *Eaſt-Gate*,
In the Year M DCC XXXI.

BIBLIOGRAPHY

Latin Translation of Pope's 'Messiah'.

A Miscellany of Poems By several Hands. Publish'd by J. {John] Husbands, A.M. Fellow of Pembroke-College, Oxon. Oxford: Printed by Leon. Lichfield, near the East-Gate, In the Year M D CCXXXI. 8°.

1731
Boswell, i. 60–2.

It is stated in the preface that 'The Translation [pp. 111–17] of Mr. *Pope's Messiah* was deliver'd to his Tutor [William Jorden], as a College Exercise, by Mr. *Johnson*, a Commoner of *Pembroke College* in *Oxford*, and 'tis hoped will be no Discredit to the excellent Original'. It was reprinted in the third volume of Edward Popham's *Selecta Poemata Anglorum Latina* (1776), pp. 16–21.

Dr. Taylor told Boswell 'that it was first printed for old Mr. Johnson without the knowledge of his son, who was very angry when he heard of it'. This is the first printed composition of Johnson, but Boswell states that there are in the library of Pembroke College four more of his college exercises, two in verse and two in prose. One of the latter two is printed by him under the date of 1728 (Hill's ed., i. 61); and one of the copies of verse under July 16, 1754 (ib. 271).

John Husbands was the son of the Rev. Thomas Husbands, of Marsh Baldon, Oxfordshire, and was baptized there on February 12, 1705/6. He matriculated from Pembroke College, Oxford, on July 28, 1721, aged 15, and graduated B.A. 1725, M.A. 1728. He entered into Holy orders and was elected Fellow of his college on June 7, 1728. Husbands died on Nov. 21, 1732. Latin verses by him are in the Oxford University set on the death of George I and the accession of George II (1727). At the time of his death 'he was preparing for the press a comparison of the Eastern and Western poetry' (*Gent. Mag.*, 1732, p. 1083; *N. & Q.*, 8th S., xii. (1897) 8, 95).

Johnson's connexion with Pembroke College is described by the Rev. Douglas Macleane in his History of the College (Oxford Hist. Soc. (1897), pp. 330–50).

The Birmingham Journal.

1733
Boswell, i. 85.

In 1732 Johnson, as the guest of his friend Edmund Hector, passed some time at Birmingham in the house of Thomas Warren, the bookseller. He contributed some numbers to the periodical Essay printed in Warren's newspaper. This was the *Birmingham Journal*, and in the office of the *Birmingham Daily Post* is preserved the number (No. 28) for May 21, 1733. It is believed to be the only copy in existence.

It is suggested by Joseph Hill (*Bookmakers of Old Birmingham*, 1907, p. 43) that Johnson's hand may be traced in the preface to 'Sermons on the Following Subjects [14 in all] . . . By the Late Reverend and Learned Mr. Edward Brodhurst. Birmingham: Printed by T. Warren. MDCCXXXIII.'

Politian.

1734
Boswell, i. 90.

Angeli Politiani Poemata Latina, quibus, Notas cum historiâ Latinæ poeseos, à Petrarchæ ævo ad Politiani tempora deductâ, et vitâ Politiani fusius quam antehac enarratâ, addidit Sam. Johnson. *Proposals issued*, August, 1734.

'The book was to contain more than thirty sheets, the price to be two shillings and sixpence at the time of subscribing, and two shillings and sixpence at the delivery of a perfect book in quires.'

Subscriptions were to be taken in by Johnson himself or his brother Nathanael Johnson, bookseller, at Lichfield, but there 'were not subscribers enough to insure a sufficient sale; so the work never appeared, and probably, never was executed'.

Lobo's Voyage to Abyssinia.

1735
Boswell, i. 87–9.

A Voyage to Abyssinia. By Father Jerome Lobo, A Portuguese Jesuit. Containing, A Narrative of the Dangers he underwent in his first Attempt to pass from the Indies into Abyssinia; with a Description of the Coasts of the Red-Sea. An Account of the History, Laws, Customs, Religion, Habits, and Buildings of the Abyssins; with the Rivers, Air, Soil, Birds, Beasts, Fruits and other natural Productions of that remote and unfrequented Country. A Relation of the Admission of the Jesuits into Abyssinia in 1625, and their Expulsion from thence in 1634. An exact Description of the Nile, its Head, its Branches, the

A VOYAGE TO ABYSSINIA.

BY

Father *Jerome Lobo*,

A PORTUGUESE JESUIT.

CONTAINING,

A Narrative of the Dangers he underwent in his first Attempt to pass from the *Indies* into *Abyssinia*; with a Description of the Coasts of the *Red-Sea*.

An Account of the History, Laws, Customs, Religion, Habits, and Buildings of the *Abyssins*; with the Rivers, Air, Soil, Birds, Beasts, Fruits and other natural Productions of that remote and unfrequented Country.

A Relation of the Admission of the Jesuits into *Abyssinia* in 1625, and their Expulsion from thence in 1634.

An exact Description of the *Nile*, its Head, its Branches, the Course of its Waters, and the Cause of its Inundations.

With a Continuation of the History of *Abyssinia* down to the Beginning of the Eighteenth Century, and Fifteen Dissertations on various Subjects relating to the History, Antiquities, Government,. Religion, Manners, and natural History of *Abyssinia*, and other Countries mention'd by Father *JEROME LOBO*.

By MR. *LE GRAND*.

From the *FRENCH*.

LONDON.

Printed for A. BETTESWORTH, and C. HITCH at the *Red-Lyon* in *Paternoster-Row*.

MDCCXXXV.

Course of its Waters, and the Cause of its Inundations. With a Continuation of the History of Abyssinia down to the Beginning of the Eighteenth Century, and Fifteen Dissertations on various Subjects relating to the History, Antiquities, Government, Religion, Manners, and natural History of Abyssinia, and other Countries mention'd by Father Jerome Lobo. By Mr. [Joachim] Le Grand. From the French. London: Printed for A. Bettesworth, and C. Hitch at the Red-Lyon in Paternoster-Row. MDCCXXXV. 8°.

Collation:—Title, p. [i]; Dedication, pp. [iii]-[v]; Preface, pp. vii-xii (Errata on p. xii); A Voyage, &c., pp. 1-42; A Description, &c., pp. 43-144; The Sequel, &c., pp. 145-83; Dissertations, pp. 185-396; Contents, pp. [397]-[404].

[There is an unnumbered dissertation (pp. 222-33) between the third and the fourth. There are thus *sixteen* dissertations. Ed.]

It is dedicated by the editor to John Warren, Esq., of Trewern, in the county of Pembroke. The volume was printed at Birmingham for Thomas Warren (see *Bookmakers of Old Birmingham*, by Joseph Hill, 1907), and Johnson received but five guineas for this anonymous work. An exact translation is given only in the dissertations; the rest is an epitome.

The manuscript account in Portuguese of Lobo's life in Abyssinia is said to be in the Monastery of St. Roque at Lisbon and to be still unprinted. Johnson's version was condensed from 'Voyage historique d'Abissinie, du R. P. Jerome Lobo de la Compagnie de Jesus. Traduite du Portugais, continuée & augmentée de plusieurs Dissertations, Lettres & Memoires. Par M. Le Grand, Prieur de Neuville-les-Dames & de Prevessin. A Paris, Chez la Veuve d'Antoine-Urbain Coustelier, & Jacques Guerin Libraires, Quay des Augustins. MDCCXXVIII.' Another edition has the imprint 'A Paris & à La Haye, Chez P. Gosse & J. Neaulme. MDCCXXVIII'. An edition was published at Amsterdam also in 1728 in two volumes.

A Voyage to Abyssinia, by Father Jerome Lobo, a Portuguese missionary. Containing the history, natural, civil, and ecclesiastical, of that remote and unfrequented country, Continued down to the beginning of the Eighteenth Century: with Fifteen Dissertations on various Subjects, relating to the antiquities, government, religion, manners, and natural history, of Abyssinia. By M. Le Grand. Translated from the French by Samuel Johnson, LL.D. To which are added, various other tracts by the same author, not published by Sir John Hawkins or Mr. Stockdale. London: Printed for Elliot and Kay, No. 332 Strand, And C. Elliot, Edinburgh. M,DCC,LXXXIX. 8°.

The dedication to Arthur Murphy is signed George Gleig (afterwards Bishop of the Scottish Episcopal Church at Brechin), and dated Stirling, Dec. 1, 1788. His preface is not devoid of interest. In it he condemns the 'uncommonly numerous' blunders of the printer in the 1735 version, and girds at the edition of the works of Dr. Johnson which was edited by Sir John Hawkins and John Stockdale in thirteen volumes (1787). He says that the memoirs of Bishop Berkeley and the preface to Dr. John Kennedy's Scripture Chronology, which are included therein as by Johnson, were certainly not written by him. A letter from the bishop's son on this matter is printed *in extenso*, and Kennedy's son, 'the present rector of Langley in Kent', is quoted as the authority for assigning only the *Dedication* to Johnson.

The 'other tracts' printed in this volume as by Johnson are: (1) pp. 382–402. The picture of human life. Translated from the Greek of Cebes, a Disciple of Socrates.—(2) pp. 403–80. A review of books (viz. Russel's *Aleppo*; Mrs. Lennox's trans. of Sully's Memoirs; *Waters*, by C. Lucas; *Essays* by Lewis Evans; [Joseph Warton's] *Essay on the writings and genius of Pope*; *Miscellanies*, by Elizabeth Harrison).—(3) pp. 481–5. The Dedication of the Evangelical History Harmonized. To the Lords Spiritual and Temporal, and Commons, in Parliament assembled. —(4) pp. 486–7. The Dedication of Kennedy's Scripture Chronology, To the King.—(5) pp. 487–93. The Story of the Cock-lane Ghost, with the account of its Detection.—(6) pp. 494–8. Letters: To Dr. Lawrence, Jan. 30, 1780; To the Reverend Charles Lawrence, Aug. 30, 1780.—(7) pp. 499–500. Nugæ Anapæsticæ in lecto cusæ Medico Ægro. S. March 21, 1782.

A Voyage to Abyssinia, &c.

Reprinted in John Pinkerton's *Collection of Voyages*, xv (1814), pp. 1–60; and in part (with the omission of the Sequel and the Dissertations) in Cassell's National Library, No. 91 (1887), with an introduction signed H. M. (Henry Morley).

The Gentleman's Magazine.

(1) 'Ad Urbanum' [i. e. the editor, Edward Cave] signed S. J. p. 156.

1738 March. Boswell, i. 113-14.

A translation of this Ode, signed Briton and dated May 22, 1738, appeared in the *Magazine* (p. 268). Both the original and the translation (which is not by Johnson) are printed in Boswell.

(2) 'Ad Ricardum Savage, Arm. Humani Generis Amatorem.' p. 210.

Boswell, i. 162.

(3) Epigram in Greek and Latin on Eliza [Miss Elizabeth Carter]. p. 210.

Boswell, i. 140.

(4) 'To a Lady [Molly Aston], who spoke in Defence of Liberty.' p. 211.

Boswell, i. 83.

(5) Debates in the senate of Magna Lilliputia: June 1738, p. 283 et seq.

Boswell, i. 115-18, 501-12.

The King's speech in Parliament was published *ib.* ii. 560 (Jan. 1732). An article entitled 'Proceedings and Debates of the last Session of Parliament' appeared in July 1732, pp. 864-7, and was continued at intervals. These articles were originally compiled by William Guthrie, but for some time before 1740 they were sent by Cave to Johnson for revision. When the House of Commons passed resolutions against the publication of their proceedings it became necessary to throw an air of fiction around the narrative. The introduction (p. 283 et seq.) was accordingly worded as 'Debates in the Senate of Magna Lilliputia', and it narrated the voyage of Captain Gulliver's grandson to Lilliputia. It was probably by Johnson; 'it bears', says Hill, 'all the marks of his early style'. [The idea, according to Hawkins, was Cave's. *Life* (1787), pp. 97-9. Ed.]

From Nov. 19, 1740, to Feb. 23, 1742-3, these articles were written by Johnson alone. They are collected in 'Debates in Parliament by Samuel Johnson, LL.D. London: Printed for John Stockdale, MDCCLXXXVII'. 2 vols. 8vo (issued both separately and as vols. xii and xiii of Hawkins's edition of Johnson's Works). [This collection substitutes 'the real for the fictitious speakers'. Boswell says that the editor was George Chalmers. Ed.] Johnson was inside the House of Commons

Boswell, i. 150.

only once. Usually nothing was communicated to him but the names of the several speakers and the part which they had taken in the debate, but sometimes scanty notes were furnished by persons employed to attend the Houses of Parliament. Often the speeches were written 'from no materials at all—the mere coinage of his own imagination', three columns of the *Magazine* in an hour being no uncommon effort. Consequently the speeches have not any historical value. When Johnson discovered that one of the Debates was translated into French, German, and Spanish (*Gent. Mag.*, xiii. 59) as authentic, he discontinued his part in the undertaking. He owned that he had taken care that the WHIG DOGS should not have the best of it.

A table showing the order of Johnson's Debates as published is printed in Hill, Appendix A, vol. i, p. 510. Particulars as to these Debates are given in the autobiography of Sylvanus Urban, chapters iv and v (*Gent. Mag.*, Nov. 1856, pp. 531–41; Dec. 1856, pp. 667–77).

Boswell, i. 140.

(6) English verses to Eliza, signed Urbanus (an imitation of the Latin epigram, *Ad Elisam Popi Horto Lauros carpentem*, on p. 372). p. 429.

Boswell, i. 136.

(7) 'To Lady F——ce [Firebrace] at Bury Assizes.' p. 486.

(8) 'The Life of Father Paul Sarpi, Author of the History of the Council of Trent; For printing a new Translation of which, by S. Johnson, we have publish'd Proposals.' Signed S. J., pp. 581–3.

(9) Greek epigram on Dr. Birch. p. 654.

(10) [Address] To the Reader. pp. iii–iv (prefixed to the collected numbers).

'Dr. Johnson and the Gentleman's Magazine', a paper by Arthur Wollaston Hutton, appeared in the *English Illustrated Magazine*, xvii (1897), pp. 663–9. It is reprinted in the *Johnson Club Papers*, 1899, pp. 93–113.

LONDON:

A

POEM,

In IMITATION of the

THIRD SATIRE of *JUVENAL.*

--------- *Quis ineptæ*
Tam patiens Urbis, tam ferreus ut teneat ſe?
JUV.

LONDON:
Printed for *R. Doddeſley*, at *Tully*'s Head in *Pall-Mall.*
MDCCXXXVIII.

London.

London: A Poem, In Imitation of the Third Satire of Juvenal. *Quis ineptæ Tam patiens Urbis, tam ferreus ut teneat se?* Juv. London: Printed for R. Doddesley, at Tully's Head in Pall-Mall. MDCCXXXVIII. folio.

1738
Boswell, i. 118–30.

Collation:—Title, p. [1]; the poem, pp. [3]–19.

Published in May; price 1*s*.

Johnson received ten guineas for it. 'Paul Whitehead had a little before got ten guineas for a poem and I would not take less than Paul Whitehead' was his statement to Boswell in later life.

The poem reflects the political views current among the 'patriots' who opposed Sir Robert Walpole.

It is a matter of doubt whether the second line of the poem

When injur'd Thales bids the Town farewell

does not refer to Richard Savage. The question is discussed in the *Gentleman's Magazine* for Dec. 1840, pp. 612–15.

Short extracts from Johnson's poem are given in the *Gent. Mag.*, 1738, vol. viii, p. 269, with the statement that it had 'become remarkable for having got to the Second Edition in the Space of a week'. Pope's satire of 1738 (afterwards called *Epilogue to the Satires*, *Dialogue I*) came out on the same morning as Johnson's *London*, but, though sold at the same price of one shilling, was longer in reaching its second edition. Pope requested Jonathan Richardson, son of the painter, to try to find out the name of the new author. On learning that he was some obscure man named Johnson, Pope remarked, 'He will soon be *déterré*'.

[There were two forms of what is called 'The Second Edition',—folio and octavo. The folio reproduces the first edition page for page, and was reset only to p. 14. In the octavo the poem runs from p. [3] to p. 20. Both have 'R. Dodsley' in the imprint. Ed.]

The third edition also came out in 1738; the fourth edition was issued in 1739. The fifth edition, still without the author's name, but with the note that *The Vanity of Human Wishes* is by the same author, is dated 1750. Nine years later, in 1759, it was included in 'Two Satires [*London* and *The Vanity of Human Wishes*]. By Samuel Johnson, A.M. Oxford. M.DCC.LIX'. 8°.

'London . . . by Mr. Samuel Johnson' was inserted in

Dodsley's *Collection of Poems*, vol. i, 1748, and in the subsequent issues of that work. Gray, in criticizing the collection, described this poem as 'one of those few imitations that have all the ease and all the spirit of an original'. It was appended, pp. 373-9, to an edition (by Vicesimus Knox) of the *Satiræ Expurgatæ in usum scholarum* of Juvenal and Persius which was published by Charles Dilly in 1784; and (pp. 63-75) to Gay's poem of *Trivia: or the art of walking the streets of London*, which was printed for Effingham Wilson in 1807. It was included (pp. 233-40) in a collection of the 'best satires of the most celebrated poets from Pope to Byron' which was published at Glasgow in 1826 (under the general title of *The British Satirist*); and Charles Badham, M.D., F.R.S., inserted it (pp. 217-24) in the appendix to his verse translation of Juvenal, 1831. [It was included in Goldsmith's *Beauties of English Poesy*, 1767, vol. i, pp. 59-68. Ed.]

It was edited with *The Vanity of Human Wishes* in 1876 by Isaac Plant Fleming, and in 1901 (Blackie's English Classics) by Frederick Ryland; and both poems are included in Henry Morley's two issues (the Reynolds and Library editions) of Boswell (1885 and 1891), iv. 371-88.

A small volume, entitled *Little Master's Miscellany, or divine and moral essays in prose and verse*, was printed at Birmingham by 'T. Warren, Book-seller in the Bull-Ring', the second edition appearing in 1748. On p. 55 a bookseller is depicted displaying his wares to a stripling, and praising the talents of Johnson—

> Here's *London* Sir! wrote in an Elegant style,
> That would make the old *Satyrist Juvenal* smile.

Warren was the printer of Johnson's translation of Lobo. This piece reached a fifth edition in two parts 1765-7.

No. 12 of the *North Briton* (August 21, 1762) was conspicuous for its violent attack by Wilkes on the pensions conferred by George the Third at the instance of Lord Bute. Johnson was in the forefront of the fray. The definitions in his Dictionary of *pension* and *excise* were dwelt on with unction. His poem of *London*, with its '*distant hints* and *dark allusions*', was satirically commented upon as the work of 'a name sacred to *George and Liberty*' and a 'friend of the public, of his [Bute's] master's family, and of the constitution of the country'.

TWO

SATIRES.

By SAMUEL JOHNSON, A.M.

OXFORD,

At the CLARENDON PRINTING HOUSE.

M.DCC.LIX.

MARMOR NÒRFOLCIENSE:

OR AN

ESSAY

ON AN

ANCIENT PROPHETICAL INSCRIPTION,

In Monkiſh Rhyme,

Lately Diſcover'd near LYNN in NORFOLK.

By PROBUS BRITANICUS.

LONDON:

Printed for J. BRETT at the *Golden-Ball*, oppoſite St. *Clement*'s Church in the *Strand*. MDCCXXXIX,

Sarpi's 'Council of Trent'.

... Just published, Proposals for printing the *History of the Council of Trent*, translated from the Italian of Father Paul Sarpi; with the Authour's Life, and Notes theological, historical, and critical, from the French edition of Dr. Le Courayer. To which are added, Observations on the History and Notes and Illustrations from various Authours, both printed & manuscript. By S. Johnson.

1738 Boswell, i. 135 *n.*

The above advertisement is said by Boswell to have appeared in the *Weekly Miscellany*, Oct. 21, 1738. The work was to be in 200 sheets, or two volumes in quarto, price 18*s.* each, but it was never brought to completion. [See Nichols's note in the *Gentleman's Magazine*, 1785, p. 6, where Boswell found the facts. Ed.]

Marmor Norfolciense.

Marmor Norfolciense: or an Essay on an Ancient Prophetical Inscription, In Monkish Rhyme, Lately Discover'd near Lynn in Norfolk. By Probus Britanicus. London: Printed for J. Brett at the Golden-Ball, opposite St. Clement's Church in the Strand. MDCCXXXIX. 8°.

1739. Boswell, i. 141-2.

Collation:—Title; the essay, pp. [5]-55.

It was advertised among the books for April 1739, and priced 1*s.* (*Gent. Mag.*, p. 220). The introduction, inscription, and translation are inserted in the *London Mag.*, May 1739, pp. 244-5.

'In this performance, Johnson, in a feigned inscription, supposed to have been found in Norfolk, the county of Sir Robert Walpole, inveighs against the Brunswick succession, and the measures of government consequent upon it.' Sir John Hawkins states that the Government endeavoured to apprehend the author, but the inquiry made at the Treasury by Boswell proved this to be an error. The pamphlet became exceedingly scarce, but was reprinted as 'A new edition, with Notes, and a Dedication to Samuel Johnson, LL.D., by Tribunus. London: Printed for J. Williams, No. 39, Fleet-Street. M.DCC.LXXV.' Tribunus, in a vein of irony, contended that Johnson could not be the author of this satire on the House of Hanover and the revolution of 1688, as he had accepted a pension from the Crown and had defended the measures of its government.

The *Monthly Review*, vol. liii, Oct. 1775, p. 360, says: 'This is a bloody Jacobitical pamphlet, on the most avowed anti-revolutional principles, prophesying the evils impending on this nation in consequence of the accession of the present R. F. [royal family] and said (*nem. con.*) to have been written by the *now notorious* Gentleman, to whom this new edition is addressed. . . . The substance of the pamphlet has been retailed in almost every newspaper.'

The pamphlet was again reprinted about 1819 with the addition of the preface and notes of Tribunus.

Brooke's Gustavus Vasa.

1739. Boswell, i. 140-1.

A Compleat Vindication of the Licensers of the Stage, from the Malicious and Scandalous Aspersions of Mr [Henry] Brooke, Author of Gustavus Vasa. With A Proposal for making the Office of Licenser more Extensive and Effectual. By an Impartial Hand. London, Printed for C. Corbett, at Addison's Head, in Fleetstreet. MDCCXXXIX. sm. 4°.

Half-title:—'A Compleat Vindication of the Licensers of the Stage, &c. [Price One Shilling.]'

Collation:—Half-title, p. [1]; title, p. [3]; the vindication, pp. [5]-31.

It was published in May 1739 (*Gent. Mag.*, p. 276).

Under the disguise of a defence of the Licensers it is an ironical attack upon them for their suppression of that tragedy.

The tragedy was based on the history of Sweden, and the character of Trollio, vicegerent to Cristiern, King of Denmark and Norway, and usurper of Sweden, was designed to represent Sir Robert Walpole. Nearly a thousand persons subscribed to its publication. Their names are not given, but the prefatory dedication is addressed 'to the subscribers'.

The Gentleman's Magazine.

(1) Letter to Mr. Urban. pp. 3-4.

1739 Boswell, i. 140.

(2) The Life of Dr. Herman Boerhaave, late Professor of Physick in the University of Leyden in Holland. pp. 37-8, 72-3, 114-16, 172-6.

This Life was drawn from the *Oratio academica in memoriam Hermanni Boerhaavii* of Albert Schultens (Leyden, 1738).

A COMPLEAT

VINDICATION

OF THE

Licensers of the Stage,

FROM THE

Malicious and Scandalous ASPERSIONS

OF

Mr. *BROOKE*, Author of GUSTAVUS VASA.

WITH

A Proposal for making the Office of LICENSER more Extensive and Effectual.

By an Impartial Hand.

LONDON:

Printed for C. CORBETT, at *Addison*'s *Head*, in *Fleetstreet*.
MDCCXXXIX.

Several of the passages in Johnson's Life of Boerhaave are reproduced in the *London Chronicle*, iv, 1758, p. 570.

(3) An Appeal to the Publick. pp. 111–12.

(4) [Address] To the Reader. p. 223.

[The letter on p. 601, dated 'Oxford, Nov. 19, 1739' and containing a criticism of the contributions of Joseph Warton and Collins, is ascribed to Johnson in Wooll's *Memoirs of Joseph Warton* (1806), p. 109, but apparently without authority. Ed.]

To this year belongs 'Considerations [by the late Dr. Samuel Johnson] on the Case of Dr. T[rapp]'s Sermons, abridged by Mr. Cave, 1739', first published in the *Gent. Mag.* of July 1787, pp. 555–7. The Considerations were occasioned by the long extract from Dr. Joseph Trapp's 'Four sermons on Ecclesias. vii. 16', which appeared in the *Magazine* for 1739, pp. 288–92.

Boswell, i. 140 *n.*

1740

(1) Life of Admiral Blake. pp. 301–7.

1740

Boswell, i. 147–8.

Reprinted in the *London Chronicle*, August 13–16, 1757, pp. 154–5; August 16–18, pp. 162–4; August 18–20, pp. 171–2.

(2) Life of Sir Francis Drake. pp. 389–96 [August 1740], 443–7, 509–15, 600–3; 1741, pp. 38–44.

The lives of Drake and Blake were appended to Johnson's account of Savage (1767 and later editions).

(3) An epitaph upon the celebrated Claudy Philips, Musician, who died very poor. Signed G. p. 464.

This was afterwards published, with some other pieces of his, in *Miscellanies in Prose and Verse*, by Anna Williams, 1766, p. 23. In consequence of the signature it had been ascribed to Garrick.

(4) An Essay on Epitaphs. pp. 593–6.

This essay is reproduced in (1) 'A Collection of Epitaphs . . . To which is prefixed [pp. v–xvi] An Essay on Epitaphs by Dr. Johnson. 1806.' 2 vols., and (2) 'Gleanings from God's acre . . . by John Potter Briscoe . . . with an Essay on Epitaphs [pp. 5–16], by Dr. Samuel Johnson. 1883'. Johnson's Essay on Epitaphs was added to the third edition of the *Idler*, 1767.

(5) Life of John Philip Barretier. p. 612; 1741, pp. 87, 88, and 93. (See also below, 1742.)

(6) Preface. pp. iii–viii.

1741

1741
Boswell, i. 149–50.

(1) A Debate between the Committee of the House of Commons in 1657, and O. Cromwell, upon the Humble Petition and Advice of the Parliament, by which he was desired to assume the Title of King. pp. 93–100, 148–54.

(2) A Dissertation on the Amazons. From the History of the Amazons, written in French by the Abbé de Guyon. pp. 202–8.

(3) A Panegyric on Dr. [Lewis] Morin, By Mr. Fontenelle. pp. 375–7.

(4) The Jests of Hierocles. pp. 477–9.

Hill states 'this piece is certainly not by Johnson'.

(5) Debates in the Senate of Lilliput.

(6) Preface. p. (iii).

1742

1742
Boswell, i. 153.

(1) A Review of the Account of the Conduct of the [Dowager] Dutchess of Marlborough [by Nathaniel Hooke]. pp. 128–31, 204–6, 256–8, 297–30.

(2) An Account of the life of Peter Burman, the late Professor of History, Poetry, &c. in the University of Leiden. pp. 206–10.

(3) Additional Account of the Life of Mr. John Philip Barretier. pp. 242–5.

Johnson's articles on Barretier were revised and reissued as 'An Account of the Life of John Philip Barretier, Who was Master of Five Languages at the Age of Nine Years. Compiled from his Father's Letters, &c. London: Printed for J. Roberts in Warwick-lane. 1744. [Price Sixpence.].'

Boswell, i. 157.

(4) Essay on the description of China in two Volumes Folio [printed by Edward Cave]. From the French of Jean Baptiste Du Halde. pp. 320–3, 353–7, 484–6.

(5) The Life of Dr. Sydenham. pp. 633–5.

The following note is subjoined, p. 635: 'The above Account of Dr. Sydenham is prefixed to the New Translation [1742] of his Works by John Swan, M.D. of Newcastle in Staffordshire.'

AN

ACCOUNT

OF THE

LIFE

OF

John Philip Barretier,

Who was Master of Five LANGUAGES at the Age of Nine YEARS.

Compiled from his Father's LETTERS, &c.

LONDON:
Printed for *J. Roberts* in *Warwick lane.* 1744.
[Price Sixpence.]

The fourth edition of Swan's Entire works of Sydenham (1763) contains this Life, and it was also included in the edition of 1788, which bore on the title-page the name of George Wallis, M.D., and was annotated by him. In neither of these editions was Johnson said to be the author.

(6) Proposals for Printing, by Subscription, the Two first Volumes of Bibliotheca Harleiana: or, a Catalogue of the Library of the Late Earl of Oxford, Purchased by Thomas Osborne, Bookseller in Gray's-Inn. pp. 636–9.

(7) Foreign History. pp. 660–1.
This little abridgement is attributed to him by Boswell.

(8) Debates in the Senate of Lilliput.

(9) Preface. pp. iii–iv.

The Harleian Catalogue.

Catalogus Bibliothecæ Harleianæ, In Locos communes distributus cum Indice Auctorum. Vol. i (–v). Londini: Apud Thomam Osborne. MDCCXLIII. (Vols. i and ii, 1743; iii and iv, 1744; v, 1745.)

1743, 4
Boswell, i. 154.

The 'Account of the Harleian Library', which had been given in Johnson's *Proposals* (*Gent. Mag.*, 1742, pp. 636–9), is reprinted at the beginning of the Catalogue, vol. i, pp. 1–8. According to Boswell, the Latin accounts of books were written by Johnson. He probably wrote the Preface to the third volume, but Boswell does not attribute it to him. [Hawkins believed that Oldys's collaboration ceased at the end of the second volume, and that Johnson was responsible for the third and fourth, but he admitted that to discriminate between Johnson's notes and those of Oldys is not easy (*Life*, 1787, pp. 133, 134). The fifth volume is 'nothing more than a catalogue of Osborne's old stock'. The Latin dedication to Lord Carteret in vol. i was by Mattaire. Ed.]

Medical Dictionary of Dr. James.

A Medicinal Dictionary; including Physic, Surgery, Anatomy, Chymistry, and Botany, In all the Branches relative to Medicine. Together with a History of Drugs; An

1743
Boswell, i. 159.

Account of their Various Preparations, Combinations, and Uses; and an Introductory Preface, Tracing the Progress of Physic, and explaining the Theories which have principally prevail'd in all Ages of the World. By R. James, M.D. 1743–5. 3 vols. folio.

Johnson was understood by Boswell to have written or assisted in writing the proposals for this work, and to have furnished some of the articles. The dedication 'To Dr. Mead' (pp. iii–iv) was certainly written by him.

The Gentleman's Magazine.

1743 Boswell, i. 157.

(1) Considerations on the Dispute between [Jean Pierre de] Crousaz and Warburton, on Pope's Essay on Man. pp. 152, 587–8.

[The English edition of Crousaz by Elizabeth Carter was sometimes erroneously ascribed to Johnson. See *Boswell*, i. 137–8. Ed.]

(2) Friendship, an Ode. p. 376.

Reprinted in the *Gentleman's Magazine*, 1785, p. 477.

(3) Ad Lauram parituram epigramma. p. 378.

This epigram was made impromptu. The first line was proposed by Dr. James, and Johnson was called upon to finish it.

Boswell, i. 54.

(4) The Young Author. p. 378.

Written about 1725. Boswell prints the original version.

(5) Letter on proposed life of Savage. p. 416.

Boswell, i. 156.

(6) Epitaph on the late R——d S——e, Esq. [Richard Savage]. p. 490.

This does not seem to have been by Johnson.

(7) Latin Translation of Pope's Verses on his Grotto. p. 550.

(8) Advertisement of the third and fourth volumes of the *Bibliotheca Harleiana*. p. 560.

Hill doubts whether (7) and (8) are by Johnson.

(9) Debates in the Senate of Lilliput.

(10) Preface. p. (iii).

AN

ACCOUNT

OF THE

LIFE

OF

Mr *Richard Savage*,

Son of the Earl RIVERS.

LONDON:

Printed for J. ROBERTS in *Warwick-Lane*.

M.DCC.XLIV.

The Harleian Miscellany.

The Harleian Miscellany, or a Collection of . . . Pamphlets and Tracts . . . found in the late Earl of Oxford's library. 1744–6. 8 vols.

1744
Boswell, i. 175.

The introduction by Johnson is in vol. i (2nd pagination), pp. i–viii. It is reprinted in the later issues: No. I (1753, 1744–6, vol. i only being second edition and dated 1753); No. II (ed. Thomas Park, 1808–13, 10 vols.); No. III (ed. John Malham, 1808–11, 12 vols.). In its first issue it did not have the title 'An Essay on the Origin and Importance of Small Tracts and Fugitive Pieces'. It is included in Davies's *Miscellaneous and Fugitive Pieces* (1744), vol. ii, pp. 1–9; and in the Pamphlet Library (1897), vol. i (ed. Ernest Rhys), pp. 41–54.

[The Miscellany was issued in monthly parts from April 1744: see the *Gentleman's Magazine*, 1744, p. 232.

The Proposals for the Miscellany were also by Johnson. They are usually bound with the third volume of the Catalogue (6 pp.), and they are also reprinted (2 pp.) at the conclusion of the *Gentleman's Magazine* for 1743. Ed.]

The Gentleman's Magazine.

Preface. 1 page.

1744
Boswell, i. 161.

The Life of Savage.

An Account of the Life of Mr. Richard Savage, Son of the Earl Rivers. London: Printed for J. Roberts, in Warwick-Lane. MDCCXLIV. 8°.

1744
Boswell, i. 161–74.

Half-title:—The Life of Mr. Savage.

Collation:—Half-title; title; the life, pp. [1]–180 (= 186).

Published in February 1744; price 2*s.* 6*d.*

Johnson had been heard to say, 'I wrote forty-eight of the printed octavo pages of the *Life of Savage* at a sitting; but then I sat up all night'. The *Life of Savage* was no sooner published than it was highly praised in the *Champion* of Feb. 21 (quoted in *Gent. Mag.*, 1744, p. 78), probably by James Ralph. In later years the Life incurred some censure: 'Reflections upon the moral and biographical writings of Dr. Johnson,' chiefly dealing with his Life of Savage, are in the *European Magazine*, vol. lxxxvii (April 1825), pp. 320–6. They were answered in the numbers for May, pp. 422–5, 426–33, and June, pp. 518–22.

1748 An Account, *etc.* [Anon.]. The Second Edition. London: Printed for E. Cave at St. John's Gate. M.DCC.XLVIII. 8°.

1767 The Life of Mr. Richard Savage, Son of the Earl Rivers. The third edition. To which are added, The Lives of Sir Francis Drake and Admiral Blake. All Written by the same Author. London: Printed for Henry and Cave, at St. John's Gate: M.DCC.LXVII. 8°.

The editor's preface says that 'The following Lives were written by the ingenious Author of the *Rambler*'.

1769 The Life of Mr. Richard Savage, Son of the Earl Rivers. The fourth edition. To which are added, The Lives of Sir Francis Drake, and Admiral Blake. All written by the Author of the Rambler. London, Printed for F. Newbery, at the Corner of St. Paul's Church Yard, Ludgate Street. M.DCC.LXIX. 8°.

The same preface, again dated '*St. John's Gate, July* 1, 1767'. Another issue, purporting to be the fourth edition, was 'Printed for F. Newbery, the corner of St. Paul's Church-Yard. 1777.' 12°. The preface dated 1767 was still retained.

The *Life of Savage* was translated into French in 'Histoires de Richard Savage et de J: Thompson [James Thomson, author of *The Seasons*]. Traduites de l'Anglois Par M. [Pierre Prime Félicien] Le Tourneur. à Paris, chez Fetil, Libraire, rue des Cordeliers, près celle de Condé; au Parnasse Italien. MDCC.LXXI. *Avec Approbation et Permission.*' 12°. The first paragraph of the *avertissement de l'éditeur anglois* is a translation into French of part of the preface dated July 1, 1767. The translation of the *Life of Savage* occupies 320 pages.

It formed, in English, vol. xi of 'The English Library', which was published at Zürich in 1881–2.

The Life is prefixed to editions of *The Works of Richard Savage, Esq., son of the Earl Rivers*, which appeared in London in 1775 in 2 vols. and in 1777; in Dublin, 1777, 2 vols.; and was inserted in Cooke's edition of *The Poetical Works of Richard Savage* (1801). It was included in:

(1) '*The Works of the English Poets*, with prefaces, biographical and critical, by Samuel Johnson' (prefaces vol. ix (1781), pp. 1–147; and in all subsequent editions of Johnson's *Lives of the Poets.*

(2) Bell's *British Poets*, vols. lxix and lxx. ['Edinburg: at the Apollo Press, by the Martins. *Anno* 1780.']

(3) *The Works of the English Poets*, with prefaces . . . by Samuel Johnson, 1790; preface, vol. iv, pp. 61–233.

(4) Robert Anderson's *British Poets* [abridged], vol. viii, 1794.

(5) Alexander Chalmers's *English Poets*, vol. xi, 1818.

(6) [Ezekiel Sanford and] Robert Walsh, jun.: *British Poets*, vol. xix, 1819.

(7) Charles Whittingham's *British Poets*, vol. xxxv, 1822.

This *Life of Savage* underwent very little alteration in the later issues. 'Mr. Page' of the original edition was altered into 'Sir Francis Page', and two sentences were added on the 'charge of very atrocious Ingratitude', which one of Orator Henley's advertisements had caused Pope to convey to Savage, when he had been six months in prison (1743).

['The Life of Richard Savage, Esq.,' in *The Lives of the Poets of Great-Britain and Ireland*, nominally by 'Mr. Cibber', but mainly by Robert Shiels, 1753, vol. v, pp. 32–66, is admittedly compiled from Johnson's *Life*. Ed.]

There appeared in 1909 a volume entitled *Richard Savage: a mystery in biography*, by Stanley V. Makower.

Observations on Macbeth.

1745
Boswell, i. 175.

Miscellaneous Observations on the Tragedy of Macbeth: with Remarks on Sir T. H.'s [Sir Thomas Hanmer's] Edition of Shakespear. To which is affix'd, Proposals for a New Edition of Shakeshear (*sic*), with a Specimen. London: Printed for E. Cave, at St. John's Gate, and Sold by J. Roberts in Warwick-lane. Price 1*s*. M.DCC.XLV. 12°.

Half-title:—Miscellaneous Observations on the Tragedy of Macbeth.

Collation:—Half-title; title; the observations, pp. [1]–64.

In the *Gentleman's Magazine* for Feb. 1745, p. 112, is the following: 'Advertisement. *Speedily will be published* (*Price* 1*s*.) Miscellaneous observations on the tragedy of MACBETH, with remarks on Sir *T. H.*'s edition of *Shakespear*; to which is affix'd, proposals for a new edition of *Shakespear*, with a specimen. Printed for *J. Roberts* in *Warwick Lane*.' The advertisement is repeated in the number for March 1745 (p. 114), with the new heading 'April 6. *will be published* (*Price* 1*s*.)'.

The register of books for April 1745 (p. 224) contains as the twenty-fifth published book of that month: 'Miscellaneous observations on the tragedy of *Macbeth*, with remarks on Sir *T. H.*'s edit. and a specimen of a new one. pr. 1*s*. *Roberts*'; but no mention is made of the Proposals.

A copy of the *Miscellaneous Observations* with the Proposals is in the library of Worcester College, Oxford; and a copy of the Proposals alone is in the Bodleian Library. They are printed on one side of a single folio sheet. A footnote says: 'Subscriptions are taken in, and Receipts signed by E. Cave at *St. John's Gate*; and by the Editor.' There is no date, and no editor's name.

[The Proposals were folded among advertisements at the end of the book, and apparently were commonly torn off by the binder. They state that 'I. This Work will be printed in Ten small Volumes, of the same Paper and Print with the following Specimen. II. The Price to Subscribers will be one Pound five Shillings in Sheets, of which half a Guinea is to be paid at the Time of Subscribing'. The specimen (Act III, Sc. i, 45–72) represents two 18mo pages in small type. The Proposals are described in Pegge's *Anonymiana*, ed. 1818, p. 23, where a letter from Tonson to Cave, dated April 11, 1745, which had the effect of stopping the edition, is given in full. See also below, p. 163. Ed.]

Warburton, in the Preface to the first volume of his *Shakespeare* (1747), p. xiii, writes of the *Miscellaneous Observations*: 'For as to all those Things, which have been published under the titles of *Essays*, *Remarks*, *Observations*, &c. on *Shakespear*, (if you except some critical Notes on *Macbeth*, given as a Specimen of a projected Edition, and written, as appears, by a Man of Parts and Genius) the rest are absolutely below a serious Notice.' Johnson remarked that Warburton praised him at a time when praise was of value.

Johnson's title probably suggested that of the anonymous 'Miscellaneous Observations on the Tragedy of Hamlet' (1752).

Boulter's Monument.

1745
Boswell, i. 318.

Boulter's Monument. A Panegyrical Poem, Sacred to the Memory Of That Great and Excellent Prelate and Patriot, The Most Reverend Dr. Hugh Boulter; Late Lord Archbishop of Ardmagh, and Primate of All Ireland. . . . London: Printed by S. Richardson: And are to be Sold by M. Cooper in Pater-noster Row *etc.* MDCCXLV. 8°.

PROLOGUE

AND

EPILOGUE,

SPOKEN AT THE OPENING OF THE

THEATRE

IN

DRURY-LANE 1747.

LONDON:

Printed by E. CAVE at St *John's Gate*; sold by]
COOPER in *Pater-Noster-Row*, and R. DODSLEY
Pall-mall. M,DCC,XLVII. (*Price 6d.*)

Boulter's Monument. . . . Dublin: Printed by George Faulkner. MDCCXLV. 8°.

[The London edition was published in October: see *Gent. Mag.*, 1745, p. 580. The Dublin edition, which is sometimes described as the original, is shown by the 'errata' on the verso of its title-page to be a reprint. The author took the opportunity to include in the 'errata' three emendations of the London text, ll. 403, 666, 1605. Ed.]

This anonymous poem of portentous length (2,034 lines) was written by the Rev. Samuel Madden, D.D. (*D. N. B.*). The author submitted it to Johnson for castigation, and he 'blotted a great many lines'. His labour was generously rewarded by the gift of ten guineas, 'which was to me at that time a great sum', said Johnson, many years later.

Debates of the House of Commons.

The 'Proposals for Publishing the Debates of the House of Commons, *From the Year 1667 to the Year 1694*. Collected by The Hon^able Anchitell Grey, Esq;' which are printed in the *Gentleman's Magazine*, March 1745, pp. 135–6, are said to be by Johnson (*Gent. Mag.*, Dec. 1856, p. 677). These debates were published in 1769 in ten volumes, probably through the instrumentality of Thomas Tyrwhitt.

The Drury-lane Prologue

1747 Boswell, i. 181.

Prologue and Epilogue, spoken at the opening of the Theatre in Drury-lane [15 Sept.] 1747. London: Printed by E. Cave at St. John's Gate; sold by M. Cooper in Pater-Noster-Row, and R. Dodsley in Pall-mall. M,DCC,LVII. (Price 6*d.*) 4°.

The Prologue (pp. 3–7) is by Johnson, and it was to have been spoken by Garrick. It was inserted in the *Gent. Mag.* for Oct. 1747, pp. 490–1, and has been often reprinted, notably in Dodsley's *Collection of Poems* (vol. i), when Gray pronounced the verses to be 'far from bad'. It was also inserted in Henry Morley's two issues (the Reynolds and Library editions) of Boswell, iv. 389–90. [The Epilogue was by Garrick. Ed.]

The favours of Coventry ribbon that were worn at the Shakespeare Jubilee, Stratford-on-Avon, in Sept. 1769, were adorned with the third line of the Prologue,—'Each Change of many-colour'd Life he drew'.

A facsimile of the Prologue and Epilogue, 'with preface by Austin Dobson and notes by A. S. W. Rosenbach', was produced at New York in 1902 in folio form, pp. xxiv and 12.

Genest (*Some Account of the English Stage*, iv. 231) reproduces the advertisement from the *General Advertiser*, Oct. 8, stating that Garrick was 'disabled by illness from speaking the Prologue', and adds that it was 'the best Prologue that was ever written'.

Plan of the Dictionary.

1747
Boswell, i. 182 et seq.

The Plan of a Dictionary of the English Language; Addressed to the Right Honourable Philip Dormer, Earl of Chesterfield; One of His Majesty's Principal Secretaries of State. London: Printed for J. and P. Knapton, T. Longman and T. Shewell, C. Hitch, A. Millar, and R. Dodsley. MDCCXLVII. 4°.

Collation:—Title, with erratum on verso; the letter, pp. [1]–34.

The *Plan* was also issued in the same year in 8°, 37 pages. [There is no difference in the wording or punctuation of the title. The erratum is corrected. Ed.]

The scheme of the Dictionary was first mentioned to Johnson by Robert Dodsley, on whose suggestion the *Plan* was addressed to Lord Chesterfield. It apparently passed through several hands before reaching Lord Chesterfield. Mr. Croker had seen the draft which contained the remarks of his lordship and of another person: 'Johnson adopted all these suggestions.' The price stipulated was £1,575, but Johnson received £100 and upwards more than his due.

Johnson, in a conversation with Boswell (March 1772), mentioned that on the publication of the *Plan* 'Lord Chesterfield told me that the word *great* should be pronounced so as to rhyme to *state*; and Sir William Yonge sent me word that it should be pronounced so as to rhyme to *seat*, and that none but an Irishman would pronounce it *grait*' (Boswell, ii. 161). The only person drawn by the *Plan* into helping Johnson was Zachary Pearce, afterwards Bishop of Rochester, who sent him twenty etymologies.

The *Plan* is reproduced in Harrison's edition of the Dictionary, 1786. The original draft of it fetched £57 at the sale (Sotheby, May 1875) of the collection of Lewis Pocock.

THE

PLAN

OF A

DICTIONARY

OF THE

ENGLISH LANGUAGE;

Addressed to the Right Honourable

PHILIP DORMER,

Earl of *CHESTERFIELD*;

One of His MAJESTY's Principal Secretaries of State.

LONDON:

Printed for J. and P. KNAPTON, T. LONGMAN and T. SHEWELL, C. HITCH, A. MILLAR, and R. DODSLEY. MDCCXLVII.

The Gentleman's Magazine.

The following pieces are commonly attributed to Johnson: **1747**

Boswell, i. 177-8.

(1) A translation of the Latin Epitaph on Sir Thomas Hanmer, Or rather a Paraphrase. p. 239.

This is included in *Miscellanies in Prose and Verse* of Miss Anna Williams (1766), pp. 94-6, and in Sir Henry Bunbury's *Correspondence of Hanmer* (1838), pp. 96-7. The Latin Epitaph was by Dr. Robert Freind, Hanmer's tutor at Oxford. The evidence for Johnson's authorship of the translation is insufficient.

(2) To Miss —— on her giving the Author a Gold and Silk Net-work Purse, of her own weaving. p. 239.

(3) Stella in Mourning. pp. 239-40.

(4) The Winter's Walk. p. 240.

(5) An Ode. p. 240.

(6) To Lyce, an elderly Lady. p. 240.

[The above pieces have all the same signature ***. (1), (2), (4), and (5) are said to be by Johnson in Pearch's *Collection of Poems*, vol. iii (1770). Ed.] Boswell has doubts in assigning any to Johnson; Malone suggests that Hawkesworth was the author.

(7) Winter, an Ode. p. 588.

Boswell assigns this to Johnson with unwarranted certainty. [It also is in Pearch's *Collection*, vol. iii. Ed.]

1748.

Life [with notes] of the Earl of Roscommon. pp. 214-17. **1748**

Boswell, i. 191-2.

It was enlarged, and the notes were incorporated in the text, for inclusion in the *Lives of the English Poets.*

Boswell also attributes to him the notes on Foreign History which are contained on p. 526.

[The letter on the Fireworks, signed O. N., January 1749, p. 8, was included in Chalmers's edition of Johnson's works in 1823. Ed.]

Dodsley's Preceptor.

The Preceptor: Containing A General Course of Education. Wherein The First Principles of Polite Learning Are laid down In a Way most suitable for trying the Genius, and **1748**

Boswell, i. 192.

advancing the Instruction of Youth. In twelve parts. London: Printed for R. Dodsley, at Tully's-Head in Pall-Mall. MDCCXLVIII. 2 vols. 8°.

Johnson furnished the Preface, vol. i, pp. ix–xxxi, and also 'The Vision of Theodore, the Hermit of Teneriffe, found in his Cell', ii. 516–26. Tom Tyers said that Johnson composed this piece in one night 'after finishing an evening in Holborn'. Bishop Percy heard Johnson say that it was the best thing he ever wrote. The 'Vision of Theodore' is printed as an appendix to 'Selections from Dr. Johnson's *Rambler*', ed. W. Hale White, 1907.

['The Picture of Human Life: Translated from the Greek of Cebes,' which forms the conclusion of the second volume, and is introduced as 'translated into *English*, by a Person considerably distinguished in the Republic of Letters', has been attributed to Johnson. The *Monthly Review* for March, 1790, p. 282, says that 'we can say, on good authority, that Johnson has been often heard to acknowledge it as his'. It was reprinted in Gleig's supplementary volume of Johnson's works, 1789 (see above, p. 4), and in Murphy's edition. But it was omitted in 1806 by Chalmers, who says definitely that 'it was translated by Mr. Spence'. It is a revised version of what had been printed in 1747 in Dodsley's *Museum*, vol. iii, pp. 233–46. Ed.]

The Preceptor, *etc.* The second edition, with Additions. MDCCLIV. 2 vols. 8°. (Preface and Vision as in first ed.)

The Preceptor, *etc.* The fourth edition, with Additions. MDCCLXIII. 2 vols. 8°. (Preface, vol. i, pp. ix–xxxi; Vision, ii. 520–30.)

The Preceptor, *etc.* The fifth edition, with Additions. MDCCLXIX. 2 vols. 8°. (Preface, vol. i, pp. ix–xxxi, with slight alterations; Vision, ii. 520–30.)

The Preceptor, *etc.* The sixth edition. MDCCLXXV.

Vanity of Human Wishes.

1749
Boswell, i. 192–5.

The Vanity of Human Wishes. The Tenth Satire of Juvenal, Imitated By Samuel Johnson. London: Printed for R. Dodsley at Tully's Head in Pall-Mall, and Sold by M. Cooper in Pater-noster Row. M.DCC.XLIX. 4°.

Collation:—Title, p. [1]; the poem, pp. [3]–28.

This was Johnson's first work that bore his name.

THE VANITY OF HUMAN WISHES.

THE

Tenth Satire of *Juvenal*,

IMITATED

By *SAMUEL JOHNSON*.

LONDON:

Printed for R. DODSLEY at Tully's Head in Pall-Mall, and Sold by M. COOPER in Pater-noster Row.

M.DCC.XLIX.

The *Gentleman's Magazine*, 1748, p. 598, has this note: 'On *Jan.* 9, was published, long wish'd, another *satire* from *Juvenal*, by the author of *London*; tho' it belongs not properly to this year, we cannot resist the pleasure of entertaining our readers with some passages from it on this *first* opportunity.

N.B. The history of *Lydiat* not being much known, we have illustrated that character, by a note, and added some lines from *Juvenal.*'

110 lines, not consecutive, are then quoted from the poem, and the advertisement ends (p. 599) with the intimation:

'*We hope to be able soon to give our readers a specimen of a tragedy, entitled* Irene, *by the same ingenious author, Mr.* Garrick *having it now in rehearsal.*'

The poem was composed in the preceding year, when his wife had lodgings at Hampstead, the first seventy lines being written 'in the course of one morning in that small house beyond the church at Hampstead' (T. J. Barratt, *Hampstead*, i. 257 et seq., iii. 299–300). Its price was one shilling a copy, and Johnson received for it on Nov. 25, 1748, the sum of fifteen guineas, assigning to Dodsley in return 'the right of copy of an imitation of the *Tenth Satire of Juvenal*, written by me; reserving to myself the right of printing one edition'; but this edition was never issued.

The Vanity of Human Wishes was included in Dodsley's *Collection of Poems*, vol. iv. It was published in 1784 in *D. Iunii Juvenalis et A. Persii Flacci Satirae expurgatae*, pp. 380–90; in J. Roach's *Beauties of the Poets*, vol. iii (1794), No. xi, pp. 33–46; in the *British Satirist* (1826), pp. 243–54; in *Juvenal*, translated by Charles Badham (1831), pp. 225–36; in *Dr. Johnson's Satires*, with notes, &c., by J. P. Fleming (1876). It was edited by E. J. Payne for the Clarendon Press, 1876, 1884, and 1906; and by F. Ryland in Blackie's English Classics, 1901.

In 1851 there was issued 'Vanity of Human Wishes. By Samuel Johnson, LL.D. Reprinted, July–August 1851. Respectfully dedicated to the dense masses of well-dressed, and most loyal subjects, male and female, adult and non-adult, from town and country, of our sovereign lady . . . Queen, Defender of the Faith. By A. M. Oxon, and J. P. for Somerset, Dorset, Middlesex, &c. [Motto.] London: John Lee, 440, West Strand. 1851.' 8vo. At the back of the title-page is printed: 'Finding during many past years, this great work not so generally read as I thought it well deserved, I have often intended to have it reprinted in a popular shape. Recent events have precipitated my taking the step. William Hoskins. Athenæum, Pall Mall, August 15, 1851.' A copy is in the library of Trinity College, Oxford.

William Hoskins, eldest son of William Hoskins, of North Perrott, Somerset, gent., matriculated from that college on Oct. 26, 1805, aged 18. He graduated B.A. 1809, M.A. 1812, was admitted at Lincoln's Inn on May 12, 1809, and was called to the bar in 1813. He died at North Perrott on Dec. 3, 1863, aged 76 (*Gent. Mag.*, 1864, pt. i, p. 132). A pedigree of the family is in several issues of Burke's *Landed Gentry*.

Irene.

1749
Boswell, i. 100–1, 106–11, 196–201.

Irene: A Tragedy. As it is Acted at the Theatre Royal in Drury-Lane. By Mr. Samuel Johnson. London: Printed for R. Dodsley at Tully's-head Pall-mall and sold by M. Cooper in Pater-noster-Row. MDCCXLIX. 8°.

Half-title:—Irene, A Tragedy. Price One Shilling and Six-pence.

Collation:—Half-title, p. [i]; title, p. [iii]; prologue, pp. [v, vi]; epilogue, p. [vii]; the persons, p. [viii]; the play, pp. [1]–86.

An edition was published in Dublin in 1749, 'Printed by S. Powell, For G. and A. Ewing,' *etc.*, 12°.

Irene . . . Second edition. MDCCLIV.

Irene . . . By Samuel Johnson, LL.D. A new edition. London: Printed for J. Dodsley, in Pall-Mall. M.DCC.LXXXI.

Half-title, &c., as before, pp. 1–8; the play, pp. 9–94. This follows the first edition page for page.

Irene. In Bell's [and Cawthorn's] *British Theatre*, vol. xiv (1796); in another issue, xxv (1797).

Irene. *Modern British Drama*, ii (1811), pp. 232–53.

Part of the tragedy had been written by Johnson at his school of Edial, near Lichfield, in 1736. He continued writing it in lodgings at Greenwich in 1737, and it was finished at Lichfield in the summer of that year. Fleetwood, the patentee of Drury Lane Theatre, declined to put it on the stage, and it slumbered in manuscript for twelve years. By this time Garrick was the manager of that theatre, and it was brought out there on Feb. 6, 1748/9 (Genest, *English Stage*, iv. 265–7). The prologue was by Johnson, the epilogue by Sir William Yonge. The profits of the

IRENE:

A
TRAGEDY.

As it is Acted at the

THEATRE ROYAL

IN

DRURY-LANE.

By Mr. *SAMUEL JOHNSON.*

LONDON:

Printed for R. DODSLEY at *Tully*'s-head *Pall-mall* and ſold by M. COOPER in *Pater-noſter-Row.*

MDCCXLIX.

piece—it was acted nine times—amounted with the copyright to 'very nearly £300'. An account of its representation on Johnson's benefit-night is in a letter by Aaron Hill, dated Feb. 15, 1749 (*Works*, ii. 355–6).

'Plan and Specimens of *Irene*', signed H. H., appeared in the *Gent. Mag.* for 1749, pp. 76–81. 'Irene at Drury Lane' is the title of a narrative by Dutton Cook in *Once a Week*, v (1861), pp. 651–6. A criticism by William Archer of *Irene* appeared in the *Tribune* for Sept. 22, 1906, p. 2, columns 4 and 5. An article on it is in J. F. Molloy's *Famous Plays* (1886), pp. 101–26. Another article is printed in *Shylock and Others*, Eight Studies by G. H. Radford, 1894, pp. 95–115.

'An Essay on Tragedy, with a Critical Examen of Mahomet and Irene. . . . London: Printed for R. Griffiths, at the Dunciad, in Ludgate-Street, 1749,' 8°, is in the Bodleian Library (Godw. Pamph. 802). Johnson's play was called *Mahomet and Irene* in the bills, but only *Irene* in the book. The author of this production, being at too great a distance from the press, could not correct the proofs. The *Essay* is very scarce; no copy is in the British Museum, and it is not mentioned by Boswell.

The Rambler.

1750 Boswell, i. 201–26.

The first paper of *The Rambler* was published on Tuesday, March 20, 1749/50; the last, No. 208, on Saturday, March 14 (in the folio edition misprinted 17th), 1752. Each number consisted of 'three half sheets (unstamped); price 2ᵈ'. The whole was written by Johnson, with the following exceptions, viz.:

No. 10, four billets by Hester Mulso, afterwards Mrs. Chapone.

No. 30 [signed Sunday], by Catherine Talbot.

No. 97, by Samuel Richardson, introduced as 'an Author from whom the Age has received greater Favours, who has enlarged the Knowledge of human Nature, and taught the Passions to move at the Command of Virtue'. Through the purchases of the admiring ladies by whom Richardson was surrounded, this was the only number of *The Rambler* which had a large sale.

Nos. 44 and 100, by Elizabeth Carter. They are reprinted (pp. 91–104) in her *Poems on Several Occasions* (1762).

The second letter in No. 15 and that signed 'Amicus' in No. 107 are from unknown correspondents.

The Rambler was at first received with little favour, but Mary, Lady Hervey, praised the numbers, while in course of publication, as 'extremely well written'. She could not ascertain the name of the writer, but suggested Melmoth (*Letters*, pp. 61–2, but the date of the letter is erroneous). An article on this neglect (No. 58 of the set called *The Ruminator*) by Sir S. E. Brydges is in *Censura Literaria*, x. 71–7 (1809), and was reproduced in the separate edition of *The Ruminator* (1813), ii. 61–8. Less than 500 copies of each number were sold on each day, and the bookseller John Payne, afterwards the chief accountant in the Bank of England, 'who paid the author four guineas a week, did not carry on a successful trade', but in the course of thirty-six years eleven editions issued from the press, and Johnson received something for his share of the profits of these issues.

No. 37 (on pastoral poetry) was inserted by Joseph Warton in his edition of *The Works of Virgil in Latin and English* (1753), i. 38–43, with the remark that he had not been able to find anything 'so rational, so judicious, and yet so new', and that it was the work of 'an excellent Writer of our own Country'. At the end Warton adds the expression: 'Thus far the learned and judicious Mr. Johnson.'

A very graceful compliment to *The Rambler* was printed by Goldsmith in his article of 'A Reverie', which appeared in No. 5 of *The Bee*, Nov. 3, 1759 (*Works*, ed. Cunningham, iii. 81–2).

The character of Suspirius in No. 59 suggested to Goldsmith the conception of Croaker in *The Good-Natur'd Man.* Garrick was the original of Prospero in No. 200, and the idiosyncrasies of Gelidus (No. 24) are said to have been drawn from the Rev. John Colson, the Lucasian Professor of Mathematics at Cambridge, or from John Coulson, of University College, Oxford. 'The man immortalised for purring like a cat was, as he told me, one Busby, a proctor in the Commons. He who barked so ingeniously, and then called the drawer to drive away the dog, was father to Dr. Salter of the Charterhouse. He who sung a song, and by correspondent motions of his arm chalked out a giant on the wall, was one Richardson, an attorney' (*Anecdotes of Johnson*, by Mrs. Piozzi, 1789, p. 49). All these entertainers are described in the last paragraph but one of No. 188. Polyphilus, in No. 19, is said by Chalmers to have been drawn from the various studies of Floyer Sydenham.

Exception was taken to the hard words used by the author—

THE

RAMBLER.

Nullius addictus jurare in verba magistri,
Quo me cunque rapit tempestas deferor hospes.
HOR.

LONDON:

Printed for J. PAYNE, and J. BOUQUET, in *Pater-noster-row.*

M.DCC.LI.

THE

RAMBLER.

VOLUME FIRST.

Nullius addictus jurare in verba magistri,
Quo me cunque rapit tempestas deferor hospes.

HOR.

LONDON:
Printed for J. PAYNE, at Pope's Head, in Pater Noster Row.
MDCCLIII.

the number for May 26, 1750, which contained in one sentence the words 'adscititious' and 'equiponderant', being especially censured. These difficult words and the diction of Johnson were satirized in an anonymous volume entitled, 'Lexiphanes, a Dialogue. Imitated from Lucian, and suited to the present Times. With A Dedication to Lord Lyttleton, a Preface, Notes, and Postscript. Being An attempt to restore the English Tongue to its ancient Purity, And to correct, as well as expose, the affected Style, hard Words, and absurd Phraseology of many late Writers, and particularly of Our English Lexiphanes, the Rambler. London: [March] MDCCLXVII.' (Two editions in 1767; 3rd ed. 1783; 4th ed. Dublin 1774, *sic.*) Sir John Hawkins, in the first edition of his *Life of Johnson*, attributed this tract to Kenrick, but in the second (1787; p. 347) correctly assigned it to 'Campbell, a purser of a man of war, who as well for the malignancy of his heart as his terrific countenance, was called horrible Campbell'. This was Archibald Campbell. He had tried when in London to read *The Rambler*, but through disgust at its pedantry and affectation had failed in his task. 'At last, during a long voyage at sea', when the volumes of *The Rambler* were the only new English books on board, he was 'in a manner obliged to read them' and did so 'with great care and attention'.

'Lexiphanes', 'The Sale of Authors', and 'Some other imitations of Lucian', were composed about three years previously (i.e. in 1764) 'in one of our American Colonies'. His attacks were not confined to Johnson; Young, Akenside, and Gordon, the translator of Tacitus, were also satirized. The criticism of Johnson showed smartness but exaggeration. Its aim was to degrade Johnson's 'words of large meaning' by applying them to insignificant and ludicrous matters.

'The Sale of Authors, A Dialogue, In Imitation of Lucian's Sale of Philosophers', also an anonymous work of Campbell, came from the press in June 1767. Johnson was again but one of the celebrities figuring in this satire. He shared its honours with Gray, Macpherson and Churchill, Shebbeare and Garrick, Hoyle on cards, and Heber on horses. This was Reginald Heber, of Fullwood's Rents, Holborn, who published for some years from 1752 'an historical list of *horse-matches Run* and of Plates and Prizes run for in *Great Britain and Ireland*', in continuation of a similar work by John Cheny.

The imperfect memoir of Archibald Campbell in the *D. N. B.*

may be supplemented by an article of Mr. R. B. Langwill in *Scottish N. & Q.* v (1892), p. 136. He was born at Larbert in 1724, being the son of Archibald Campbell, Minister of Larbert and afterwards professor of church history in St. Mary's College at St. Andrews. 'His morals were as bad as his principles, so that he died wretched and unlamented', it is believed in 1780 (John Ramsay, *Scotland and Scotsmen in 18th cent.*, i. 268). Dr. Currie, in his *Works of Robert Burns, with an account of his Life*, ii. 289–90, states, on the authority of a surgeon of a man-of-war, that Campbell befriended William Falconer (subsequently author of the poem entitled *The Shipwreck*) when he was a seaman in his ship. He communicated to Falconer, who acted as his servant, what knowledge he himself possessed, a circumstance of which he used in after-life to boast, but some doubt has been thrown by Joseph Moser on this statement (*European Mag.*, May 1803, p. 344). An anecdote as to his conduct in a sea-fight, which did not redound to his credit, is contained in the 'Journal of a Naval Surgeon, 1758–1763' (*Naval Yarns*, ed. W. H. Long, 1899, pp. 89–91).

Two essays by the Rev. Robert Burrowes, 'On the stile of Doctor Samuel Johnson', are contained in the *Trans. of the Royal Irish Academy*, 1787 (Section of Polite Literature, pp. 27–56). An article by Dr. Hill on 'Dr. Johnson's Style' is in *Macmillan's Magazine*, lvii (1888), pp. 190–4. An anonymous paper, 'On a neglected book' (i. e. *The Rambler*), appeared in *Macmillan's Magazine*, Sept. 1883, pp. 414–23, and elicited from Dr. Hill an article in the *Saturday Review* for Sept. 15, 1883, pp. 333–4, on 'Johnson's *Rambler*'.

Bonnell Thornton's imitation of *The Rambler*, which originally appeared in his paper entitled 'Have at you all, or the Drury-Lane Journal. By Madam Roxana Termagant', No. 3, January 30, 1752, pp. 67–71, was reprinted in Isaac Reed's collection of *The Repository*, 2nd ed., 1790, iii. 216-20.

There was published in 1802, price 3*s.* 6*d.*, a volume entitled 'A critical inquiry into the Moral Writings of Dr. Samuel Johnson. In which the tendency of certain passages in the Rambler, and other publications of that celebrated writer, is impartially considered. To which is added an Appendix containing a dialogue between Boswell and Johnson in the shades. By Attalus.' These 'essays' had originally appeared in *The Porcupine*, a London newspaper. The first of them was in the number for October 3, 1801, and No. 12 appeared in that for Dec. 26. An article by Laicus on the same subject was in the issue of Dec. 30. The dialogue between Boswell and Johnson (Boz and Poz in the second edition) purports to be by another contributor to that paper. Boswell, in this dialogue, acknowledged that he had died of *Mahogany* (the Cornish drink, a compound of gin and treacle, referred to in his life of Johnson, *sub* March 30, 1781), and the Doctor hoped that in Erebus Boswell might be hailed 'no longer *Corsica*, but *Mahogany* Boswell'. Attalus was William Mudford, and the second edition, with an altered title-page and with his name as the author, appeared in 1803.

A communication signed W. K. [? Kenrick] in the *Westminster Mag.*, iii (1775), pp. 260–1, contains eleven passages from *The Rambler* and *The Idler* satirically applied to their author.

The works of Milton were criticized without severity in Nos. 86, 88, 90, 94, 139 and 140. 'The Impropriety of imitating Spencer (*sic*)' was one of the subjects in No. 121. H. T. Buckle stigmatizes No. 122 as containing Johnson's 'foolish notions about history' (*Miscell. Works*, i. 209).

No. 170, the first part of the letter of Misella, was printed in *Beauties of the Magazines*, vol. i (1762), pp. 194–7, as an original piece sent by W. R., the name of Misella being altered to Infelix, and was reproduced in the *London Chronicle*, xi (1762), p. 570, and in the *Lady's Magazine* for June and July, 1762. The second part of Misella's narrative appeared in the same volume of the *Beauties*, pp. 248–51, as sent from Oxford on June 16, 1762, but an editorial note was added, announcing that although the piece had been sent as original, it was written by the author of *The Rambler.*

Two volumes in 12°, price 6*s*., of 'The narrative companion containing . . . novels and allegories from the *Spectator*, *Rambler*, etc.', were published by T. Becket in February 1760 (*London Chronicle*, 1760, pt. i, p. 159).

Many of Johnson's articles in the periodical papers were included in 'The Life and Writings of Samuel Johnson, LL.D., by Rev. William P. Page, New York, 1842', 2 vols., 8°; in 'The Wisdom of the *Rambler*, *Adventurer*, and *Idler*, by Samuel Johnson, LL.D., London: Longman 1848', 8°; in 'The Essays of Samuel Johnson selected from *The Rambler*, *The Adventurer*, and *The Idler*. With biographical introduction and notes by Stuart J. Reid, London, 1888' (Camelot Series, ed. Ernest Rhys); 'Select Essays of Dr. Johnson, edited by George Birkbeck Hill, 1889,' 2 vols. 8°; and in 'Samuel Johnson: Little Masterpieces, edited by William Stead, Jr., 1905'. Two pieces—Nos. 102 and 65—are included in *Every Boy's Stories*, London, James Hogg and Sons (1860), pp. 533–41.

A volume of 'Passatempi morali; ossia Scelta di novelle e storie piacevoli da autori celebri inglesi e francesi' was printed at 'London, MDCCCXXVI', with a dedication signed A. M. D. It purported to contain two translations from Johnson: (1) 'Assano, ossia la religione il fondamento del vero contento', pp. 1–12; and (2) 'Storia della bella Vittoria', pp. 59–77. The second piece is No. 130 of *The Rambler*, but the first piece is No. 32 of *The Adventurer*, and it is by John Hawkesworth.

Ruskin's father, on his foreign journeys, took with him 'four little volumes of Johnson—*The Idler* and *The Rambler*'—as containing 'more substantial literary nourishment than could be, from any other author, packed into so portable compass'. The volumes were read and re-read 'in spare hours and on wet days'. Their style entered into the youth's being, and it was long before he could rid himself from their mastery (*Praeterita*, vol. i, 1899, pp. 344–5).

EDITIONS

1750
Boswell, i. 201–26.

The Rambler. Volume First (Second). *Nullius addictus jurare in verba magistri, Quo me cunque rapit tempestas deferor hospes.* Hor. London: Printed for J. Payne, at Pope's Head, in Pater Noster Row. MDCCLIII. folio.

Collation:—Vol. i: title, p. [1], with publisher's advertisement of *The Adventurer* on verso; contents, pp. [iii, iv]; 'mottos' of Nos. 1–104, pp. [v–x]; essays, pp. [1]–622. Vol. ii: title, p. [i]; contents, pp. [iii, iv]; 'mottos' of Nos. 105–208, pp. [v–ix]; essays, pp. [623]—1244. In general 104 numbers are contained in each volume.

[There was an earlier title-page for the collected numbers without 'Volume First' and with the imprint 'London: Printed for J. Payne, and J. Bouquet, in Pater-noster-row. M.DCC.LI.' Neither the table of contents nor the collection of mottoes accompanies this title-page. Ed.]

The separate numbers, 208 in all, were said to be printed for J. Payne and J. Bouquet in Pater-noster-Row, 'where Letters for the Author [after No. 1 'for the RAMBLER'] are received'.

After No. 4 is added 'and the preceding Numbers may be had'. Edward Cave had also some interest in it.

A copy in the British Museum has 100 numbers in the first volume and 108 in the second. The special title-page to vol. i runs as in the preceding copy, but the note to No. 1 says: 'London: St. John's Gate. Printed for J. Payne, and J. Bouquet, in Pater-noster-row, where Letters for the RAMBLER are received, and the preceding Numbers may be had' (*sic*). [This copy of No. 1 was not the original issue, but a reprint made to complete the set for binding. Ed.] The words 'St. John's Gate', which emphasize the connexion of Edmund Cave, do not appear again until No. 67. They then continue (with the exception of Nos. 77 and 94) to No. 118 inclusive, when they cease altogether. Nos. 2, 3, and 4 are without the addition 'and the preceding Numbers may be had'. There are other slight variations in the notes. Vol. ii of this copy has the title-page dated MDCCLI, but the last number of *The Rambler* was issued on March 14, 1752.

Mr. D. Nichol Smith has a copy of the original issues of *The Rambler* in four volumes, all dated 1751. His collation of the two issues of the first number has shown several variations in the text, some of which are not to be attributed to the printer.

The Mottoes of 'The Rambler'. Translations of the mottoes and of the quotations are printed together at the beginning of each volume with the title-page dated MDCCLIII. They were taken from Addison, W. Bowles (two quotations from his translation of Juvenal's fifth satire in Dryden's *Juvenal*), Catcott, Cowley, Creech, E. C. (i.e. Edward Cave), Dryden, J. Dryden jun. (two quotations from his translation of Juvenal's fourteenth satire in Dryden's *Juvenal*), Rev. Philip Francis, Stephen Harvey (from his translation of Juvenal's ninth satire in Dryden's *Juvenal*), F. Lewis, Earl of Orrery, Pope, Roscommon, Rowe, Stepney, Miss A. W. (Anna Williams), Leonard Welsted (two of the lines of Welsted's translation of part of the fifteenth book of Ovid's *Metamorphoses,* translated by Dryden and others, 1717; reproduced in Welsted's *Works*, 1787, p. 108), Gilbert West (from his translation of Pindar's seventh Olympic ode), Dr. Young, and from Elphinston's Edinburgh edition. Some of them are reproduced in the *Gent. Mag.*, 1750, pp. 406–9, and 1752, pp. 468–70.

Of some of these authors our knowledge is scanty or deficient. William Bowles (1659–1705) was an Eton boy, who graduated B.A. 1681, M.A. 1685, from King's College, Cambridge. Three of his poems are reproduced in the John Nichols's *Select Collection of Poems* (1780), i, pp. 21, 92, where there is a short account of his life; cf. also Harwood, *Alumni Etonenses*, p. 263. The Christian name of Catcott, and the poem from which the quotation is taken, I cannot identify. Stephen Harvey was no doubt the barrister and bencher of the Middle Temple (*d.* 1707), who matriculated from St. John's College, Oxford, on June 27, 1671 (Foster, *Alumni Oxon.*). Lewis was thus described by Johnson to Malone: 'Sir, he lived in London and hung loose upon society.' Chalmers calls him the Rev. F. Lewis, of Chiswick. The lines given as from Miss A. W. are not in the volume of *Miscellanies by Anna Williams*, but we know that her poetical effusions were not infrequently corrected out of existence by Johnson, and the mottoes were probably from her pen.

The anonymous versions are 65 in number. Francis was responsible for 42, Elphinston (Edinburgh edition) for 36, Lewis for 34, Dryden for 32, Pope for 15, and Creech for 14.

Elphinston's edition. Mr. James Elphinston took charge of an edition of *The Rambler* which was printed at Edinburgh, and followed progressively the London publication. The advertisement in which he announced its publication is printed in the *Monthly Magazine*, xxviii (1809), pp. 485–6, and the *European Magazine*, lvi (1809), p. 363. The first number was to appear on June 1, 1750, price one penny each number, and Elphinston plumed himself over the probable sales of the Edinburgh issue, as he had prevailed on this new writer 'to renew in Scotland his Rambles at half the London price'. No copy of this edition is in the British Museum. Boswell says: 'It was executed in the printing office of Sands, Murray, and Cochran, with uncommon elegance, upon writing paper, of a duodecimo size, and with the greatest correctness; and Mr. Elphinston enriched it with translations of the mottos. When completed, it made eight handsome volumes. It is, unquestionably, the most accurate and beautiful edition of this work; and there being but a small impression, it is now become scarce, and sells at a very high price.' Cf. also Elphinston, *Forty Years' Correspondence*, i. 34–5. [The *Scots Magazine* shows that the volumes appeared in June and Sept. 1750, Jan., March, July, and Nov. 1751, and (vols. vii and viii) July 1752. There was a second edition of the first four volumes, dated 1751 (August), 1752, 1753, 1753. Elphinston's 'Version of the Mottoes' was printed at the end of each volume. Ed.]

THE

RAMBLER.

VOLUME THE FIRST.

Nullius addictus jurare in verba magistri,
Quo me cunque rapit tempestas, deferor hospes.
HOR.

LONDON:

Printed for J. PAYNE and J. BOUQUET,
IN PATER-NOSTER-ROW.
M.DCC.LII.

THE
RAMBLER.

VOLUME I.

Nullius addictus jurare in verba magistri,
Quo me cunque rapit tempestas, deferor hospes.

EDINBURGH:
Sold by W. GORDON, C. WRIGHT,
and the other Booksellers.
MDCCL.

The Rambler. Volume the First (–Fourth). *Nullius addictus* . . . London: Printed for J. Payne and J. Bouquet, in Pater-noster-row. M.DCC.LII. 12°. **1752**

This collected edition (Nos. 1–136) appeared while *The Rambler* was still in progress. 'A correct and beautiful edition of the RAMBLER in 4 volumes in 12mo. *Pr.* 12*s.* *Payne and Bouquet*' is announced in the *Gentleman's Magazine* for January 1752, p. 47. Johnson 'multiplied' his essays to six volumes (see No. 208).

The Rambler. Volume the Fifth (Sixth). *Nullius addictus* . . . London: Printed for J. Payne, at Pope's-Head, in Pater-noster-Row. M.DCC.LII. 12°.

[At the end of vol. vi were bound the tables of contents of each of the six volumes, and the translations of the 'mottos'. Announced in the *Gentleman's Magazine* for July 1752, p. 338. Ed.]

The Rambler. Volume the First (–Sixth). *Nullius addictus* . . . London: Printed for J. Payne, at Pope's-Head in Pater-noster-row. M.DCC.LII. 12°.

[This is a reissue of the first collected edition, with Payne's name alone in all the six imprints, and with the contents and the 'mottos' prefixed to each volume. Ed.]

Alexander Chalmers states that the alterations made by Johnson in the second and third editions came to 6,834. His copy of the first edition of *The Rambler*, with his marginal additions and corrections, came into the possession of James Crossley. In April 1913 it was on sale by Sotheran & Co. for £5 15*s.* 6*d.* Crossley thought that Johnson's alterations were not always for the better.

The Rambler. Volume the First (–Sixth) . . . Dublin: Printed by George Faulkner, in Essex-Street. MDCCLII. 12°.

[This unauthorized edition is the first to incorporate the translations immediately below each motto and quotation. The copy in the British Museum lacks vols. v and vi. Ed.]

The Rambler. Third edition. MDCCLVI. 4 vols. 12°. **1756**

The Rambler. Fourth edition. London: Printed for A. Millar, J. Hodges, J. and J. Rivington, R. Baldwin, and B. Collins. MDCCLVI. 4 vols. 12°.

The Rambler. Fifth edition. London: Printed for A. Millar, J. Rivington, J. Newbery, *etc.* MDCCLXI. 4 vols. 12°. **1761**

The Rambler. Sixth edition. MDCCLXIII. 4 vols. 12°. **1763**

1767 The Rambler. Seventh edition. London: Printed for A. Millar, W. Strahan, J. Rivington, J. Newbery, *etc.* MDCCLXVII. 4 vols. 12°.

1772 The Rambler. Eighth edition. Printed in the year MDCCLXXII. 4 vols. 12°.

1776 The Rambler. Ninth edition (*sic*). Printed in the Year MDCCLXXVI. 4 vols. 12°.

1779 The Rambler. Ninth edition. London: Printed for W. Strahan, J. Rivington, *etc.* MDCCLXXIX. 4 vols. 12°.

1784 The Rambler. Tenth edition. London: Printed for W. Strahan, J. Rivington, *etc.* MDCCLXXXIV. 4 vols. 12°.

The editions from 1756 were furnished with an index compiled by the Rev. Roger Flexman, a dissenting minister. In response to a compliment of George Steevens on Flexman's 'exact memory in chronological matters', Johnson growled out: 'Let me hear no more of him, Sir. That is the fellow who made the index to my *Ramblers*, and set down the name of Milton thus: Milton, *Mr.* John.' He did the same for Shakespeare, Spenser, and Cowley.

Flexman [*d.* 1795] compiled the general index to the Journals of the House of Commons for the period 1660–97.

The Rambler. Eleventh edition. London: Printed for J. Rivington, T. Longman, B. Law, *etc.* MDCCLXXXIX. 4 vols. 12°.

The Rambler. Twelfth edition. London: Printed for W. Osborne, *etc.* MDCCLXXXIII (*sic*). 4 vols. 12°.

The Rambler, by Dr. Samuel Johnson, *etc.* London: Printed for J. Parsons, No. 21, Paternoster-Row. 1793. 4 vols. 12°. (Parsons's edition of Select British Classics.)

The Rambler, by S. Johnson, LL.D. Sixteenth edition. 1810. 3 vols. 8°. Seventeenth edition. 1816. 3 vols. 8°.

The Rambler, by Samuel Johnson, LL.D. *etc.* London: Printed for F. C. and J. Rivington, *etc.* 1820. 2 vols. 18°.

The Rambler, by S. Johnson, LL.D. Glasgow. 1824.

The Rambler, by S. Johnson, LL.D. London: Printed for Thomas Tegg, 73 Cheapside. 1826. 3 vols. 12°.

The Rambler, by Samuel Johnson, LL.D., with a sketch of the author's life by Sir Walter Scott, Bart. In two volumes. London: William Tegg. *n. d.* [1876]. 2 vols.

The Rambler and Idler, by Dr. Johnson; The Adventurer and The Connoisseur. 1877 [1876]. 8°.

It was also included in James Harrison's *British Classics*, 1785–7, and vol. i (1796); *The British Classics*, vols. xv–xviii (1809); *The British Essayists*, 1792–7, 4 vols.; *The British Essayists*, ed. Alexander Chalmers, vols. xix–xxii (eds. of 1803 and 1817), vols. xvi–xviii (1823), vols. xvi–xviii (Boston, U.S., 1856); *The British Essayists*, ed. Rev. L. T. Berguer (1823); *The British Essayists*, ed. James Ferguson, vols. xvi–xviii (2nd ed. 1823); *The British Essayists*, ed. R. Lynam, vols. xii, xiii (1827).

A French translation, *Le Rôdeur*, by C. G. Lambert, baron de Chamerolles, was published in 1827. 5 vols.

The Greenland tale of Anningait and Ajut (in Nos. 186 and 187) is reprinted in 'The Romancist and Novelist's Library', vol. i, No. 25 (1839). It was 'versified by a lady' (Anne Penny) in 1761, pp. 23, 1*s.*; and was included (pp. 91–115) in 'Poems, with a dramatic entertainment. By **** *****' (i.e. Anne Penny), in 1771, the dedication from the author to Jonas Hanway being dated Bloomsbury Square, May 13, 1771. It was also reproduced in an anonymous edition (1780) of her poems (pp. 85–106).

Kearsley published in 1788 (2 vols. 12mo) 'Beauties of the *Rambler*, *Adventurer*, *Connoisseur*, *World*, and *Idler*'. Selections from *The Rambler* were inserted in vol. iii, pp. 156–216, of *Classic Tales*; London, printed and published for John Hunt and Carew Reynell, 1807; and a volume of Selections, 'edited with preface and notes by W. Hale White' (*d.* March 1913), was published by the Clarendon Press at Oxford in 1907. Nathan Drake, M.D., brought out in 1809–10 two volumes of 'Essays . . . illustrative of *The Rambler*, *Adventurer*, and *Idler*', *etc.* They contained in vol. i, pp. 111–499, the 'Literary Life of Dr. Johnson'; and in vol. ii, pp. 35–236, 'Sketches of the occasional contributors to *The Rambler*, *Adventurer*, and *Idler*'.

Mr. Herbert Vivian produced (1901–2) *The Rambler* (intended as a continuation of Dr. Johnson's *Rambler*, the numeration and pagination following on). The luxurious edition, Nos. 209–221 (Saturday, June 29, 1901—Saturday, Sept. 21, 1901), was priced £2 10*s.* yearly, and copies were only sold to subscribers. The public edition ran from No. 222 to No. 260 (Saturday, Sept. 28, 1901—Thursday, June 26, 1902, No. 249 et seq. being issued on Thursdays), and was priced 6*d.*

Prologue for Milton's 'Comus'.

1750
Boswell, i. 227.

A New Prologue [by Samuel Johnson] spoken by Mr. Garrick, Thursday, April 5, 1750. At the Representation of Comus, for the benefit of Mrs. Elizabeth Foster, Milton's Grand-Daughter, and only surviving Descendant. London: Printed for J. Payne and J. Bouquet in Pater-Noster-Row. M,DCC,L. For Mrs. Elizabeth Foster. folio.

Collation: Title, p. [1]; Prologue, pp. [3]–5.

Johnson published in *The General Advertiser* for April 4 a letter drawing attention to the performance. Elizabeth Foster was the daughter of Abraham Clarke, who married Deborah Milton, the poet's youngest daughter. Her husband, Thomas Foster, was a 'weaver in Spitalfields', but in 1750 they kept a small chandler's shop in Cock Lane, Shoreditch. The profits of the performance amounted to £67 14*s.* 6*d.*, and the sum was made up to £130 by contributions from various persons (Genest, *English Stage*, iv. 298–9). Mrs. Foster died on May 9, 1754, at Islington, in her sixty-sixth year, and with her Milton's line is believed to have become extinct (Masson's *Life of Milton*, vi. 750–61).

The Prologue is inserted in the *Gent. Mag.* for April 1750, p. 183, and in Pearch's *Collection of Poems* (1770), i. 313–14.

Lauder and Milton.

1750
Boswell, i. 228–31.

An Essay on Milton's Use and Imitation of the Moderns, in his Paradise Lost. *Things unattempted yet in prose or rhime.* MILTON. London: Printed for J. Payne and J. Bouquet, in Pater-noster-row. MDCCL. 8°.

The dedication 'To the learned Universities of Oxford and Cambridge' is signed William Lauder. He had been engaged for several years, by communications in the *Gent. Mag.*, in endeavouring to convict Milton of wholesale plagiarism. To this volume Johnson contributed the Preface of four pages on the labours of Lauder, and the Postscript of three pages soliciting contributions for Milton's grand-daughter. The greater part of this Preface had appeared in the *Gent. Mag.* for Aug. 1747, p. 404, in support of Lauder's 'Proposals for printing, by Subscription, Hugonis Grotii Adamus Exsul, Tragoedia: With an *English*

A NEW

PROLOGUE

SPOKEN BY

Mr GARRICK,

THURSDAY, *April* 5, 1750.

AT THE

REPRESENTATION of COMUS,

FOR THE BENEFIT OF

Mrs ELIZABETH FOSTER,

MILTON's

Grand-Daughter, and only ſurviving Deſcendant.

LONDON:

Printed for J. PAYNE and J. BOUQUET in Pater-noſter-Row.
M,DCC,L.

For Mrs ELIZABETH FOSTER.

AN

ESSAY

ON

MILTON'S USE

AND

IMITATION

OF THE

MODERNS,

IN HIS

PARADISE LOST.

THINGS UNATTEMPTED YET IN PROSE
OR RHIME. MILTON.

LONDON:

Printed for J. PAYNE and J. BOUQUET,
IN PATER-NOSTER-ROW.

MDCCL.

version, and notes, and the lines imitated from it by *Milton* subjoined'.

Richard Richardson, late of Clare Hall, Cambridge (B.A. of Camb. 1745), brought out in 1747 a pamphlet, 'Zoilomastix, or a vindication of Milton from all the invidious charges of Mr. William Lauder'; but the decisive exposure of his fabrications was by John Douglas, afterwards Bishop of Salisbury, in 'Milton vindicated From the Charge of Plagiarism, Brought against him by Mr. Lauder, and Lauder himself convicted of several Forgeries and gross Impositions on the Public [Nov. 1750] 1751', the second edition of which, with postscript, appeared in 1756 as 'Milton no Plagiary'.

Johnson dictated to the culprit a confession, published as 'A Letter to the Reverend Mr. Douglas, occasioned By his Vindication of Milton.... By William Lauder, A.M. [Dec. 1750], 1751', in which he acknowledged his fraud, but had the effrontery to append to it 'testimonies concerning Mr. Lauder' and a disingenuous postscript. Lauder published on his own account 'An Apology for Mr. Lauder, in a Letter most humbly addressed to his Grace the Archbishop of Canterbury, MDCCLI', in which he owned the charge of Douglas to be just, but put forward some inadequate pleas in defence of his conduct.

The publishers, John Payne and Joseph Bouquet—it was probably through Johnson's influence that they had undertaken the publication—inserted in the papers an advertisement dated Nov. 28, 1750, that Lauder had on that day admitted his fault, and that they should for the future 'sell his Book only as a Master-piece of Fraud'. To the copies afterwards issued were prefixed 'A new Preface by the Booksellers', dated Dec. 1, 1750, consisting of four pages, and a Postscript dated Jan. 2, 1750–51, pp. v–viii.

An article by A. H. Millar on 'William Lauder, the literary forger', which sets out his various contributions in the *Gent. Mag.* from Jan. 1747, and the replies made to him both therein and in separate publications, appeared in *Blackwood's Edinburgh Magazine* for Sept. 1899, pp. 381–96. Lauder was perhaps attracted to the subject by an anonymous essay of 62 pp., probably the work of Richard Meadowcourt, upon 'Milton's imitations of the ancients in his Paradise Lost', which came out in 1741.

It is an interesting circumstance that Johnson, who was thus connected with Lauder's attempt to injure Milton's poetical reputation, cherished a lock of the blind poet's hair which at one time was the property of Addison. It afterwards belonged to Leigh Hunt, who gave it to Robert Browning. See Sotheby's Browning Sale Catalogue, May 1913, p. 157.

The Student.

1751
Boswell, i. 228.

The Student, or the Oxford and Cambridge Monthly Miscellany. Oxford. MDCCL (MDCCLI). 2 vols.

To this periodical Johnson contributed 'The Life of Dr. Francis Cheynel', ii. (1751) 260–69, 290–94, 331–4. The last part is signed 'S. J—n.' It is reproduced in the *Gentleman's Magazine*, xlv (1775), pp. 117–21, 176–8.

The Female Quixote.

1752
Boswell, i. 367.

The Female Quixote; or, the Adventures of Arabella. [Anon.: by Mrs. Charlotte Lennox.] MDCCLII. 2 vols. 12°.

Johnson wrote the dedication (pp. iii–vi), 'To the Right Honourable the Earl of Middlesex'. It was reproduced in the second edition, 1752, 2 vols.; in the 1783 edition (Harrison and Co.), and in the two issues of 1810 (one of them being vols. xxiv and xxv of *The British Novelists*, with a preface by Mrs. Barbauld).

Hill attributes to Johnson the short notice of the book in *Gent. Mag.*, March 1752, p. 146.

The Rev. John Mitford pointed out in the *Gent. Mag.* for 1843, pt. ii, p. 132, the praises of the author of *The Rambler* which are contained in this work (ii. 119, 314), and expressed the opinion that the eleventh chapter of the ninth and concluding book, which is described in the heading as 'being in the author's opinion the best chapter in this history', was written by Johnson. He reproduced this chapter in the next volume of the *Magazine* (1844, pt. i, pp. 41–8). Cf. also *Sylvanus Redivivus* (the Rev. John Mitford), by M. Houstoun (1889), pp. 115–16.

Shakespeare Illustrated.

1753
Boswell, i. 255.

Shakespear Illustrated: or the Novels and Histories, On which the Plays of Shakespear Are Founded, Collected and Translated from the Original Authors. With Critical Remarks. . . . By the Author of the Female Quixote. MDCCLIII. 2 vols.: third and last volume, MDCCLIV. 12°.

The dedication 'To . . . John, Earl of Orrery', vol. i pp. iii–xii, is by Johnson.

THE

ADVENTURER.

VOLUME the FIRST.

—Tentanda via est; quâ me quoque possim
Tollere humo, victorque virûm volitare per ora.

VIRG.

LONDON:

Printed for J. PAYNE, at POPE'S HEAD in PATER-NOSTER ROW.

MDCCLIII.

The Adventurer.

The Adventurer. Volume the First.... London: Printed for J. Payne, at Pope's Head in Pater-noster Row. MDCCLIII. Volume the Second. MDCCLIV. folio.

1753, 4
Boswell, i. 234, 252–5.

First number dated 'Tuesday, November 7,' 1752; last, 'Saturday, March 9, 1754'. No. XXXIX on Sleep, which appeared on March 20, 1753, is believed to have been in part, if not entirely, written by Johnson. It is signed T, the signature which he used throughout this periodical. The other numbers marked in this way are XLV (April 10, 1753), L (April 28), LVIII (May 26), LXVII (June 26), LXIX (July 3), LXXIV (July 21), LXXXI (Aug. 14), LXXXIV (Aug. 25), LXXXV (Aug. 28), XCII (Sept. 22), XCV (Oct. 2), XCIX (Oct. 16), CII (Oct. 27), CVII (Nov. 13), CVIII (Nov. 17), CXI (Nov. 27), CXV (Dec. 11), CXIX (Dec. 25), CXX (Dec. 29), CXXVI (Jan. 19, 1754), CXXVIII (Jan. 26), CXXXI (Feb. 5), CXXXVII (Feb. 26), CXXXVIII (Mar. 2).

Those signed by the letter T and the word Misargyrus [XXXIV (Mar. 3, 1753), XLI (Mar. 27), LIII (May 8), LXII (June 9)] may also be by Johnson, but it is suggested by Boswell that they are the composition of Richard Bathurst, M.D. Joseph Warton's services for the periodical were obtained by Johnson. John Hawkesworth was the editor, and the final article was signed by him and dated from Bromley in Kent, March 8, 1754. *The Adventurer* was included in the Collections of *The British Essayists*.

An article on *The Adventurer* in Willis's *Current Notes*, 1857, p. 13, contains some fresh information.

[On Johnson's authorship of LXXXI, see Hawkins, *Life of Samuel Johnson*, 1787, pp. 294, 309. An original copy of LXXXIV in the possession of the editor lacks the signature T. Ed.]

The Gentleman's Magazine.

An Account of the Life of the late Mr. Edward Cave. pp. 55–8.

1754
Boswell, i. 256.

The Dictionary.

In the second paragraph of his preface Johnson speaks of the dictionary-maker as the 'humble drudge that facilitates' the progress 'of Learning and Genius'. He accumulated in time his materials and then reduced them to method. In the domain of

ORTHOGRAPHY he found that 'caprice has long wantoned without control and vanity sought praise by petty reformation'. Our 'primitives' are derived from the Roman and Teutonic. Under the Roman he comprehended 'the *French* and provincial tongues, and under the *Teutonick* range the *Saxon*, *German*, and all their kindred dialects'. For the Teutonic etymologies he was 'commonly indebted to Junius and Skinner', to whose aid he rendered 'one general acknowledgment'.

The words which Johnson included in his Dictionary were mostly obtained from the dictionaries of his predecessors. Others were added 'by fortuitous and unguided excursions into books, and gleaned as industry should find, or chance should offer it, in the boundless chaos of a living speech'. Many words 'stand supported only by the name of *Bailey*, *Ainsworth*, *Philips*, or the contracted *Dict.*'. But he omitted a great number of words given in these dictionaries and never found by him in any book. Others he inserted upon his own attestation, claiming the same privilege with his predecessors 'of being sometimes credited without proof'.

Johnson expected that 'malignity would most frequently fasten' on his Explanations, for he could not hope 'to satisfy those who are perhaps not inclined to be pleased, since I have not always been able to satisfy myself'. His purpose was to exclude the testimony of living authors, and he had omitted them save when 'some performance of uncommon excellence excited my veneration, when my memory supplied me from late books with an example that was wanting, or when my heart, in the tenderness of friendship, solicited admission for a favourite name'. He had studiously endeavoured to collect his examples from writers before the Restoration, as after that date the 'original *Teutonick* character' had been 'deviating towards a *Gallick* structure and phraseology'. Sidney's work was his boundary, and he had made few excursions into the works of remoter writers. 'From the authours which rose in the time of *Elizabeth*, a speech might be formed adequate to all the purposes of use and elegance. If the language of theology were extracted from *Hooker* and the translation of the Bible; the terms of natural knowledge from *Bacon*; the phrases of policy, war, and navigation from *Raleigh*; the dialect of poetry and fiction from *Spenser* and *Sidney*; and the diction of common life from *Shakespeare*, few ideas would be lost to mankind, for want of *English* words, in which they might be expressed.'

He had devoted 'this book, the labour of years, to the honour of my country, that we may no longer yield the palm of philology to the nations of the continent. The chief glory of every people arises from its authours: whether I shall add anything by my own writings to the reputation of *English* literature, must be left to time: much of my life has been lost under the pressures of disease; much has been trifled away; and much has always been spent in provision for the day that was passing over me; but I shall not think my employment useless or ignoble, if by my assistance foreign nations, and distant ages, gain access to the propagators of knowledge, and understand the teachers of truth; if my labours afford light to the repositories of science, and add celebrity to *Bacon*, to *Hooker*, to *Milton*, to *Boyle*.'

Animated by this wish, he looked with pleasure on his book. 'A few wild blunders, and risible absurdities . . may for a time furnish folly with laughter, and harden ignorance in contempt; but useful diligence will at last prevail.' He wished the world to know 'that the *English Dictionary* was written with little assistance of the learned, and without any patronage of the great; not in the soft obscurities of retirement, or under the shelter of academick bowers, but amidst inconvenience and distraction, in sickness and in sorrow'. Horne Tooke could never read this part of the preface without tears.

When Johnson regarded the fate of previous dictionaries in ancient or foreign languages, 'I may surely be contented,' he says, 'without the praise of perfection, which, if I could obtain, in this gloom of solitude, what would it avail me? I have protracted my work till most of those whom I wished to please, have sunk into the grave, and success and miscarriage are empty sounds: I therefore dismiss it with frigid tranquillity, having little to fear or hope from censure or from praise.'

It was in the *Grammar of the English Tongue* that Johnson embodied the sentence, 'H seldom, perhaps never, begins any but the first syllable', which Wilkes fastened on with eagerness. In an essay (said by Boswell to have been inserted in the *Public Advertiser*, but I have not been able to find it) his sarcastic pen wrote the remark that 'the authour of this observation must be a man of quick *appre-hension* and of a most *compre-hensive* genius'. Johnson must have felt the force of the sneer, but he took no public notice of the ribald wit. In the third edition of the Dictionary, which came out in 1765, he inserted after 'never' the limitation 'except in compounded words', and in the fourth edition (1773) he omitted the words 'perhaps never except in compounded words', and added the sentence: 'It sometimes begins middle or final syllables in words compounded, as *blockhead*; or derived from the Latin, as *comprehended*.'

The Dictionary was reviewed with high praise by Adam Smith in the *Edinburgh Review*, No. 1, 1755, appendix, Article III, pp. 61–73. This review is reprinted in the *European Magazine*, xli (1802), pp. 249–54. The title-page of the 'abridgement' (1758, 2 vols., 8º), by Mr. [N.] Thomas, of Ainsworth's *Dictionary of the Latin Tongue* stated that in order to make the work more useful 'care has been taken to compare the English part with Mr. Johnson's celebrated Dictionary of the English Language'. The Rev. John Whitaker gave in his *History of Manchester*, Book II (1775), pp. 240–326, 'a specimen of an English-British dictionary', inserting in it between crotchets quotations which he described as 'the property of Dr. Johnson or his author'. Garrick's verses on the Dictionary are printed in the *Public Advertiser*, April 22, 1755, p. 2, col. i; in the *London Magazine*, April, 1755, p. 187. [Cf. the *Gentleman's Magazine*, April 1755, p. 190. Ed.]

The history of English dictionaries is contained in Henry B. Wheatley's 'Chronological Notices of the Dictionaries of the English Language' (*Trans. of the Philological Soc.*, 1865, pp. 218–93); Sir James A. H. Murray's *Evolution of English Lexicography* (Romanes Lecture, 1900); History of English Lexicography and a Catalogue of English Dictionaries, prefixed to *The Dictionary of the English Language*, by Joseph E. Worcester, 1863, pp. liii–lxv; and in 'English Dictionaries before Webster', by Percy W. Long, 1910 (reprinted from Bibliog. Soc. of America, Papers, vol. iv). The three dictionaries specified by Johnson are by Nathaniel Bailey (1721: numerous later editions), for whose dictionary see the volumes of *N. and Q.* from 1874 to 1877, and the paper of Mr. W. E. Axon (English Dialect Soc. 1883); Robert Ainsworth (*Latin Dictionary*, 1736; numerous editions); and Edward Phillips, Milton's nephew (1658; seventh edition, 1720); of all of whom memoirs are in the *D. N. B.* An interleaved copy of Bailey was used by Johnson as the repository for his articles. He marked his books with a black-lead pencil to show his amanuenses the quotations which he wished to make; they then transcribed each sentence on a separate slip of paper and arranged them in order. There was on view in the Exhibition of

Printing at Stationers' Hall, in June 1912, a copy of the first volume of *The Works of the most celebrated Minor Poets* (1749). It was from Dr. Johnson's library, and contained his marginal notes throughout the works of the Earl of Dorset, Earl of Halifax, and Sir Samuel Garth, particularizing the quotations to be made for the Dictionary.

Six amanuenses were employed, five of them being 'natives of North-Britain'. 'There were two Messieurs Macbean; Mr. Shiels who . . . partly wrote the *Lives of the Poets* to which the name of Cibber is affixed; Mr. Stewart . . . and a Mr. Maitland. The sixth . . . was Mr. Peyton, who, I believe, taught French and published some elementary tracts' (Boswell, *sub anno* 1748). He may have been the V. J. Peyton entered in the Catalogue of the British Museum Library as the author of some works of this nature. The fate of all of them was sad; they had no resource save the sympathy of Johnson. The elder Macbean, Alexander Macbean, became librarian to the third Duke of Argyll, on whose death he was left without a shilling. After struggling for his living by literature and receiving frequent guineas from Johnson and his friends, Macbean, through Johnson's influence with Lord Thurlow, was admitted into the Charterhouse on April 11, 1781. There he died on June 25, 1784, and was buried three days later. Robert Shiels died of consumption in May's Buildings (on the east side of St. Martin's Lane, London) on Dec. 27, 1753. Some particulars of 'Frank' Stewart, son of George Stewart, the Edinburgh bookseller, are given in Hone's *Year Book*, pp. 1043–7, but his authority for the notice is not specified. Stewart furnished the specimens of slang and the explanations of the words used in card-playing, and helped in the business part of the undertaking. Of Maitland, I know nothing. Peyton was steeped in poverty for many years. He died on April 1, 1776, a few days after his wife, and both were buried at Johnson's expense. The brutal Baretti called him 'a fool and a drunkard'.

The work was begun in Holborn, and ended in No. 17 Gough Square, on the north side of Fleet Street, the amanuenses working at their desks in 'an upper-room fitted up like a counting-house'. A description of a visit to it made more than eighty years ago (1832), 'not without labour and risk', is given by Thomas Carlyle in his essay on Croker's edition of Boswell (*Miscellanies*, iv. 82–3). Articles describing the house appeared in *The Times*, Oct. 15

and 17, 1887, the *Daily News*, Oct. 21, and the *Pall Mall Gazette*, Oct. 21. 'A Garret in Gough Square' is the title of an article in Mr. Austin Dobson's first series of *Eighteenth-century Vignettes* (1892), pp. 93–103.

When the Dictionary was upon the eve of publication, Dodsley informed Lord Chesterfield of its approaching appearance after many years of toil, and no doubt reminded him of the fact that the Plan of the work had been addressed to him. The scheming peer may have hoped that the Dictionary itself would be dedicated to him. At all events he sent to the fashionable paper of the day, *The World*, two essays (Nov. 28 and Dec. 5, 1754), lauding the enterprise and flattering the compiler, whom he had neglected for seven years. Johnson was not to be cajoled: he answered on Feb. 7, 1755, 'the honeyed words' with that terrible letter which was known to the town as soon as it was composed, but was not formally communicated to the world in print until it appeared in 1790, priced half a guinea, as 'The celebrated Letter from Samuel Johnson, LL.D., to Philip Dormer Stanhope, Earl of Chesterfield; now first published, with notes, by James Boswell, Esq. London: Printed by Henry Baldwin; for Charles Dilly in the Poultry.'

An entertaining volume entitled 'Leisure Moments in Gough Square, on the beauties and quaint conceits of Johnson's Dictionary, by the author of Shakspere's Draughts from the Living Water' (i. e. George Alfred Stringer), was published at Buffalo, N.Y., by Ulbrick and Kingsley in 1886. An article by Mr. Henry B. Wheatley on 'The Story of Johnson's Dictionary' is in *The Antiquary*, xi (1885), pp. 11–17. I have made an independent study of its volumes.

Johnson utilized the labours of many of his predecessors. Not infrequently he gives as his authority nothing but the abbreviation *Dict.*, which more often than not conceals the identity of Bailey. He quotes from the dictionary of Ephraim Chambers, the free-thinker, and from that compiled by the Jesuit priests at Trévoux; from the English translation of the *Universal Dictionary of Trade and Commerce* which was begun by Jacques Savary des Bruslons and augmented by Philémon Louis Savary, and from the *Mathematical Dictionary* of Edmund Stone. For special words he goes to the *Farrier's Dictionary*, the *Builder's Dictionary*, the *Military Dictionary*, Kane's *Campaigns*, and the *Lexicon Technicum* of John Harris. The definition of Becafico, 'a bird like a nightingale, feeding on figs and grapes: a fig-pecker', a word to be found in the poems of Pope, he cites from the *Spanish-English Dictionary* (1740) of Pedro Pineda.

Extracts from the Sermons of South,[1] Sprat, Atterbury, Bentley, Rogers,[2] and others, are to be found throughout Johnson's ponderous tomes. The religious treatises called *Decay of Piety* and *The Government of the Tongue*, which supply many instances of words, are by the author of *The Whole Duty of Man.* Medical terms are taken from the treatises of Quincy, Arbuthnot, Wiseman, Samuel Sharpe, Harvey (on consumption), Floyer[3] (on the humours), and Cheyne, who dealt with the gout and the maladies which spring from over-eating and over-drinking. Those relating to mathematics are mainly derived from Bishop Wilkins's treatise on *Mathematicall Magick.* Law phrases are illustrated from the writings of John Cowell and John Ayliffe, gardening and husbandry from the works of Philip Miller and John Mortimer, and scientific terms in general find their authorities in the volumes of Bacon and Boyle, Grew (*Cosmologia Sacra*) and Glanvill (*Scepsis Scientifica*), Woodward and Moxon (*Mechanical Exercises*), and in Sir Isaac Newton's *Treatise on Opticks.* Among the masters of English literature Dryden was an especial favourite with Johnson. His name is to be found on every page. But still he is not without chastisement. Two instances of the verb *perfectionate* are taken from his writings, but its use is sternly condemned: 'This is a word proposed by Dryden, but not received, nor worthy of reception.' Dryden gave a new meaning to the word *falsify* ('to pierce', 'to run through') and defended it at some length. The defence is embodied in the Dictionary with the keen comment

[1] I saw, in October, 1912, in the library at Lichfield Cathedral, a copy of 'Twelve Sermons preached upon Several Occasions by Robert South, D.D.', 1694, 2 vols. It is marked in the margin by Johnson to show the words which he wished to insert as illustrations in his Dictionary. It was bought from Francis Barber's daughter, and passed by gift to the Cathedral library.

[2] There were several persons called Rogers who published sermons. Hill thought (*Miscellanies of Johnson*, i, p. 6) that the writer was John Rogers, D.D. Johnson records in his Prayers that he read these sermons in 1734 (ib., p. 6) and about 1770 (ib., p. 124).

[3] Floyer, in his time the chief physician at Lichfield, overcame the terrors of asthma for many years, and was not defeated by his enemy until he reached the age of 85. Johnson, in the hope of finding a remedy against the same disease, borrowed from the Cathedral library at Lichfield, on July 17, 1784, Floyer's *Treatise of the Asthma*, and kept it until November 9. It was in vain. He arrived in London on November 16, and died on December 13.

that 'Dryden, with all this effort, was not able to naturalise the new signification, which I have never seen copied, except once by some obscure nameless writer, and which indeed deserves not to be received'. Spenser, under the word *quaid*, is said to have taken 'great liberties . . . for the poor convenience of his rhyme', and his use of *quaint* (meaning 'quailed') is condemned as a 'very licentious irregularity'. Not a few works which were at that time outside the reading of the ordinary man of letters, or now appear to be forgotten, came into the scope of Johnson's citations. Chapman's version of the *Iliad* and Richard Carew's charming *Survey of Cornwall* were carefully perused by him. Boyle against Bentley, Broome's notes on the *Odyssey*,[1] Henry Felton on the classics, are not often in these days taken from their shelves by the student, but Johnson had read them through and through. Who can now rival him in knowledge of Sir Kenelm Digby's *Nature of Bodies*, or Sir Henry Wotton's *Elements of Architecture*? How many of the younger generation have skipped through Bramston's *Man of Taste*, from which Johnson culled the word 'baubee'? I do not remember to have met in his Dictionary the name of Daniel Defoe, but *Robinson Crusoe* is the authority for 'awning'.

Malone, in his copy of the Dictionary which is now in the British Museum, gives references to sixteen contemporary writers who are quoted by Johnson. I doubt whether the list is complete, and whether any student will take the trouble to revise it. Johnson himself is inserted among the authorities by a quotation from *The Vanity of Human Wishes* of the verb *to lacerate*, and his tragedy of *Irene* furnishes the example of the verb *to intimidate*. An epilogue by Garrick is cited for *giggle*, while *plication* and *quaggy* are said to be 'somewhere in *Clarissa*'. Johnson's friend, the Rev. Francis Wise, of Elsfield, near Oxford, suggested the etymology for the Scotch word *warluck*; and the name of *Macbean*, probably his assistant, is appended to the lengthy explanation of the word *loord*, found in Spenser's *Pastorals*. [Mrs. Mulso is quoted from memory under *quatrain*: see *Gent. Mag.*, 1775, p. 88. Ed.]

Instances of Johnson's political and personal antipathies have often been extracted. *Excise* is the most notorious of them. The

[1] Strange to say, although Broome's 'Notes on the *Odyssey*' are often referred to in the Dictionary, a perfunctory notice only is given of them in the *Lives of the Poets*. Felton is referred to in the last paragraph but one of Johnson's Life of Cowley in that collection, and in the third paragraph of the very meagre notice of Duke.

tax was favoured by Sir Robert Walpole, the leader of the Whigs, and was consequently obnoxious to a high Tory. Johnson denounced it as 'a hateful tax levied upon commodities, and adjudged not by the common judges of property, but wretches hired by those to whom excise is paid'. This definition was known to have been submitted by the Commissioners of Excise to the Attorney-General, Murray, afterwards Lord Mansfield, for his opinion whether the words should not be brought into the law courts as a libel. Boswell was not allowed to have a copy of the case: Croker was more fortunate. Murray thought it a libel, but suggested that the author should be allowed 'an opportunity of altering his definition'. It was not changed. Time has taken the sting out of this derivation, but what victim of dabbling in the City will not heartily accept the lexicographer's definition of a *stockjobber* as 'a low wretch who gets money by buying and selling shares in the funds'?

Whig was defined as 'the name of a faction'. *Tory* was 'a cant term, derived, I suppose, from an Irish word signifying a savage'. But one of his rolling sentences then elevated this species of politician into 'One who adheres to the antient constitution of the state, and the apostolical hierarchy of the church of England'. *Oats* was 'a grain, which in England is generally given to horses, but in Scotland supports the people'; and the then Lord Elibank retorted, 'Very true, and where will you find such *men* and such horses?' *Renegado* is explained as 'One who deserts to the enemy; a revolter'; but Johnson, with an allusion to Lord Gower, who abandoned the Jacobite cause, had added in the manuscript 'sometimes we say a Gower'. The printer, William Strahan, wiser than the author, struck the words out.

Johnson could not abide the astute scribbler known as David Mallet. The instance which he gave in his unabridged dictionary of the word *alias* was 'Simpson *alias* Smith, *alias* Baker; that is, *otherwise* Smith, *otherwise* Baker'. When he was condensing his two folio tomes into the two volumes in octavo which he brought out in 1756 he pilloried the object of his dislike in the example: 'Mallet *alias* Malloch; that is, *otherwise* Malloch'; but even Johnson did not hate enough to repeat the words of the old definition, 'often used in the trials of criminals, whose danger has obliged them to change their names'.[1]

[1] Many years later, when writing the Life of James Thomson in the *Lives of the Poets*, he took the trouble to point out that the lines prefixed to *Winter* were signed Malloch.

If he attacked others he did not spare himself. His own profession of *lexicographer* was degraded into the business of 'a harmless drudge, that busies himself in tracing the original, and detailing the signification of words'. Johnson had many places of abode, but his permanent address for many years was that of *Grub Street*. This he defines as 'originally the name of a street in Moorfields in London, much inhabited by writers of small histories, dictionaries, and temporary poems; whence any mean production is called *grubstreet*'. He adds two lines of Greek—

> Χαῖρ' Ἰθάκη μετ' ἄεθλα μετ' ἄλγεα πικρὰ
> Ἀσπασίως τεὸν οὖδας ἱκάνομαι.

Which may be thus translated—

> 'Hail Ithaca, after strife and after bitter trials,
> Gladly I approach thy threshold.'

This quotation is taken, as I learn from Professor Bensley of Aberystwyth, from *Epigrammatum Anthologia Palatina* IX 458 (Vol. II. p. 95 of the edition of 1872). Johnson omitted the word θαλάσσης at the end of the first line as unsuitable for his purpose.[1]

Johnson's interpretation of the word *pension*, 'an allowance made to any one without an equivalent. In England it is generally understood to mean pay given to a state hireling for treason to his country', was often brought up against him when he had accepted one for himself. It formed the main topic of the twelfth number of Wilkes's *North Briton* (see above, p. 8), and those who imitated Wilkes in attacking Johnson did not neglect to revive it.

Johnson's notions of words which should not fall from the lips of the learned or the polite were extensive and peculiar. A *dab* for 'a man expert at something' was confined to 'low language'. Still it has been adopted in recent years by Thackeray and Helps, although the latter prints it in inverted commas and qualifies the use by the words 'as we used to say at Eton'. *Death's-door* 'is now a low phrase'; *deft* is declared 'obsolete', but alas! I find it still used in the works of Carlyle, Charlotte Brontë, and George

[1] A second Greek quotation is introduced under *To rest*, viz.:

> Ἱερὸν ὕπνον
> Κοιμᾶται· θνήσκειν μὴ λέγε τοὺς ἀγαθούς.

[He sleeps a holy sleep; say not that the good die.]

This is taken from the epigrams of Callimachus, No. 10, line 2 (Blomfield, ed. 1815, p. 56).

Eliot. *Fib* is 'a cant word among children', *flirtation* 'a cant word among women', *fuss* 'a low cant word' everywhere, and *fidge* is 'a cant word', implying, in Scotland, agitation. *Finesse* is 'an unnecessary word which is creeping into the language'; so successfully, indeed, that it is now used daily by thousands of card-players, and has found its way into the works of our best writers.

Johnson tells us that the *l* in *fault* 'is sometimes sounded, and sometimes mute. In conversation it is generally suppressed'; this was the regular pronunciation in the time of Swift and Pope. *Flimsy* baffled him. He confessed 'of this word I know not any original, and suspect it to have crept into our language from the cant of manufacturers'. *Fraischeur*, for freshness, coolness, was 'a word foolishly innovated by Dryden'. Johnson was incorrect. It had been used before that age; since then it has been adopted by Thackeray. To *freak*, that is, to variegate, was, 'I suppose, Scotch, brought into England by Thomson'.

To giggle 'is retained in Scotland', but Cowper spoke of Thurlow and himself as 'giggling and making giggle' with his feminine cousins in Southampton Row. *Gratefulness*, set down as 'now obsolete', has come since 1755 from the pen of Charles Lamb and from many others. *Guerdon*, 'a word now no longer in use', will be found in the works of Cowper, Scott, and Tennyson, and in the popular hymns of John Mason Neale. 'A barbarous term of heraldry' is the stigma attached to the word *Gules*.

I pass on to other letters. *Ignoramus*, though finding favour in the eyes of South, is 'a low word'. To *ignore*, in the sense of being ignorant of, occurs frequently in the works of Boyle. Johnson contended that 'it has not been received', but since 1830, as De Quincey pointed out, the word has passed into more frequent currency. To *jeopard* is 'obsolete'. *Jeopardy* is 'not now in use'. *Job* becomes 'a low word now much in use, of which I cannot tell the etymology'; *kidney*, as in the Shakespearian phrase, 'a man of my kidney', is only employed 'in ludicrous language'.

Leeward and *Windward*, though of opposite meaning, are both described as 'towards the wind'. When Johnson came to the word *Lich*, a carcase, he thought of the beloved city of his birth and inserted in the definition the glowing apostrophe, *Salve magna parens*. The word *Shaw*, a thicket, brought before his eyes the scenes of his youth; he pens the words, 'a tuft of trees near Lichfield is called Gentle *shaw*'. He would, too, say a word for his early friends. *Magazine* had come to signify 'a miscellaneous pamphlet, from a periodical miscellany named the *Gentleman's Magazine* by *Edward Cave*'. Another of these early friends made a suggestion to Johnson which it is difficult to account for. This was Derrick, who is said for some unknown reason to have proposed the omission of the word *ocean*. The advice, if given, was not adopted, and the word occurs both as noun and adjective, with quotations in the first case from Shakespeare and Locke, and in the second from Milton. The authority for Derrick's suggestion is John Taylor in *Records of My Life*, i. 7, but the story seems to be an inaccurate version of the anecdote recorded in Mr. John Murray's *Johnsoniana*, 1836, p. 423, No. 653.

Loon is 'now used only in Scotland', yet Coleridge, and Barham of *The Ingoldsby Legends*, two very different spirits, have both condescended to adopt it. *Lesser* is stigmatized as 'a barbarous corruption of less'. *Lingo* is characterized as 'a low cant word', but Kingsley and Jowett have both embodied it in their writings. *Monsieur* becomes 'a term of reproach for a Frenchman'. The example is from Shakespeare's *Cymbeline*; nowadays we should quote Johnson's own line, 'All sciences a fasting Monsieur knows'. *Nonplus*, *plaguy*, *prog*, *rantipole*, and *slapdash* are all of them low words. *Prig* is cant; *piping*, Shakespeare's *piping* time of peace, is 'only used in low language'. The word *precarious* elicits the comment that 'no word is more unskilfully used than this with its derivatives. It is used for uncertain in all its senses', and under *precariousness* Johnson gives an instance of this impropriety from Sharp's *Surgery*, 'a book otherwise elegantly written'. *Predal* is 'not countenanced from analogy', and the sole instance of its use is that repeated in the N.E.D. Sometimes, says Johnson, *preeminence* is 'written to avoid the junction of *ee*, *preheminence*', but no citation of such spelling is appended to this statement. *Raiment* is little used 'but in poetry'; the *ready*, for money in hand, is a 'low word', and so it remains. To *reck* is 'out of use' but 'still retained in Scotland'.[1]

Johnson assigns to the word *relevant* one meaning only, that

[1] Dugald Stewart comments (*Works*, v. 230) on the fact that although Johnson uses the word *picturesque* in his definition of love, it does not find a place in the Dictionary.

of 'relieving', which he takes from Bailey's Dictionary, and he gives no example of its use. *Restrict* he labels as 'a word scarce English'. Of *revenue* he remarks that 'its accent is uncertain': in this year (1913) it is pronounced revēnue in official circles, revĕnue in ordinary speech. *Ruse* is heartily damned as 'a French word neither elegant nor necessary'. To *sconce*, in the sense of 'to mulct, to fine', is condemned as 'a word used in the universities', 'a low word which ought not to be retained', but Johnson used it himself and Hill inserted it (I. 59) in the notes to his edition of Boswell. Harsh treatment is assigned to *shabby*. It is 'a word that has crept into conversation and low writing, but ought not to be admitted into the language'. To *sham* and to *squabble* are 'low' words; to *sojourn* is 'almost out of use'. *Souvenance* is dismissed as 'a French word which with many more is now happily disused'. *Spick and span* meets with a harsh fate. Johnson did not expect to have found it 'authorised by a polite writer'. It is 'a low word', but he quotes it from Butler, Burnet, and Swift. *Stingo* for 'old beer' is 'a cant word' and *stingy* a 'low cant word'. The *sublime* is 'a Gallicism, but now naturalized'; *succumb*, on the other hand, is 'not in use, except among the Scotch'.

Tea,—who does not associate the name of Johnson with tea-drinking?—tea is 'a Chinese plant, of which the infusion has lately been much drunk in Europe'. *Tiff* is treated as 'a low word', illegitimate almost, for it is 'I suppose without etymology'. 'A burlesque word' is the note pinned to *tiny*; the use of *wee* in Scotland is illustrated by 'a *wee* bit'. 'Two slip-shod muses traipse along' is a line of Pope, yet *traipse* is 'a low word, I believe, without any etymology'. It is given again under *trape*, and then said to be 'used only of women'. To *transpire* for 'to escape from secrecy to notice', a word much debated even in this century, is denounced as 'a sense lately innovated from France, without necessity'. Lord Marchmont in 1778 confided to Boswell the reason of this condemnation. The word was first used by Bolingbroke, whom Johnson hated, and it was therefore denounced by him. That peer had a mania for introducing French words into the language of his native land. Writing to Swift on Sept. 12, 1724, he speaks of the 'architects et les *concierges*—we want that word in English' (*Swift's Letters* (1912), iii. 208). *Twittle-twattle*, 'a ludicrous reduplication of *twattle*', is sent to Hades as 'a vile word'. The examples of these words are taken from

L'Estrange, in whose writings the slang phrases of the day abound.[1]

Usquebaugh finds a place in the Dictionary with a commendation of the 'Irish sort' for 'its pleasant and mild flavour', and a disparagement of the 'Highland sort' through being 'somewhat hotter; . . . in Scottish they call it whisky'. The quotation of *wheedle* from Locke couples it with *sham* and seems to include it among 'cant' words. *Wont* for custom, habit, is described as 'out of use'.

The definitions of Johnson have often formed the subject of jest through his love of explaining an ordinary word in grandiloquent terms. *Network* is the best known of these portentous descriptions. The definition runs: 'any thing reticulated or decussated, at equal distances, with interstices between the intersections'. In its turn *reticulated* becomes 'made of network; formed with interstitial vacuities'. Another good sample of this high and mighty language is *blister*, a harmless trouble in ordinary life, but to Johnson 'a pustule formed by raising the cuticle from the cutis, and filled with serous blood'. So, too, the *cough* of daily life is magnified into 'a convulsion of the lungs, vellicated by some sharp serosity', and *dross* is nought but 'the recrement or despumation of metals'.

Pastern, as every one knows, was to him 'the knee of an horse', and equally familiar to every one is the frank confession of the blunder which he made to a lady at Plymouth, 'ignorance, Madam, pure ignorance'. *Loll* and some other words drove him into a public confession of inability. 'Perhaps it might be contemptuously derived from *lollard*, a name of great reproach before the reformation; of whom one tenet was, that all trades not necessary to life are unlawful.' *Pitman* is confined to the labourer 'that in sawing timber works below in the pit'. The earliest example of its use for a collier which is given in the N.E.D. is dated in 1761. The word *top-sawyer*, the opposite to Johnson's *pitman*, I do not find in his work. *Scavenger* is magnified to the dignity of 'a petty magistrate, whose province is to keep the streets clean'. 'As much as the mouth will hold' is the quantity allotted to a *sip*, but enormous indeed would the sip of Johnson's 'capacious mouth' seem to the nymphs of Pope.

[1] *Wiggle-waggle* is a word said to have been used by Johnson in conversation (*Madame d'Arblay*, ed. Dobson, i. 113), but it is not in his Dictionary.

The time that I have spent in the annotation of the Dictionary —I have done my reading in *sips* and have spread the pleasure over many days of delight—has been well expended. Every page possesses a joy. Let me give a few more—necessarily a very few more—instances of the Dictionary's singularities. Even in those days the word *absentee* was 'used commonly with regard to Irishmen living out of their country'. *Bursars* are defined as 'students sent as exhibitioners to the universities in Scotland by each presbytery', but these small emoluments are not necessarily in the gift of the presbyteries; and the word *exhibitioner* is not in the Dictionary. *Anachorite* is 'sometimes viciously written *anchorite*'. Addison is responsible for the spelling *aisle*, but he wrote the word thus 'perhaps improperly'; it should be written *aile*. *Antiquary*, as an adjective, is 'improper'. In Johnson's time the adjective *antiquarian* does not seem to have been in existence. *Balliards* is now, he says, 'corruptly called *billiards*'. 'Perhaps a fortuitous and cant word, without etymology' is the punishment inflicted on *chouse*.

The spelling of *diocess* was, a generation ago, compulsory in the columns of *The Times*. It is supported by the authority of Johnson's *Dictionary*. An odd and unnoticed blunder occurs among the illustrations of this word. The quotation from Raleigh's *Essays* speaks of 'Constance in Normandy'. This error for Coutances occurs in the passage in the 1650 edition of Sir Walter Raleigh's *Essays*, G 6, and it was perpetuated in all the subsequent editions of the Dictionary, even in that of Todd. 'Publisher' is the first meaning assigned to the word *editor*, but no example of that sense is given.

The great value of Johnson's Dictionary lay in the excellence of its definitions. Henry Thomas Buckle, the author of *The History of Civilization in England*—you will look in Johnson in vain for that word *civilization*, and when he was revising his work for the fourth edition (March 23, 1772) he refused the suggestion of Boswell for its admission—read it 'to enlarge his vocabulary' (*Life*, by A. H. Huth, i. 40). When Robert Browning adopted literature as his profession 'he qualified himself for it by reading and digesting the whole of Johnson's Dictionary. We cannot be surprised to hear this of one who displayed so great a mastery of words, and so deep a knowledge of the capacities of the English language' (*Life*, by Mrs. Orr, 1908 ed., p. 50). 'Had Johnson left nothing but his *Dictionary*', says Carlyle in his *Heroes, Hero-*

Worship and The Heroic in History (Collected Works, vol. xii Lib. ed., pp. 215–16), 'one might have traced there a great intellect, a genuine man. Looking to its clearness of definition, its general solidity, honesty, insight, and successful method, it may be called the best of all Dictionaries.' The great defect of the Dictionary was in the etymologies. Johnson was no philologer. Macaulay, in his downright way, dubbs him 'a wretched etymologist'.

Truly the undertaking was sublime, and its fulfilment noble. Nothing like it, nothing within measurable distance of it, had hitherto appeared in the English language. We should all bow down before such a monument of industry and talent, and the world at large did make its obeisance unto the author as the king of English literature. The work was urgently called for and eagerly devoured. No similar dictionary has passed through so many editions, abridged, unabridged, and revised, as the language expanded and researches into the past went deeper; and it remained for a century the unrivalled authority for the English language.

THE FIRST EDITIONS.

1755
Boswell, i. 182–90, 256–301.

A Dictionary of the English Language: in which The Words are deduced from their Originals, and Illustrated in their Different Significations by Examples from the best Writers. To which are prefixed, A History of the Language, and An English Grammar. By Samuel Johnson, A.M. In Two Volumes. Vol. I (II). Cum tabulis animum censoris sumet honesti: Audebit quæcunque parum splendoris habebunt, Et sine pondere erunt, et honore indigna ferentur. Verba movere loco; quamvis invita recedant, Et versentur adhuc intra penetralia Vestæ: Obscurata diu populo bonus eruet, atque Proferet in lucem speciosa vocabula rerum, Quæ priscis memorata Catonibus atque Cethegis, Nunc situs informis premit et deserta vetustas. Hor. London, Printed by W. Strahan, For J. and P. Knapton; T. and T. Longman; C. Hitch and L. Hawes; A. Millar; and R. and J. Dodsley. MDCCLV.

2 vols. folio, price 90*s.* *Collation*:—Vol. I. Title-page; Preface, 10 pp.; The History of the English Language, 27 pp.; A Grammar of the English Tongue, 13 pp.; Directions to the Book-Binder, 1 p.; General Dictionary (A–K inclusive) in rest of vol.

A

DICTIONARY

OF THE

ENGLISH LANGUAGE:

IN WHICH

The WORDS are deduced from their ORIGINALS,

AND

ILLUSTRATED in their DIFFERENT SIGNIFICATIONS

BY

EXAMPLES from the beſt WRITERS.

TO WHICH ARE PREFIXED,

A HISTORY of the LANGUAGE,

AND

AN ENGLISH GRAMMAR.

BY SAMUEL JOHNSON, A. M.

IN TWO VOLUMES.

VOL. I.

Cum tabulis animum cenſoris ſumet honeſti:
Audebit quæcunque parum ſplendoris habebunt,
Et ſine pondere erunt, et honore indigna ferentur.
Verba movere loco; quamvis invita recedant,
Et verſentur adhuc intra penetralia Veſtæ:
Obſcurata diu populo bonus eruet, atque
Proferet in lucem ſpecioſa vocabula rerum,
Quæ priſcis memorata Catonibus atque Cethegis,
Nunc ſitus informis premit et deſerta vetuſtas. HOR.

LONDON,
Printed by W. STRAHAN,
For J. and P. KNAPTON; T. and T. LONGMAN; C. HITCH and L. HAWES;
A. MILLAR; and R. and J. DODSLEY.
MDCCLV.

Vol. II. Rest of Dictionary (L–Z inclusive). The whole unpaged. Published on April 15 [see *Monthly Review*, April, 1755, p. 324. Ed.].

Of the three copies in the British Museum, one has on the title-page the stamp of Edmund Burke, Beaconsfield, and at the end of each volume are some inserted leaves with MS. notes. Horne Tooke's copy of the Dictionary, with his annotations, produced at the sale of his books the sum of £200.

The degree of A.M. was granted by the University of Oxford on Feb. 20, 1755. The diploma, which belonged to Boswell, is now Addit. MS. 38,063 in the British Museum.

1755–6 A Dictionary of the English Language, *etc.* The Second edition. London: Vol. I: MDCCLV. Vol. II: MDCCLVI.

1765 A Dictionary of the English Language, *etc.* In Two Volumes. The Third Edition. Cum tabulis *etc.* London, Printed by W. Strahan, For A. Millar, T. Longman, J. Dodsley, W. Strahan, J. Rivington, R. Baldwin, L. Hawes and W. Clarke and R. Collins, R. Horsfield, W. Johnston, W. Owen, T. Caslon, B. Law, J. Fletcher, Z. Stuart, D. Wilson, T. Becket and P. A. De Hondt, and W. Nicoll. MDCCLXV.

Collation as in first edition. An imperfect copy of the portion ranging from 'A' to 'Jailer' of this edition, interleaved and containing additions and corrections by Johnson and others, is in the Library of the British Museum.

1773 A Dictionary of the English Language, *etc.* ... By Samuel Johnson [*without the letters* A.M.]. In Two Volumes. The Fourth Edition, revised by the Author. Cum tabulis *etc.* ... London, Printed by W. Strahan, For W. Strahan, J. & F. Rivington, T. Davies, J. Hinton, L. Davis: Hawes, Clarke & Collins; W. Johnston, W. Owen, T. Caslon, S. Crowder, T. Longman, B. Law, E. & C. Dilly, J. Dodsley, Z. Stuart, Becket & De Hondt, J. Knox, T. Cadell, Wilson & Nicoll, W. Nicoll, G. Robinson, Jo. Johnson, J. Robson, Richardson & Urquhart, and M. Hingeston. MDCCLXXIII.

2 vols. folio. One copy of this edition at the British Museum is in three volumes, although the title-page of each volume says that the work is 'in two volumes'. The explanation probably is that it was found too bulky for general use when bound

in two volumes only, and that it was forgotten to alter the title-page.

An additional leaf was inserted after the Preface (or after the Directions to the Book-binder) with the following undated 'Advertisement to the Fourth Edition':

'Many are the works of human industry, which to begin and finish are hardly granted to the same man. He that undertakes to compile a Dictionary, undertakes that, which, if it comprehends the full extent of his design, he knows himself unable to perform. Yet his labours, though deficient, may be useful, and with the hope of this inferior praise, he must incite his activity, and solace his weariness.

'Perfection is unattainable, but nearer and nearer approaches may be made; and finding my Dictionary about to be reprinted, I have endeavoured, by a revisal, to make it less reprehensible. I will not deny that I found many parts requiring emendation, and many more capable of improvement. Many faults I have corrected, some superfluities I have taken away, and some deficiencies I have supplied. I have methodised some parts that were disordered, and illuminated some that were obscure. Yet the changes or additions bear a very small proportion to the whole. The critic will now have less to object, but the student who has bought any of the former copies, needs not repent; he will not, without nice collation, perceive how they differ, and usefulness seldom depends upon little things.

'For negligence or deficience, I have perhaps not need of more apology than the nature of the work will furnish; I have left that inaccurate which never was made exact, and that imperfect which never was completed.'

Johnson's corrected copy of the fourth edition, formerly the property of Sir Joshua Reynolds, passed to Lord Spencer's library, and is now in the John Rylands Library at Manchester.

Boswell (ii. 155) on March 23, 1772, found him busy on it, and suggested some additions, but he would not admit *civilization.* Peyton was again acting as amanuensis.

A Dictionary of the English Language, *etc.* Dublin: Printed for Thomas Ewing, in Capel-Street, M.DCCLXXV.

2 vols. quarto. *Collation.* Vol. I. Title-page, 1 p.; Advertisement (as in 1773 ed., but signed S. Johnson); Subscribers' names, 4 pp.; Preface, 12 pp.; History of the English Language, 31 pp.;

Grammar of the English Tongue, 18 pp.; General Dictionary, letters A–K inclusive, in rest of vol. Vol. II. Rest of Dictionary.

Malone's copy of this edition, bound in three volumes, is in the British Museum. Inserted in it are two portraits of Johnson and a sheet, published in 1793, containing facsimiles of his handwriting. A memorandum, characteristic of the owner, on the second prefatory leaf of the first volume, says, 'August 18, 1809. 1052 manuscript remarks in the three volumes of this most valuable Dictionary.' Another note on the third leaf records the facts: 'For the greater part of the Manuscript Observations I am answerable; those to which D. is subscribed were written by Samuel Dyer, the principal author of Junius.' Malone gives references to sixteen moderns quoted by Johnson, among them being Garrick, under *giggle*.

A Dictionary of the English Language, *etc.* By Samuel Johnson, LL.D. In two volumes. The fifth edition. London. MDCCLXXXIV.

A Dictionary of the English Language, *etc.* By Samuel Johnson, LLD. In two volumes. The sixth edition. . . . London. Printed for J. F. and C. Rivington, L. Davis, T. Payne and Son, *etc.* M.DCCLXXXV.

2 vols. quarto. Prefixed are the original Preface, History of the English Language, &c., and the Advertisement to the fourth edition. Malone says that this edition was published both in folio and quarto.

[James] Harrison's edition, with his Life of the Author. A Dictionary of the English Language, *etc.* By Samuel Johnson, LL.D. Cum tabulis, *etc.* London: Printed for Harrison and Co. N° 18 Paternoster Row. MDCCLXXXVI.

1 vol. folio. Prefixed to title-page is a portrait of Johnson, 'Engraved by Heath, from an Original Painting by Opie, in the Possession of Mr. Harrison. The Sarcophagus, and other Ornamental Parts, designed by Mr. R. Smirke.' Then follow (i) Advertisement to Mr. Harrison's life of the author; (ii) The Life; (iii) Editor's Preface; (iv) Plan of the Dictionary; (v) Original Preface, &c.

This edition purports to 'comprehend the Genuine Original Edition, printed verbatim, without the hosts of typographical inaccuracies multiplied in subsequent impressions; and retains some hundred elucidations injudiciously struck out from all other editions; while it furnishes, in a Supplement of barely three pages, the boasted additional words, not only in the copy bequeathed to Sir Joshua Reynolds, whose name has been so shamefully prostituted on the occasion, but in all the other editions taken together.' This 'Supplement of additional words, introduced by Dr. Johnson, subsequent to his original edition, from which the foregoing work has been literally reprinted', consists of a title-page and three pages of Dictionary.

A Dictionary of the English Language, *etc.* By Samuel Johnson, LL.D. In two volumes. The eighth edition; corrected and revised... London. Printed for J. Johnson, C. Dilly, G. G. and J. Robinson [and others]. 1799.

2 vols. quarto. With the original Preface, History of the English Language, &c., and Advertisement to the fourth edition. The Dictionary is said to have been published by Campe, of Hamburg, in this year (two vols. 8vo).

A Dictionary of the English Language, *etc.* By *Samuel* Johnson, LL.D. In four volumes. The ninth edition; corrected and revised. London. Printed for Longman, Hurst, Rees, and Orme, Paternoster-Row [& others]. 1805.

4 vols. octavo. Prefixed is a 'Life of Dr. Samuel Johnson, by J[ohn] Aikin, M.D., extracted from the General Biography'.

A Dictionary of the English Language, *etc.* By Samuel Johnson, LL.D. In two volumes. The tenth edition, corrected and revised. . . . London. Printed for F. & C. Rivington, J. Walker, W. Lowndes [& others]. 1810.

2 vols. quarto. With original Preface, History of the English Language, &c., and Advertisement to fourth edition, dated 1773. Malone says that the 'Tenth edition was published in Nov. 1810, price £5 5s. od., probably more incorrect than any of the preceding'.

A Dictionary of the English Language, *etc.* By Samuel Johnson, LL.D.

Philadelphia, 1818. First American edition.

A Dictionary of the English Language, *etc.* By Samuel Johnson, LL.D. With numerous corrections, and with the addition of several thousand words, as also with additions to the history of the language, and to the grammar. By the Rev. H. J. Todd, M.A., F.S.A., Chaplain in ordinary to his majesty, and keeper of the Archbishop of Canterbury's records. In four volumes. London: Printed for Longman, Hurst, Rees, Orme, and Brown [& others]. 1818.

4 vols. quarto. Prefixed to vol. i are: (1) Dedication to George, Prince of Wales, 2 pages; (2) Advertisement, four pages, signed H. J. Todd and dated August 1, 1814; (3) Introduction, pp. iii–viii, signed Henry John Todd and dated May 29, 1818; (4) the original Preface of Dr. Johnson, pp. ix–xxvi; (5) The History of the English Language, by Dr. Johnson, with additions by the Rev. Mr. Todd. Some 'Additions and corrections', and the 'Grammar of the English Tongue' with notes by Todd, are printed at the end of the fourth volume. Last of all comes two appendixes (6 pp.) and a list of most of the authors and their writings quoted in the Dictionary (18 pp.). The Introduction shows that Todd had the use of Malone's interleaved copy; the second copy annotated by the Rev. Mr. Bagshaw, of Bromley (references to whom are given in *N. and Q.*, 11th S., viii. 50, 97, 157; this may have been the copy with his notes which came into the possession of Sion College, through the bequest of the Rev. William Clements, its librarian, who died April 8, 1799. *Gent. Mag.*, 1799, pt. i, p. 375; E. H. Pearce, *Sion College*, 1913, pp. 75, 85, 158, 297–302, 357–8); an interleaved copy with notes by the Rev. Mr. [Samuel] Henshall,—see the *D. N. B.*; another copy with marginal remarks by the Rev. Mr. Eyre; and several books and papers belonging to Horne Tooke. It also names several friends from whom he had assistance.

Eyre was the Rev. James Eyre, an account of whom is given in the Memoirs of Samuel Parr, *Works*, vol. i, pp. 601–6. The booksellers gave £50 for his copy of Johnson's Dictionary.

A Dictionary of the English Language, *etc.* . . . In three volumes. The second edition. London: Printed for Longman, Rees, Orme, Brown, and Greene. 1827.

Title-page, p. i; Dedication to the King, pp. iii–iv, and Preface, pp. v–vi, both dated Feb. 12, 1827; Advertisement, to his first edition, pp. vii–x; his Introduction with some new notes, pp. xi–xv; Dr. Johnson's preface, pp. 1–14; History of the English Language, &c., pp. 15–99; Grammar of the English Tongue, pp. 101–26; two Alphabets, pp. 127–8; Words considered by Mr. Horne Tooke as false English, pp. 129–30.

There also appeared, in connexion with Todd's edition:

(1) A Supplement to Dr. Johnson's Dictionary of the English Language; adapted both to the common editions, and to that of the Rev. H. J. Todd. By the Rev. John Seager, B.A. London. 1819.

Dedicated to George Isaac Huntingford, D.D., Bishop of Hereford.

(2) A Dictionary of the English Language . . . by Samuel Johnson, LL.D. Abridged from the Rev. H. J. Todd's corrected and enlarged quarto edition. By Alexander Chalmers, F.S.A. London, 1820.

(3) Todd's Johnson's Dictionary of the English Language in miniature, *etc.* . . . By Thomas Rees, LL.D., F.S.A. London, 1826.

(4) Johnson's English Dictionary, as improved by Todd, and abridged by Chalmers; with Walker's Pronouncing Dictionary, combined: [ed. J. E. Worcester]. Boston, 1828.

(5) Johnson's Dictionary improved by Todd, abridged for the use of schools. With the addition of Walker's pronunciation . . . and an appendix of Americanisms; Boston, 1839. Preface dated June 1828.

Later Editions.

A Dictionary of the English Language, *etc.* By Samuel Johnson, LL.D. In two volumes. London: Printed for G. & J. Offor, W. Allason, R. Akerman [& others]. 1824.

2 vols., quarto. Prefixed are Dr. Johnson's original Preface, History of the English Language, &c.

Dictionary of the English Language, by Samuel Johnson. . . . Heidelberg, 1827. 2 vols.

A Dictionary of the English Language, *etc.* By Samuel Johnson, LL.D. In two volumes, 1835–7. 4°.

Dictionary of the English Language, by Samuel Johnson. Verbatim from the author's last folio edition. 1852.

1866–70 Latham and Todd.

A Dictionary of the English Language. By Robert Gordon Latham . . . Founded on that of Dr. Samuel Johnson as edited by the Rev. H. J. Todd, M.A. With numerous emendations and additions. In two volumes. Vol. I, pt. i. London: Longmans, Green & Co. [and others], 1866.—Vol. I, pt. ii, 1866, Vol. II, pt. i, 1870. Vol. II, pt. ii, 1870. Issued in 36 parts, price 3*s.* 6*d.* each.

Title-page; Author's [*i. e.* Dr. Johnson's] Preface, pp. v–xxii; History of the English Language, with continuation by Todd, pp. xxiii–lxxi; Notes on Dr. Johnson's History, pp. lxxii–lxxxvi; Editor's Preface, pp. lxxxvii–cxxxiii; Abbreviations, &c., 1 p. The 'Preliminary remarks' (temporary) of Dr. Latham follow the title-page of the first part (March 1864). There appeared in 1876: 'A Dictionary of the English Language, abridged by the editor from that of Dr. Samuel Johnson as edited by Robert Gordon Latham, M.A., M.D., &c.' The Preface is signed R. G. Latham and dated June 1, 1876.

Eyre's copy of the Dictionary, and Horne Tooke's copy, came under Latham's examination.

The review of the first six parts of 'Latham's Johnson's Dictionary' by Sir George Webb Dasent, which appeared in the *North British Review* for December, 1864, is reprinted in his *Jest and Earnest* (1873), ii. 1–109.

The review of vol. i of Latham's Dictionary of Johnson, in which the reviewer (F. J. Furnivall) mistook the Preface of Johnson for one by Latham, is in the last number of *The Reader*, Jan. 12, 1867, pp. 24–5. It is headed: 'First notice—The Preface.' His mistake may have arisen from the fact that Latham's title-page is immediately followed (pp. v–xxii) by the 'Author's Preface' without any indication that it is by Johnson, and that this in turn was succeeded by the 'History of the English Language', which was specifically assigned to Johnson. See Henry Morley, *English Literature in the Reign of Victoria* (Tauchnitz, vol. 2000), 1881, p. 248; T. H. S. Escott, *Platform, Press, Politics and Play* (1895), p. 241; *N. and Q.*, 11th S., vii. 468, &c.).

Abridged Editions.

1756 A Dictionary of the English Language: in which The Words are deduced from their Originals, Explained in their Different Meanings, and Authorized by the Names of the Writers in whose Works they are found. Abstracted from the Folio Edition, By Samuel Johnson, A.M. To which is prefixed, A Grammar of the English Language. In Two Volumes. London, Printed for J. Knapton; C. Hitch and L. Hawes; A. Millar; R. and J. Dodsley; and M. and T. Longman. [January] MDCCLVI.

2 vols. octavo. Vol. I; Title-page, 1 p.; Preface, 2 pp.; Grammar of the English Tongue, 29 pp.; Alphabets, 1 p.; Dictionary, letters A–K; Vol. II, rest of dictionary.

The quotations are omitted, the explanations are abridged and a great number of words are left out. The celebrated definition of the word *Excise* is, for instance, limited to 'A hateful tax levied upon commodities, and adjudged not by the common judges of property'. In the concluding paragraph of the preface, Johnson claims that 'The words of this dictionary, as opposed to others, are more diligently collected, more accurately spelled, more faithfully explained, and more authentically ascertained. Of an abstract it is not necessary to say more; and I hope, it will not be found that truth requires me to say less.'

1760 A Dictionary of the English Language . . . Abstracted from the Folio Edition, By the Author Samuel Johnson, A.M. . . . In two volumes. The Second Edition, corrected. London. [August 14] MDCCLX.

2 vols. octavo. Collation as in first edition.

1766 A Dictionary of the English Language, *etc.* Third edition, corrected. London. MDCCLXVI. 2 vols.

An edition of the abridged Dictionary was issued at Dublin in 1768.

1773 A Dictionary of the English Language, *etc.* Fifth edition, corrected. London. MDCCLXXIII.

2 vols. octavo. Collation as in first edition.

1778 A Dictionary of the English Language, *etc.* Sixth edition, corrected by the author. London. MDCCLXXVIII.

2 vols. octavo. Collation as in first edition.

A Dictionary of the English Language, *etc.* Eighth edition. London. MDCCLXXXVI.

2 vols. octavo. Collation as in first edition.

A Dictionary of the English Language, *etc.* Tenth edition. London: 1792. 2 vols. 8°.

A Dictionary of the English Language, *etc.* Twelfth edition, corrected and revised; With considerable Additions from the Eighth Edition of the Original. London, 1807. 8°.

A Dictionary of the English Language, *etc.* Fourteenth edition, corrected, *etc.* London. 1815. 8°.

A Dictionary of the English Language, *etc.* London, Stereotype edition. 1823. 8°.

CONTINUATIONS OF THE DICTIONARY.

A Spelling-Dictionary of the English Language. For the Use of Young Gentlemen, Ladies, and Foreigners. Published by the King's Authority. The Twelfth Edition, with the Addition of several Thousand Words. The Whole Revised and Accented By Dr. Johnson's New Dictionary of the English Language. To which is prefixed, A Compendious English Grammar; With a concise historical Account of the Language. Dublin: Printed for P. Wilson, J. Exshaw & H. Saunders. M.DCC.LXIX.

Johnson's Dictionary of the English Language in Miniature. To which are added, An alphabetical account of the heathen deities; A list of the cities, boroughs, and market towns in England and Wales; A copious chronology; And a concise epitome of the most remarkable events during the French Revolution. By the Rev. Joseph Hamilton, M.A., Master of the Academy at Hemel Hemsted, Herts. Ninth edition. London: Printed for T. N. Longman . . . 1798. —New edition. 1809.

The words 'Ninth edition' on the title-page do not refer to Hamilton's work but to the editions of Johnson's unabridged Dictionary. The preface to the 1809 edition speaks of the rapid sale of thirteen former editions. A tablet on the north wall of the north transept of Hemel Hempstead Church records the death of four children of the Rev. Joseph Hamilton and Mary Ann his wife (Cussans, *History of Hertfordshire*, vol. iii, pt. 1, p. 159).

There appeared at Montrose in 1807, 'printed by D. Buchanan and sold by him and the booksellers of Edinburgh, Glasgow, &c.', an octavo ed. of 'Johnson's Dictionary of the English Language in Miniature' with lists of the Heathen deities, English market-towns, and other information. It was called the 'Eighteenth edition improved'.

The Union Dictionary, containing all that is truly useful in the Dictionaries of Johnson, Sheridan, *and* Walker, the orthography and explanatory matter selected from Dr. Johnson, the pronunciation adjusted according to Mr. Walker, with the addition of Mr. Sheridan's pronunciation of *Those Words wherein these two eminent Orthoëpists differ*. ... By Thomas Browne, A.M. London: Printed for G. Wilkie [and others]. 1800. 8°.

The Synonymous, Etymological and Pronouncing English Dictionary, in which the words are deduced from their originals, *etc.* Extracted from the Labours of the late Dr. Samuel Johnson; being an attempt to Synonymise his Folio Dictionary of the English Language. ... By William Perry, surgeon of the royal navy. 1805.

His *Royal Standard English Dictionary* (1775) had by this date passed through ten editions, each consisting of 10,000 copies. He had compiled other dictionaries and was the author of an anonymous *Abridgment of the Account of the Embassy to the Emperor of China* (1797), which was compiled by Sir George Staunton.

Johnson's English Dictionary: To which is Annexed, the pronunciation ... with an Appendix containing several thousand words omitted by Dr. Johnson, *etc.* By William Maver. In two volumes. Glasgow. 1809.

The Appendix has a separate title-page, and the additional words are contained in pp. 1–64.

In its compilation the Editor was principally indebted to George Mason.

The Union Dictionary, *etc.* ... with about Two thousand additional words, deduced from the best modern authorities.

By Thomas Browne, LL.D. The Third edition, with numerous additions and improvements. London. 1810. 8°.

The Advertisement, signed Thomas Browne, is dated 'Private Seminary, Wright's Buildings, Kensington, August 3, 1810'. See Faulkner's *Kensington*, p. 321.

The Union Dictionary, *etc.* By Thomas Browne, LL.D. The Fourth edition. London: 1822. 8°.

The Advertisement, which is the same as in the previous edition, is undated.

Johnson's Dictionary of the English Language in miniature. Improved and enlarged. By George Fulton, &c. Third edition. Edinburgh, 1823. [Another ed.] Edinburgh, 1861. [Another ed.] London, [1887].

A Dictionary of the English Language: By Samuel Johnson, LL.D., and John Walker. With the pronunciation greatly simplified and on an entirely new plan: and with the addition of several thousand words. By R. S. Jameson, Esqr., of Lincoln's Inn. Second edition, revised and corrected. London: M.DCCC.XXVIII. 8°.

A Dictionary of the English Language, compiled from Dr. Johnson; with the addition of many hundred words. A new edition. London [1843].

Johnson's Dictionary. [No title-page to copy in British Museum.] [1845?]

Diamond edition. Dr. Johnson's Comprehensive Pocket Dictionary of the English Language, improved by the addition of many thousand words. . . . London [1853].

Johnson's Dictionary of the English Language, for the use of schools and general students. A new edition. By P. Austin Nuttall, LL.D. London: 1855.

Preface signed P. A. N. and dated London, June 1855.

Johnson's Dictionary of the English Language, *etc.* . . . A new edition. . . . By P. Austin Nuttall, LL.D. . . . London 1856.

The Preface much enlarged, signed P. A. Nuttall and dated London, June 1855.

An illustrated Dictionary of the English Language, for the use of schools and general students. By Dr. Johnson. London: [1872]. Stamped on cover as Routledge's Illustrated Dictionary of the English Language, ed. by Dr. Nuttall.

Johnson's English Dictionary: New edition. Improved from the best authorities. Preceded by an Abstract of Walker's pronunciation. London: [1856].

Johnson's Dictionary of the English Language: containing many additional words not to be met with in former pocket editions. Accentuated for pronunciation on the basis of Walker; . . . Glasgow, 1856.

Johnson's Pocket Dictionary of the English Language. Greatly improved by an Augmentation of some thousand words and technical terms. . . . London MDCCCLX.

Advertisement practically identical with that of the Glasgow edition of 1856.

Johnson's Dictionary of the English Language. Carefully condensed from the larger editions. London. [1862.]

Johnson's Dictionary Modernized; with numerous additions from the latest lexicographers. Edited by Alex. Charles Ewald, F.S.A. London. 1868.

The unsigned Preface is dated The Temple, July, 1867.

The Library Dictionary of the English Language . . . founded on the labours of Johnson, Walker, Webster, Worcester, with numerous important additions, and an Appendix. London and Glasgow, 1871.

Johnson's Dictionary with numerous additions from the most eminent authorities. Edited by James Henry Murray. London & N. York. 1874.

Stamp on cover asserts that it contains 36,000 words.

Johnson's Pocket Dictionary of the English Language. Entirely new edition, based upon Worcester and Webster's Standard Editions with 2,000 additional words. London. 1876.

Johnson's Pocket Dictionary of the English Language.

An entirely new edition, with two thousand additional words. London. MDCCCLXXXIII.

The publisher's note states that 'This Dictionary is now well-known as "The Reporter's Dictionary", and as such is used in the Gallery of the House of Commons'.

Johnson's Pocket Dictionary of the English Language. Greatly improved by the addition of some thousand words. . . . Glasgow [1883].

FOREIGN EDITIONS, &c., OF THE DICTIONARY.

German.

Neues grammatisch-kritisches Wörterbuch der Englischen Sprache für die Deutschen; vornehmlich aus dem grössern englischen Werke des Hrn. Samuel Johnson nach dessen vierten Ausgabe gezogen, und mit vielen Wörtern, Bedeutungen und Beyspielen vermehrt. Leipzig, im Schwickertschen Verlage, 1783–96. 2 vols. [by J. C. Adelung]. Vol. I, A–J, 1783; Vol. II, K–Z, 1796.

Taschenbuch der englischen Aussprache [based on Dr. Johnson], by F. E. Feller. Third issue. Leipzig, 1852.

Italian and French.

The new Italian, English and French pocket-dictionary. Carefully compiled from the Dictionaries of La Crusca, Dr. S. Johnson, *etc.* By F. Bottarelli. London: MDCCLXXVII. 3rd ed. 1795. 2 vols.

Italian.

Paralello del vocabolario Della Crusca con quello della lingua Inglese compilato da Samuele Johnson e quello dell'Accademia Spagnuola ne' loro principi costitutivi. Lavoro inviatoci dalla cortesia del celebre vocabolarista e filologo G. G.; Vol. II, pt. i, *of the* Proposta di alcune correzioni ed aggiunte al vocabolario Della Crusca [by Vincenzo Monti]; Milano, 1819.

French.

General English and French Dictionary, newly composed, from the English Dictionaries of Johnson, Webster, Richardson, *etc.*, and from the French Dictionaries of the French Academy, &c. . . . By A. Spiers. London: Whittaker & Co., 1846.

Bengalee.

An Abridgement in English and Bengalee, peculiarly calculated for the use of native as well as European students. To which is subjoined a short list of French and Latin words and phrases in common use among English authors.... By John Mendies. Serampore, 1822.

The second improved edition was published at Calcutta in 1851. It was re-issued at Calcutta in 1872.

A Companion to Johnson's Dictionary in English and Bengalee. To which is prefixed an Introduction to the Bengalee language. Vol. II. By John Mendies. Serampore, 1828.

The Advertisement stated that 'Not long hence the second edition of his Abridgement, &c., will be published upon a more improved plan, so as to give general satisfaction. It is to be volume first to match this volume.' A third improved edition of 'A Companion', &c., came out in 1856.

A Dictionary in English and Bengalee, translated from Todd's edition of Johnson's English Dictionary. In two volumes. By Ram Comul Sen. Serampore Press. 1834.

2 vols. folio. The dedication is to Lord William Cavendish Bentinck, and is dated Calcutta, Feb. 10, 1834.

Works connected with the Dictionary.

October 15, 1755. A Letter from a friend in England to Mr. Maxwell [John Maxwell, M.A.] complaining of his Dilatoriness in the Publication of his so-long-promised work: With a character of Mr. Johnson's English Dictionary, lately published, and Mr. Maxwell's Justification of himself. Also, a Specimen of the Work which he has in Hand, In an Explanation of the Words, Nature and Assises. Dublin: Printed by S. Powell in Crane-lane. MDCCLV.

A criticism of Johnson's work, containing a list of omissions and several pages of comments on the words *Nature* and *Assises*. For John Maxwell see Cotton, *Fasti Eccl. Hibernicae*, iii. 270.

A New Dictionary of the English Language, *etc.* By William Kenrick, LL.D. London: MDCCLXXIII.

'With respect to the etymology, explanation of words, and illustration of idiom and phraseology, . . . I have generally followed the celebrated dictionary of the learned Dr. Johnson.' (Introduction, p. viii.)

An unfinished Letter to the Right Honourable William Pitt, concerning the New Dictionary of the English Language. By the Rev. Herbert Croft, LL.B. London: Printed in March, 1788, but neither finished nor published.

On page 44 is the following note: 'As the Printer was not able to put together any more of what I wrote yesterday se'nnight than these forty-four pages, and the following seven pages of the Postscript; and as I found, in writing this Letter to Mr. Pitt, how much is to be said, and must be said, concerning Johnson's book and mine; it was thought better not to print the remainder of this Letter. Of these pages I have had a few copies pulled for my particular friends. In the course of the Summer, I hope to lay before the Public all I have to say.

'Those friends, who wish to see all that I have hitherto said concerning the MSS. of my Dictionary, are desired to look at the Gentleman's Magazine for August 1787 and February 1788.

'HERBERT CROFT.

'No. 36, Wigmore Street,
Saturday, 15 March, 1788.'

An analysis of this letter is in the *Analytical Review*, i (1788), pp. 512–16. Numerous communications on the progress of Croft's work appeared in vols. lvii–lxiii of the *Gentleman's Magazine*. In 1787 his manuscripts on this dictionary amounted to 200 quarto volumes, and in 1790 he claimed to have amassed 11,000 words used by the highest authorities, but not in Johnson, a number which three years later had more than doubled. Proposals for a new edition of Johnson's Dictionary were issued by Croft in 1792, and the work was to have been published in four large volumes priced at twelve guineas (*D. N. B.*), but through want of subscribers the scheme was abandoned.

It appears from the letter to Dr. Priestley, which Croft subjoined to his reprint of 'Reason and Faith . . . by John Norris, A.M., Rector of Bemerton' (1790), that the Doctor had favoured him with 'papers, conversations, and correspondence about my dictionary'.

Croft dwelt still further on Johnson's Dictionary and his own collections in his rambling 'Letter from Germany to the Princess Royal of England' (1797).

A Letter to James Boswell, Esq. With some Remarks

on Johnson's Dictionary, and on Language. London, 1792. 8°.

Cf. the *Monthly Review*, 1792, N.S. viii, pp. 570–1.

Three Philological Essays, chiefly translated from the German of John Christopher Adelung, by A. F. M. Willich, M.D. London, 1798.

The third essay is 'On the relative merits and demerits of Johnson's English Dictionary', pp. clxix–clxxxvi.

A Supplement to Johnson's English Dictionary: of which the palpable errors are attempted to be rectified, and its material omissions supplied. By George Mason, Author of the Glossary to Hoccleve, and of an Essay on Design in Gardening. London: Printed by C. Roworth, for John White, *etc.* MDCCCI.

This work is dedicated to George John, Earl Spencer. The Preface is contained in five pages, and is dated December, 1800. An Appendix of 16 pp. was printed shortly after the Supplement, and was given gratis, 'both to those who had already purchased, or might purchase the Supplement.' Mason first attacked Johnson in his edition of 'Poems by Thomas Hoccleve, MD.CCXCVI', pp. 105–7, where he says: 'One should really suspect, that the lexicographer had not collected his authorities for himself, nor even revised them when collected for him. Such a supposition might clear him of downright stupidity, but to the impeachment of his common honesty in dealing with the public.' He then printed a coarse epitaph on Johnson, 'written very soon after his death', which dubbed Johnson 'the Snarler general', and ended with the words, 'To the *manes* of poets august whom Johnson slandered in their graves, be this an expiatory offering'. Mason's language on Johnson and this epitaph are censured in the *British Critic*, Dec. 1797, pp. 610–12.

An Essay on the Elements, Accents, & Prosody of the English Language; Intended to have been printed as an Introduction to Mr. Boucher's *Supplement to Dr. Johnson's Dictionary*. By J. Odell, M.A. London; Printed for Lackington, Allen, and Co., Temple of the Muses, Finsbury-Square, 1806.

This was possibly by the Rev. Jonathan Odell, who introduced the American Bishop White to Johnson.

A Review of the Proposals of the Albion fire-insurance: also a continuation of the portentous Globe's History, from where Mr. Stonestreet's ends. To these is added, a Narrative of gross misbehaviour towards the public, in the *British Critic*, by long persisting in a sulky silent prevarication on the Subject of the Appendix to the Supplement to Johnson's Dictionary. By George Mason, Author of Earl Howe's Life; also a director and auditor of the Sun Fire-Office: The Majority of which Office's Managers are so far from being a Party either to this Review, or to the Globe-History, that (abhorring the very idea of Paper War, even with opponent Penmen, who never TRAVERSED the meanest outshed of sensible diction) they have strenuously, though ineffectually, endeavoured to make the writer abstain from this Publication. London: Printed for Robert Bickerstaff, 210 Strand, corner of Essex Street. 1806.

The review of Mason's supplement appeared in the *British Critic*, Oct. 1803, pp. 377–84.

A letter to Dr. David Ramsay, of Charleston (S.C.), respecting the errors in Johnson's Dictionary, and other lexicons. By Noah Webster, Esq. New-Haven [Connecticut]: Printed by Oliver Steele & Co., 1807.

A Supplement to Dr. Johnson's Dictionary; or a Glossary of Archaic and Provincial Words, by Jonathan Boucher. Part I, 1807.

Proposals for printing this glossary by subscription (4 guineas) in 2 vols. quarto, under the direction of Sir F. M. Eden, were issued in 1802. Part I, including letter A, was published in 1807, but did not obtain sufficient encouragement to justify the continuance of the work. See also below, *sub* 1832.

Illustrations of English Philology. By Charles Richardson, Esq., consisting of I. A critical examination of Dr. Johnson's dictionary, II. remarks on Mr. Dugald Stewart's Essay 'On the tendency of some late philological speculations'. London: Printed for Gale & Fenner, 1815.

The work was republished in 1826 by J. Mawman, Ludgate Street, and to it was prefixed an advertisement of 16 pp. containing 'Extracts from the English lexicon, publishing in the *Encyclopædia Metropolitana*, and from the English Dictionary of Dr. Johnson'.

1820 Philology on the English Language. By Richard Paul Jodrell. London: 1820.

The words not to be found in Johnson are marked by an asterisk. Jodrell has also given illustrations to many words inserted by Johnson but not furnished with citations of their use.

1832 Boucher's Glossary of Archaic and Provincial Words. A Supplement to the Dictionaries of the English Language. particularly those of Dr. Johnson and Dr. Webster. . . . By the Late Rev. Jonathan Boucher, A.M. & F.S.A. . . . edited jointly by The Rev. Joseph Hunter, F.S.A., and Joseph Stevenson, Esqr. London, MDCCCXXXII.

This contained the introduction to the whole work and the glossary as far as *Blade*. See above, *sub* 1807.

1833 An English Dictionary, exhibiting a complete view of the verbs, nouns and adjectives governing the various prepositions; comprehending 12,000 examples, illustrated by quotations . . .: principally extracted from the larger Dictionaries of Webster and Johnson. By T. S. Williams. . . . With a preface by Dr. Krafft. Hamburg, 1833.

Williams's 'Longitude at Sea'.

1755 Boswell, i. 301–2. An Account of an Attempt To ascertain the Longitude at Sea, by an Exact Theory of the Variation of the Magnetical Needle. With A Table of Variations at the most remarkable Cities in Europe, from the Year 1660 to 1860. By Zachariah Williams. London: Printed for R. Dodsley, in Pall-Mall; and J. Jefferies, opposite to Northumberland-House; and sold by J. Bouquet, in Pater-noster-Row. MDCCLV. 4°.

This was written for Williams by Johnson. It is printed on the left-hand page, and on the opposite page is an Italian translation by Joseph Baretti. In the copy presented by Johnson to the Bodleian Library is pasted 'a paragraph cut out of a newspaper, containing an account of the death and character of Williams, plainly written by Johnson'. This paragraph is reproduced by Boswell, i. 302. [The copy contains also three notes about Williams in Johnson's hand. Ed.]

*Mary Masters's 'Letters and Poems'.

Familiar Letters and Poems on Several Occasions. By Mary Masters. London: Printed for the Author, by D. Henry and R. Cave. M.DCC.LV. 8°. 1755 Boswell, iv. 246.

According to Boswell, Johnson 'illuminated' her work 'here and there with a ray of his own genius'. The extent of his help is not known. His name is in the list of subscribers. Ed.

Baretti's 'Introduction to Italian'.

An Introduction to the Italian Language, containing Specimens both of Prose and Verse . . . with a literal Translation and Grammatical NOTES, by Giuseppe Baretti. MDCCLV. 1755

Mr. James Crossley was of opinion (*N. and Q.*, 1st S., v. 101) that the Preface, the note on p. 48, and the remarks on p. 198 on Macchiavelli's *Life of Castruccio Castracani*, were by Johnson.

Browne's 'Christian Morals'.

Christian Morals: by Sir Thomas Browne, Of Norwich, M.D. and author of Religio Medici. The Second Edition. With a life of the author, by Samuel Johnson; and explanatory notes. London: Printed by Richard Hett, For J. Payne, at Pope's Head, in Pater-noster row. MDCCLVI. sm. 8°. 1756 Boswell, i. 308.

This is the second edition of the work of Browne, which was first published by John Jeffery, D.D., Archdeacon of Norwich, in 1716, with a dedication by Elizabeth Littleton, Browne's daughter, to David, Earl of Buchan. The copy at the British Museum has on the fly-leaf the words: 'Tho. Birch, 20 March 1756. Donum Samuelis Johnsoni.' Malone's copy, with notes, is in the Forster Library at South Kensington. The life occupies pp. i–lxi.

The third edition, with Browne's life 'written by the celebrated Author of the *Rambler*, and explanatory notes', was 'printed for and sold by Z. Stuart at the Lamb in Paternoster Row, MDCCLXI'. The life was reproduced by Simon Wilkin in his edition of the *Works of Sir Thomas Browne* (1836), i, pp. xvii–liv, and in Rivington's edition of the *Christian Morals* (1863), pp. ix–lxxiii. Two pages are quoted in the *Literary Magazine* (1756), i. 141.

Johnson's 'explanatory notes' are appended by Wilkin to his reprint, erroneously called the third edition, of the *Christian Morals* (*Works of Sir Thomas Browne*, iv. 59 et seq.).

Rolt's 'Dictionary of Trade'.

1756
Boswell, i. 358–9.

A New Dictionary of Trade and Commerce, compiled from the information of the most eminent merchants and from the works of the best writers on commercial subjects in all languages. . . . By Mr. Rolt, with the assistance of several eminent Merchants. London: MDCCLVI.—The second edition. MDCCLXI.

The Preface was written by Johnson.

Payne's 'Game of Draughts'.

1756
Boswell, i. 317.

An Introduction to the Game of Draughts. Containing fifty select games, Together with Many critical situations for Drawn Games, Won Games, and Fine Strokes. . . . By William Payne, Teacher of Mathematics. London, Printed for the Author at the Golden Ball in Bedford-street, Covent-Garden: &c. MDCCLVI.

The Dedication 'To the Right Honourable William-Henry Earl of Rochford', &c. (3 pp.), and the Preface were written by Johnson. This Preface is not in the copy of the 1756 edition which is in the British Museum. Both the Preface and the Dedication are reprinted in the account of the books on draughts by Richard Twiss (*Miscellanies*, in two volumes, 1805, ii. 140–3).

Payne was the author of an anonymous volume, published in 1773, and often reprinted, on the game of whist (W. P. Courtney, *English Whist*, pp. 360–1). He was a brother of Thomas Payne, the bookseller, in whose shop the chief book-lovers of the day used to assemble.

The Universal Visiter.

1756
Boswell, i. 306.

The Universal Visiter and Memorialist. For the Year 1756. *Sounding with Moral Virtue was his Speech, And gladly would he learn, and gladly teach.* Chaucer. London: Printed for T. Gardner, at Cowley's Head, facing St. Clement's Church, in the Strand. [1756].

Twelve monthly parts, sixpence each. Johnson's friend Christo-

CHRISTIAN
MORALS:

BY

Sir THOMAS BROWNE,

Of NORWICH, M. D.

AND AUTHOR OF

RELIGIO MEDICI.

THE SECOND EDITION.

WITH

A LIFE OF THE AUTHOR,

BY

SAMUEL JOHNSON,

AND

EXPLANATORY NOTES.

LONDON:

Printed by RICHARD HETT,

For J. PAYNE, at POPE'S HEAD, in PATER-NOSTER ROW.

MDCCLVI.

pher Smart was one of its undertakers, and it was to assist him that Johnson contributed. 'All the essays marked with two *asterisks* have been ascribed to him', but Boswell was confident that 'The Life of Chaucer', 'Reflections on the State of Portugal', and an 'Essay on Architecture' were not written by him.

The articles which Boswell accepts as authentic are:

(1) 'Further Thoughts on Agriculture.' pp. 111–15.

(2) 'Reflections on the Present State of Literature.' pp. 159–66.

(3) 'A Dissertation on the Epitaphs written by Pope.' pp. 207–19. This Dissertation Johnson afterwards added to the third edition of the *Idler* and to his *Life of Pope*.

Two asterisks are also subjoined to the Latin poem (p. 142) beginning 'Nequicquam Danaen includit ahenea turris'.

The Literary Magazine, or Universal Review.

1756
Boswell, i. 307–16.

The Literary Magazine: or Universal Review: For the Year MDCCLVI. [Quotation from Virg. *Georg*. ii.] London: Printed for J. Richardson in *Pater-noster Row*. [MDCCLVI.]

Vol. I consisted of nine numbers, running from May 1756 to Jan. 15, 1757. Vol. II included Nos. X–XX, ending with December 1757. Vol. III ran to July 1758 (seven numbers).

Johnson superintended and contributed largely to this magazine, his last contribution appearing in the fifteenth number.

JOHNSON'S ARTICLES.

Preliminary Address to the Public. No. I, pp. iii–iv.

An Introduction to the Political State of Great-Britain. No. I, pp. 1–9.

The Militia Bill, with remarks. No. II, pp. 57–64.

Observations on his Britannick Majesty's Treaties with the Empress of Russia and the Landgrave of Hesse Cassel. No. III, pp. 113–21.

Observations on the present State of Affairs. No. IV, pp. 161–5.

Memoirs of Frederick III, King of Prussia. No. VII, pp. 327–33. No. VIII, pp. 383–90. No. IX, pp. 439–42.

These memoirs were reprinted in the *London Chronicle*, May 21–24, 1757, pp. 491–3; May 24–26, pp. 498–500; May 26–28, pp. 507–8; May 28–31, pp. 516–18. There appeared thirty years later a volume of 'Memoirs of Charles Frederick, King of Prussia, by Samuel Johnson, LL.D., with notes and a continuation, by Mr. [James] Harrison, editor of the British Classics, &c., 1786'. Johnson's share consisted of a reprint of the above Memoirs.

JOHNSON'S REVIEWS.

Birch's *History of the Royal Society*. No. I, pp. 30–2.

Murphy's *Gray's Inn Journal*. No. I, pp. 32–5.

[Joseph Warton's] *Essay on the Writings and Genius of Pope*. Vol. i. No. I, pp. 35–8.

Hampton's Translation of Polybius. No. I, pp. 39–41.

Blackwell's *Memoirs of the Court of Augustus*. No. I, pp. 41, 42.

Russell's *Natural History of Aleppo*. No. II, pp. 80–6.

Sir Isaac Newton's *Arguments in Proof of a Deity*. No. II, pp. 89–91.

Borlase's *History of the Isles of Scilly*. No. II, pp. 91–7.

Francis Home's *Experiments on Bleaching*. No. III, pp. 136–41.

Browne's *Christian Morals*. No. III, pp. 141–3.

Hales on Distilling Sea-Water, Ventilators in ships, and curing an ill taste in Milk. No. III, pp. 143–5.

Lucas's *Essay on Waters*. No. IV, pp. 167–8. No. V, pp. 225–9. No. VI, pp. 288–93.

Keith's *Catalogue of the Scottish Bishops*. No. IV, pp. 171–6.

Patrick Browne's *History of Jamaica*. No. IV, pp. 176–85.

Philosophical Transactions. Vol. xlix, part I. No. IV, pp. 193–7.

Mrs. Lennox's Translation of *Sully's Memoirs*. No. VI, pp. 281–2.

Miscellanies by Elizabeth Harrison. No. VI, pp. 282–8.

Lewis Evan's *Map and Account of the Middle Colonies in America*. No. VI, pp. 293–9.

Letter on the Case of Admiral Byng and *An Appeal to the People concerning Admiral Byng*. No. VI, pp. 299–309.

[Short notice of] Jonas Hanway's *Journal of Eight Days journey*, and *Essay on Tea*. No. VII, pp. 335–42.

The Cadet, a Military Treatise. No. VII, p. 335 (*sic*).

Some further Particulars in relation to the Case of Admiral Byng, by a Gentleman of Oxford. No. VII, pp. 336 (*sic*)–40 (*sic*).

The Conduct of the Ministry impartially examined. No. VII, pp. 340 (*sic*)–51.

[Extended notice of] Jonas Hanway's *Journal of Eight Days Journey* and *Essay on Tea.* No. XIII, pp. 161–7.

A Free Inquiry into the Nature and Origin of Evil [by Soame Jenyns]. No. XIII, pp. 171–5. No. XIV, pp. 251–3. No. XV, pp. 301–6.

Tom Davies ascribed to Johnson the review of Burke's *Philosophical Enquiry into the Origin of our Ideas of the Sublime and Beautiful* (vol. ii, No. XIII, pp. 182–9), and Sir John Hawkins inserted it in his collection of Johnson's *Works*, but Boswell declares it to have been written by Arthur Murphy. Boswell attributes to Johnson the short passage appended to a long extract from *An authentic account of the present state of Lisbon* (vol. i, pp. 20–2).

The article on Jonas Hanway's *Journal* drew forth an angry answer in the number of the *Gazetteer* for May 26, 1757, to which Johnson replied in No. XIV, vol. ii, pp. 253-6, of the *Literary Magazine.*

Soame Jenyns also resented the review of his work, and after Johnson's death published a petulant epitaph upon him which is printed in C. N. Cole's edition of his works (1790), i. 222. Johnson is said to have 'reprinted this review in a small volume by itself' (*Works*, Oxford, 1825, vi. 47), but I am not able to corroborate this assertion. The 'Review of a Free enquiry into the Nature and Origin of Evil' (1759) is a different composition, the work of a different writer. Mr. Norman Pearson, in his *Society Sketches in the Eighteenth Century* (1911), gives a pleasant delineation of Jenyns as 'a male blue-stocking', with the conclusion that 'as a metaphysician he was decidedly superior to Johnson'. The epitaph, as Jenyns originally wrote it, consisted of six lines, concluding with 'A Christian and a Scholar, but a brute'. Four more were subsequently added; two of them pointed out that—

Boswell and Thrale, retailers of his wit,
Will tell you how he *wrote* and talk'd and cough'd and spit.

Proposals for Edition of Shakespeare.

1756
Boswell, i. 318–9.

Proposals for Printing the Dramatick Works of William Shakespeare.

Printed, with a preliminary puff, in the *London Chronicle*, April 12–14, 1757, pp. 358–9. They are included in Tom Davies's *Miscellaneous and Fugitive Pieces*, vol. ii (1774), pp. 87–94, and are there described as 'printed in the year 1756'. Malone gives them in full at the beginning of the preface to his edition of Shakespeare, vol. i, pt. 1 (1790), pp. i–x. They are reprinted in the collected editions of Johnson's works, and in Sir Walter Raleigh's *Johnson on Shakespeare* (1908). [A letter from Johnson to Birch proves that they had been printed before June 22, 1756, and suggests that they had then been just completed (*Letters of Johnson*, ed. Hill, vol. i, p. 64). No copy of the original Proposals appears to be known. Ed.]

The London Chronicle.

1757
Boswell, i. 317.

The London Chronicle [or Universal Evening Post] for the year 1757. Volume I. From January 1 to June 30. To be continued. London, Sold by J. Wilkie, behind the Chapter-House in St. Paul's Church-Yard [1757].

The 'Preliminary Discourse', occupying the first page of the first number (Saturday, Jan. 1, 1757), is by Johnson. For this contribution he received a guinea from Robert Dodsley. See also, below, 1764 (p. 103) and 1769 (p. 113).

The Evangelical History Harmonized.

Boswell, iv. 383.

The Evangelical History of our Lord Jesus Christ, harmonized, explained, and illustrated with variety of notes. . . . By a Society of Gentlemen [really by the Rev. John Lindsay]. London: MDCCLVII.

Robert Anderson, editor of *The British Poets*, believed that the dedication 'To the Lords spiritual and temporal and Commons in Parliament assembled' was by Johnson and 'written in the excellent dedicator's best style of dignified remonstrance and sublime piety' (Nichols, *Illustrations of Lit.*, vii (1848), p. 161). [See also Anderson's *Life of Johnson*, 1815, pp. 257–8. Ed.]

LONDON, *June* 1. 1756.

PROPOSALS

For PRINTING, by SUBSCRIPTION,

THE

DRAMATICK WORKS

OF

WILLIAM SHAKESPEARE,

CORRECTED AND ILLUSTRATED

BY

SAMUEL JOHNSON.

SUBSCRIPTIONS are taken in by

J and R. TONSON, in the Strand; J. KNAPTON, in Ludgate-Street; C. HITCH and L. HAWES, and M and T. LONOMAN, in Pater-nofter Row.

Chambers's 'Chinese Buildings'.

Designs of Chinese buildings . . . Engraved by the best hands from the Originals drawn in China by Mr. [William] Chambers, architect. London: MDCCLVII.

1757
Boswell, i. 21. iv. 188.

The first two paragraphs of the Preface were written by Johnson.

Payne's Tables of Interest.

New Tables of INTEREST, by John Payne, of the Bank of England. . . . London: Printed by D. Leach for J. Payne at Pope's Head in Pater-noster-row. MDCCLVIII.

1758

The Preface (pp. iii–vii) is attributed in the Catalogue of the British Museum Library to Johnson. This is the John Payne who published *The Rambler*.

The Idler.

The Universal Chronicle, or [and] Weekly Gazette for the year 1758. Volume I. From April 8 to December 30. Det ille veniam facile, cui venia est opus. To be continued. London. Printed for R. Stevens, at Pope's-Head, in Pater-noster Row. [This is the imprint to Volume I, but the colophon to the first number is 'London, Printed for *J. Payne* in *Pater-noster-Row*'.]

1758–61
Boswell, i. 330–5, 345.

The paper had many changes, from which Hill draws the inference that it was not successful. No. 5, erroneously headed as for week ended April 29 [should be May 6], was called *Payne's Universal Chronicle or Weekly Gazette*. Payne's name was dropped in the issue for Jan. 6, 1759, and the colophon ran, 'London, Printed for *R. Stevens* at *Pope's-head*, next Door to the *Chapter Coffee-house*'. Subsequent changes need not be mentioned.

The first number of Johnson's paper, 'The Idler. Vacui sub umbra Lusimus. *Hor.*', appeared in the second number of the *Universal Chronicle*, Saturday, April 15, 1758. Each weekly issue of this paper consisted of eight pages, and Johnson's articles came first, in larger type. They lasted until April 5, 1760 (No. 104 of *The Idler*, No. 105 of the paper), 'in the solemn Week which the Christian World has always set apart for the Examination of the Conscience and Review of Life, for the Extinction of earthly Desires and the Renovation of holy Purposes'. Nos. 9,

15, 33, 42, 54, 67, 76, 79, 82, 93, 96, 98,[1] twelve in all, were not by Johnson. Of these, Nos. 33, 93, 96 were by Thomas Warton; No. 67 by Bennet Langton; and Nos. 76, 79, and 82 by Sir Joshua Reynolds. The concluding words of No. 82, 'and pollute his canvas with deformity', were added by Johnson. 'Pollute' was one of the Doctor's favourite expressions: *Boswell*, ed. Hill, iv. 404, 440; *Miscellanies*, ed. Hill, 149. These three articles were struck off from the first collected edition and paged consecutively as a gift to Reynolds by Johnson, in a little volume of twenty pages, called 'Three Letters to *The Idler*' [1761]. It was given by Reynolds to Malone on January 18, 1789, came into the hands of Mr. C. E. Doble, and on the dispersal of his library by B. H. Blackwell, of Oxford (Catal. No. 151 (1913), art. 472), was acquired by Mr. D. Nichol Smith. They were also reprinted, with the omission of a connecting sentence or two, in 'A letter on Painting, first published in the weekly paper called *The Idler*', which appeared in the *London Chronicle*, May 12–14, 1761, pp. 460–1.

The essays in *The Idler* are for the most part of a lighter and brisker nature than those in *The Rambler*. Many eccentric personages, Tom Tempest, Jack Sneaker, Dick Minim, and Jack Whirler—the original of whom was John Newbery the publisher—for example, are described with much humour in its pages. Sober (No. 31) was Johnson himself; and much of the three days' journal of a student (No. 67), though written by Langton, is said to have been prompted by the habits of Johnson.

The letters of Betty Broom (Nos. 26 and 29), 'a poor girl, bred at a charity-school', are believed to have been suggested by the ladies' charity-school for girls then in St. Sepulchre's parish, in which Johnson was much interested through the influence of his old friend Mrs. Gardiner, 'wife of a tallow-chandler on Snowhill'. The death of Mrs. Gardner (*sic*) of Snow-hill, on Sept. 13, 1789, in her seventy-fourth year, 'a widow-lady', is chronicled with unusual warmth of sentiment in the *Gentleman's Magazine* for 1789, pt. ii, p. 956, but the entry should have been inserted among the deaths in October 1789. The burial of Ann Hedges Gardiner, of Snow Hill, aged 73, is entered in the registers of St. Sepulchre under the date of October 18.

[1] [This is the numbering in the collected edition, in which the original No. 22 is omitted. Ed.]

The volume of *Letters concerning Mind* (1750), which is referred to in No. 36, was the posthumous work of the Rev. John Petvin, M.A., late Vicar of Ilsington in Devon. The Preface states that the *Letters* had been corrected by 'the author of a Book called Three Treatises'. This was 'Hermes' Harris, and the treatises appeared first in 1744 as by J. H. (i. e. James Harris). The passage criticized by Johnson is in Letter VI, p. 40. Petvin graduated at St. John's College, Cambridge, B.A., 1711, M.A., 1719. He was born at Haslebury, Plucknett, Somerset, son of John Petvin, husbandman, and was baptized there on Dec. 26, 1691, as 'son of John Petven (*sic*) Junr and Catherine his wife'. He was educated at Crewkerne School under Mr. Leaves, and admitted at St. John's College on February 21, 1706/7, aet. 16, as sizar for Mr. Bosvile, tutor, and surety Mr. Anstey (*Admissions*, pt. ii, 1903, p. 183).

A volume of *Remarks on Letters concerning Mind* was printed in 1752, and was said to be taken 'from the original characters of the author of the Letters concerning Mind'. The Catalogue of the British Museum Library attributes to Petvin 'A Letter concerning the use and method of studying History. By the author of Letters concerning Mind' (1753). He was licensed to the curacy of Ashburton on October 19, 1720, and was instituted to the vicarage of Ilsington, Devon, on June 29, 1739 (*Notes and Gleanings*, Exeter, iii (1890), pp. 89, 139). He, however, continued to live at Ashburton as curate, and was buried there on October 12, 1745.

A note by James Harris in the third edition (1771) of his *Hermes* (p. 172) mentions Petvin as 'a person who, though from his retired situation little known, was deeply skilled in the Philosophy both of the Antients and Moderns, and more than this, was valued by all that knew him for his virtue and worth'.

The lady who undertook to ride 'on one horse, a thousand miles, in a thousand hours' within six weeks and finished the task within a month, after resting for two days at Newmarket, was Miss Pond. She arrived at her goal on May 3, 1758, and the news was published in the *London Chronicle* for May 6. Johnson made it the subject of the article (No. 6) which appeared on May 20. She was the daughter of John Pond (d. Nov. 11, 1779), who sold horses by auction at Newmarket and prints at James Street, Covent Garden, and published *The Sporting Calendar* for the years 1751 to 1757.

Her mother, Sarah Pond, died in the parish workhouse of St. Paul, Covent Garden, in May 1786 (*Gent. Mag.*, 1779, p. 567; 1786, pt. i, p. 528). John Taylor (*Records of My Life*, i. 176) knew Miss Pond well, when she was advanced in years. Tall of stature, not handsome, but well-bred and accomplished, she played well on the pianoforte. Her manners were grave, even melancholy, and were thought to have been affected by an attachment for William O'Brien the actor, who married Lady Susan Fox-Strangways, daughter of the Earl of Ilchester. Arthur Pond, the artist, was a relation; John Pond, whose portrait in a round hat was painted by T. Parkinson and engraved by B. Smith in 1787, is suggested as a brother; and she was probably the Miss Pond whose portrait by Spilsbury was published in a mezzotint by John Spilsbury on Dec. 1, 1766 (Bromley, *Portraits*, pp. 410, 443).

Johnson's feelings led him here and elsewhere into indiscretions, and occasionally he wandered into political subjects. He contrasted in the same paper (No. 20) the capture of Louisburg from the point of view of the English and of the French. The varying announcements in the newspapers, morning and evening, for a whole week, on the taking of a French ship of war are set out in No. 7. His reference in No. 65 to the probable lamentations of Sir Matthew Hale over the 'mutilations' which his *Pleas of the Crown* had suffered from the hands of the editor, Sollom Emlyn, brought forth a letter of remonstrance from an anonymous contributor, signing himself A. B., to the *Gent. Mag.*, 1760, pp. 271–2. In the same paper Johnson spoke of 'the two lowest of all human beings, a scribbler for a party and a commissioner of excise'. The persons thus stigmatized were John Oldmixon and George Duckett. When writing on the condition of those confined in jails (Nos. 22 and 38, collected edition), he thought their number was 'more than twenty thousand', but he afterwards added a note (No. 38) questioning the accuracy of the calculation. These two papers were reprinted on pp. 29–35 of 'Enquiries respecting the Insolvent Debtors Bill, with the opinions of Dr. Paley, Mr. Burke, and Dr. Johnson upon imprisonment for debt. Second edition. By Basil Montagu. 1816.'

Fewer alterations were made in *The Idler* when reprinted than in *The Rambler*. After the sixth paper no mottoes were prefixed to the articles, with the exception of Nos. 33, 41, 52, 89, and 103. Mrs. Thrale once asked him the reason for

THE

IDLER.

In Two Volumes.

Duplex libelli dos eſt, quod riſum movet,
Et quod prudenti vitam conſilio monet.
Phaedrus.

Χάρις μικροῖσι.

VOLUME I.

LONDON,
Printed for J. Newbery, at the *Bible* and *Sun* in *St. Paul's Church Yard.*

MDCCLXI.

this departure from the established custom. His answer was that he wished to conceal his identity. The pair then sat down to settle the fitting mottoes for the other numbers, and in about five minutes had fixed on nine (Mrs. Piozzi, *Letters to and from Johnson*, ii. 388–9).

The second essay in *The Idler*, that for April 22, 1758, was reproduced in the *London Chronicle*, April 22–25, 1758, pp. 387–8, and it was followed by many others. No. 7 (May 27, 1758), was inserted as a 'specimen of a new paper' in the *Grand Magazine*, i (June 1758), pp. 227–9, and three more numbers (27, 30, and 47 of the original issue) were reproduced at later dates. An essay in the same periodical, i (September 1758), pp. 471–2, consisted of 'Remarks on the *Idler*'. Twenty of the essays were printed in the *Grand Magazine of Magazines* (vols. i–iii). No. 104 (the farewell paper) was inserted in the *London Magazine*, April 1760, pp. 189–90. Several of Johnson's articles, including No. 6, which commemorates Miss Pond, were embodied in the second volume of what purports to be the second edition—printed at Dublin in 1758—of the Rev. Thomas Francklin's paper *The Centinel*. The article on that lady appears therein as No. 125, December 14, 1757. Such wholesale piracies were the cause of the whimsical advertisement from Johnson's pen which was dated January 5, 1759, and inserted in the *Universal Chronicle*.

Collected Editions.

The Idler. In Two Volumes. Duplex libelli dos est, quod risum movet, Et quod prudenti vitam consilio monet. Phaedrus. *Χάρις μικροῖσι.* Volume I. (II.) London, Printed for J. Newbery, at the Bible and Sun in St. Paul's Church Yard. MDCCLXI. 12°. **1761**

103 numbers only, that for September 9, 1758 (the original No. 22, On Vultures and their instruction of their young), having been omitted. This edition was published in October 1761, price 5*s*. sewed, or 6*s*. bound. 1,500 sets were printed, and Johnson had two-thirds of the profits, his share being £84 2*s*. 4*d*.

This was the first collected edition. The advertisement prefixed to vol. i (p. iii) names the twelve numbers not by Johnson.

The Idler. By The Author of the Rambler. The third edition. With Additional Essays. London: Printed for **1767**

T. Davies, J. Newbery, and T. Payne. MDCCLXVII. 2 vols. 12°.

The additional essays (vol. ii, pp. [285]–330) consisted of Johnson's articles: (1) Essay on Epitaphs (see above, p. 11); (2) Dissertation on the Epitaphs written by Pope (see above, p. 75); (3) Bravery of the English Common Soldiers.

1783 The Idler. By the Author of the Rambler. With Additional Essays [as above]. 4th ed. London: Printed for J. Rivington and Sons, T. Carnan, T. Payne, T. Cadell, *etc.* MDCCLXXXIII. 2 vols. 12°.

The Idler. By the Author of the Rambler. With Additional Essays [as above]. 5th ed. London: Printed for J. Rivington and Sons, and F. Power, *etc.* MDCCXC. 2 vols. 8°.

The Idler; by the Author of the Rambler. With Additional Essays [as above]. In two volumes. A new edition, &c. London: Printed for J. Cuthell, Middle-row; and J. & J. Fairbairn, Edinburgh. M.DCC.XCV.

The Idler: by the Author of the Rambler, *etc.* A new edition. London: Printed by R. Taylor & Co., Shoe-Lane; For J. Johnson, T. Payne, *etc.* 1807.

This did not contain the 'additional essays', but included at the end (pp. 333–6) the original No. 22.

The Idler: A series of essays by Samuel Johnson, LL.D. Complete in one volume. London: John Bumpus, Holborn Bars, and Richard Griffin & Co. Glasgow. M,DCCC,XXIV.

Contained original No. 22, but not the 'additional essays'.

The Idler was included in *The British Classics*, 1785–7; [James] Harrison's *British Classics*, vol. viii (1795); C. Cooke's *Pocket Edition of Select British Classics* (1799); *The British Classics*, vols. xxiii and xxiv (1810); *The British Essayists*, ed. Alexander Chalmers, vols. xxxiii and xxxiv (eds. of 1803 and 1817), vol. xxvii (1823), vol. xxvii (Boston, U.S., 1856); *The British Essayists*, ed. Rev. L. T. Berguer, 1823; *The British Essayists*, ed. James Ferguson, vol. xix (2nd ed. 1823); *The British Essayists*, ed. Robert Lynam, vol. xx (1827).

A French translation, *Le Paresseux*, by J. B. Varney, was published in 1790. 2 vols.

The details of Nathan Drake's 'Essays illustrative of *The Idler*' are set out under *The Rambler* (above, p. 35).

An anonymous poem (of 156 lines, 8 pp.) entitled 'The Fatal Effects of Luxury and Indolence Exemplified in the History of *Hacho* King of Lapland. A Tale [in *The Idler*, No. 96] of Dr. S. Johnson's versified', was printed by J. Bradley at Chesterfield in 1778.

Angell's 'Stenography'.

STENOGRAPHY, or Short-hand improved . . . by John Angell. London: [1759?] 8°.

1759?
Boswell, ii. 224.

This man came to Johnson 'to write for him a Preface or Dedication', but I doubt whether either the published Preface or Dedication was his composition.

Rasselas.

Johnson's mother died in January, 1759, and he wanted the money to pay for her burial and to discharge some little debts which she had incurred. He began the composition of this novel, finished it 'in the evenings of one week, sent it to the press in portions as it was written, and had never since read it over' until 1781, and this rapidity of execution is said to have been due to the fact that all his life long he had been pondering over its chief topics. These are the accepted statements of Strahan and Sir Joshua Reynolds as told by Boswell. But Oliver Farrar Emerson claims to have proved in the introduction to his edition of *Rasselas* (New York, 1895), that Johnson did not write it to pay the funeral expenses of his mother, and that he did not send it to the press in portions as it was written. In a subsequent article in *Anglia* (vol. xxii, 1899, pp. 499–509) he showed in a tabular statement that in the second edition of *Rasselas* there were 61 variations from the text of the original edition, and that many of them were of importance. The price which the publishers paid was £100, but when the book came to a second edition Johnson received £25 more. 'The Story of Rasselas' is the subject of an article in *Book-lore*, i (1885), pp. 5–11.

The name Rasselas, which signifies 'chief', and was taken from 'Rassela' in Lobo's *Voyage* (p. 102), did not appear on the title-page of Johnson's first edition. 'Abissinia' was the spelling adopted by him, but in Lobo the more usual form of 'Abyssinia' is used. Imlac was written by Johnson without the final *k*, because in this way it was 'less like English, which should always have the Saxon *k* added to the *c*'. Very little of the Oriental life of Lobo is reproduced in *Rasselas*, though that narrative, as his first labour in literature, must have been embedded in the author's mind. The circumstances in which *Rasselas* was composed would not inspire cheerfulness of feeling in its author, and Johnson was always predisposed to melancholy. A veil of sadness is cast over its pages. A long account of the work was inserted at the time in the *Gent. Mag.* for April 1759, pp. 184–6.

Voltaire's *Candide*, with which *Rasselas* is often contrasted, was issued in England in May, 1759. Both of these tales are described in Miss Martha's Pike Conant's monograph on *The Oriental Tale in England in the Eighteenth Century* (New York, 1908).

An abstract omitting 'all the reflections' was inserted by Thomas Kinnersly, of St. Paul's Church Yard, in the *Grand Magazine of Magazines*, ii (1759), 217–22, 301–4, whereupon Dodsley brought an action against him for infringement of copyright. Sir Thomas Clarke, the Master of the Rolls, gave judgement against the plaintiff (June 5, 1761) as 'a fair abridgement is not piracy'. The case is set out in Charles Ambler's *Reports of Chancery Cases*, 1790, pp. 403–6, second edition 1828, vol. i, pp. 402–5, and is reproduced in the *Bibliographer*, iii (1883), pp. 173–5.

'The History of Imlac' is reprinted in the *London Chronicle*, April 19–21, 1759, pp. 378–80 (when *Rasselas* was described as 'just published'). Further extracts from it are given in the same paper, April 28–May 1, pp. 410–11; May 3–5, p. 423; and May 10–12, p. 418.

Some lines by a Warwickshire poetess describing the Happy Valley in *Rasselas* are printed in the *London Chronicle*, Dec. 26–29, 1761, p. 628. Cf. also ib., Feb. 6–9, 1726, p. 134. This was Mary Whateley, who married, on Nov. 4, 1766, as his second wife, the Rev. John Darwall, of Walsall. The verses are reprinted, with some slight alterations, as 'Liberty, an Elegy. Inscrib'd to Miss Loggin. Feigned to be written from the Happy Valley of Ambara' in her *Original Poems* (1764), pp. 17–20; second edition, 1764, pp. 6–9; but were not included in the 1794 edition of her poems. Cf. Simms, *Bibliotheca Staffs.*, pp. 131–2.

THE PRINCE OF ABISSINIA.

A TALE.

IN TWO VOLUMES.

VOL. I.

LONDON:
Printed for R. and J. DODSLEY, in Pall-Mall;
and W. JOHNSTON, in Ludgate-Street.
MDCCLIX.

EDITIONS.

The Prince of Abissinia. A Tale. In two volumes. Vol. I. (II.) London: Printed for R. and J. Dodsley, in Pall-Mall; and W. Johnston, in Ludgate-Street. MDCCLIX. 2 vols. sm. 8°. **1759** Boswell, i, 340–4.

Collation:—Vol. I. Title, p. [i]; contents, pp. [iii]–viii; chaps. i–xxv, pp. 1–159. Vol. II. Title, p. [i]; contents, pp. [iii]–viii; chaps. xxvi–xlviii, pp. 1–165.

[The name 'Rasselas' is not in the title of any edition published during Johnson's lifetime, but the heading on p. 1 of both volumes of the first edition is 'The History of Rasselas, Prince of Abissinia'. All the editions during his lifetime were anonymous. Ed.]

Rasselas was published in April 1759, in two duodecimo volumes, the price being 5*s*. 'None of his writings has been so extensively diffused over Europe; for it has been translated into most, if not all, of the modern languages' (*Boswell*).

The Prince of Abissinia. A Tale. The second edition. London: MDCCLIX. 2 vols. sm. 8°. **1759**

[This follows the first edition page for page, but has corrections in the text: e. g. vol. i, pp. 8, 11, 18, etc. Ed.]

An edition, in two volumes, appeared at Dublin in 1759.

The Prince of Abissinia. A Tale. The third edition. MDCCLX. 2 vols. sm. 8°. **1760**

* The Prince of Abissinia. A Tale. The fourth edition. MDCCLXVI. 2 vols. sm. 8°. **1766**

[Rasselas. An American edition.] **1771**

A copy was sent to Johnson, early in 1773, by the Rev. William White, afterwards Bishop of the Protestant Episcopal Church in Pennsylvania. The Doctor wrote in reply: 'I received the copy of *Rasselas*. The impression is not magnificent, but it flatters an authour, because the printer seems to have expected that it would be scattered among the people. The little book has been well received, and is translated into Italian, French, German, and Dutch. It has now one honour more by an American edition.' Boswell, ii. 207

The Prince of Abissinia. A Tale. The fifth edition. London: Printed for W. Strahan, J. Dodsley, and E. Johnston. MDCCLXXV. 12°. 1 vol. **1775**

1783 The Prince of Abissinia. A Tale. The sixth edition. London: Printed for W. Strahan, J. Dodsley, and T. Longman. MDCCLXXXIII. 12°. 1 vol.

Rasselas, Prince of Abissinia. A Tale by S. Johnson, L.L.D. (*sic*). London: Printed for Joseph Wenman, No. 144 Fleet-Street. MDCCLXXXVII.

An edition, calling itself the eighth edition, appeared at Dublin in this year.

The History of Rasselas, Prince of Abissinia. A Tale. By Dr. Johnson. London: Printed for Harrison & C°, N° 18 Paternoster Row. MDCCLXXXVII. 2 vols.

The History of Rasselas, Prince of Abbissinia (*sic*). By Samuel Johnson, L.L.D. (*sic*). A new edition. Edinburgh: Printed for William Creech. MDCCLXXXIX.

The Prince of Abissinia. 8th ed. 1790.

The Prince of Abissinia. A Tale. The ninth edition. London: Printed for J. F. and C. Rivington, *etc.* MDCCXCIII. 12°.

The History of Rasselas, Prince of Abissinia. A Tale. By Dr. Johnson. . . . London: Printed under the inspection of the Literary Association . . . 1795. 8°. Portrait.

The Prince of Abissinia. A Tale. The tenth edition. London: Printed for F. and C. Rivington, *etc.* MDCCXCVIII. 12°.

* The History of Rasselas, Prince of Abissinia. A Tale. By Dr. Johnson. Two volumes in one. London: Printed for the Booksellers. 1799.

The History of Rasselas, *etc.* Cooke's *Pocket Edition of Select Novels, or Novelist's Entertaining Library.* [1799.]

With a Life of Dr. Johnson, L.L.D. (*sic*), pp. 3–36.

The History of Rasselas, Prince of Abyssinia. A Tale. By Samuel Johnson, LL.D. London: Printed by C. Whittingham, Dean Street, Fetter Lane, for F. and C. Rivington, &c. 1801. 8°. Portrait and five engravings.

Rasselas, Prince of Abissinia. A Tale by S. Johnson, L.L.D. (*sic*). Bristol; Printed by J. Mills, Castle Street. 1802.

The History of Rasselas, by Samuel Johnson, LL.D. Hartford, U.S.A. 1803.

The History of Rasselas, Prince of Abissinia. A Tale by Dr. Johnson. Cork: Printed for Edward Henry Morgan . . . 1803 (Life as in Cooke's edition prefixed).

New Mode of Printing. Rasselas, Prince of Abissinia. By Dr. Johnson. Printed with patent types in a manner never before attempted. Banbury: Printed for P. Rusher; *etc.* 1804. Cheney, Printer, High-Street, Banbury. 8°.

At p. 136 are 28 verses 'To a friend. By Dr. Johnson'. [Johnson's authorship of these verses, commonly entitled 'The Vanity of Wealth', is doubtful: first printed in *Gent. Mag.*, 1750, p. 85. Ed.]

Rasselas, by Samuel Johnson, LL.D. With engravings by A. Raimbach, from pictures by R. Smirke, R.A. London: Published by William Miller, Albemarle-Street; And sold by Manners and Miller, and Archibald Constable and Co. Edinburgh. The Letter Press by James Ballantyne, Edinburgh, 1805. 4°.

Four full-page engravings, and a vignette on p. 1. The plates were issued separately in the same year. See also *sub* 1819. Raimbach lost by this venture. See *Memoirs and Recollections of the late Abraham Raimbach*, 1843, p. 106.

Rasselas, a tale by Dr. Johnson. London: Printed by C. Whittingham, 1806.

Rasselas, a tale by Dr. Johnson. London: Printed by W. Wilson, St. John's Square, for J. Walker, *etc.* 1807, 12°.

Frontispiece by T. Uwins, engraved by Finden. Vignette on title.

Rasselas. Classic Tales, Vol. III. London. Printed and Published by and for John Hunt & Carew Reynell in Brydges Street, Strand. 1807. 8°.

Essay on Rasselas by Leigh Hunt, pp. 1-13.

Rasselas. In *System of Notation*, by William Pelham. Boston, 1808, 12°.

Mentioned in James Macaulay's bibliography.

The History of Rasselas, Prince of Abissinia. By Samuel Johnson, LL.D. British Novelists, ed. Mrs. Barbauld, vol. xxvi, 1810.

Preface by Mrs. Barbauld, pp. i–viii.

Rasselas, Prince of Abissinia. A Tale. By S. Johnson, LL.D. Frederick-Town: Printed at the Herald Press by and for John P. Thomson. 1810. 12°.

The History of Rasselas, Prince of Abyssinia. A Tale. By Samuel Johnson, LL.D. Printed at the Chiswick Press, by C. Whittingham for J. Carpenter, *etc.* 1812. 12°.

Rasselas, a Tale. By Samuel Johnson, L.L.D. (*sic*). Edinburgh: Printed by Walker and Greig for John Greig, 261 High Street . . . 1812. 12°.

'Some account of the life and writings of Dr. Johnson,' pp. v–xii.

Rasselas. By Samuel Johnson, LL.D. Leeds: 1814.

Rasselas, a Tale by Dr. Johnson. London: Published by Suttaby, Evance & Fox, and Crosby & C°. . . . 1815. 12°. Frontispiece. Life of Dr. Johnson, pp. i–xx.

Rasselas, Prince of Abyssinia. A Tale. By Samuel Johnson, LL.D. London: Printed for F. C. and J. Rivington, &c. 1816. 8°.

Extra leaf 'Rasselas, a Tale', on verso of which is imprint: 'T. Davison, Lombard-street, Whitefriars, London.' 'Some account of the life and writings of Dr. Johnson,' pp. v–xiv (identical with that in 1812 ed.).

Rasselas; A Tale. By Dr. Johnson. Dinarbas; a Tale: being a continuation of Rasselas. London: Printed for Walker and Edwards, F. C. and J. Rivington, *etc.*, by S. Hamilton, Weybridge, Surrey, 1817. 12°.

Rasselas, by Samuel Johnson, LL.D. With engravings by A. Raimbach, from pictures by R. Smirke, R.A. London: Published by Hector M^c^Lean, No. 8 Soho Square: And sold by Manners and Miller, and Archibald Constable and Co., Edinburgh. 1819. 4°.

On verso of title-page and last page is 'Printed by J. Brettell, Rupert Street, Haymarket, London'. Reissue of 1805 ed.

Rasselas, by Dr. Johnson. Novelist's Library . . . Printed by James Ballantyne and Company, at the Border Press, Edinburgh. Vol. V. 1823.

With novels by Goldsmith, Sterne, and others, and with brief memoirs by Sir Walter Scott.

[General Title] The British Novelist . . . London: Printed for J. Limbird, 355, Strand . . . 1823. [Special Title] The History of Rasselas, Prince of Abyssinia. A Tale. By Samuel Johnson, LL.D. London: Printed and Published by J. Limbird, 143 Strand . . . 1824.

Memoirs of Dr. Johnson, pp. iii–viii.

* Rasselas: A Tale. By Samuel Johnson, LL.D. London: Jones & Company. 1825. (Diamond Classics.)

The History of Rasselas, Prince of Abyssinia, A Tale. By Samuel Johnson, LL.D. London: Charles Tilt, Fleet Street . . . MDCCCXXXV. 32°. Frontispiece. (Tilt's Classical Library.)

The History of Rasselas. By Samuel Johnson. New York. 1841.

Raselas and Select Poems. Bi Samuel Jonsun . . . Lundun: Fred. Pitman . . . 1849. Edited by A. J. E. [A. J. Ellis.]

Another phonetic edition was published by Pitman in 1867.

Rasselas, a Tale. By Samuel Johnson, LL.D. [Cabinet Edition of] Classic Tales . . . London: Henry G. Bohn, York Street, Covent Garden. 1852.

Rasselas. A Tale. By Dr. Johnson. New York. 1853.

Rasselas: A Tale. By Samuel Johnson, LL.D. London: Thomas Nelson and Sons, Paternoster Row. 1855. 32°.

Rasselas. A Tale. By Dr. Johnson. London: Groombridge. 1858. 32°.

Rasselas, A Tale. By Samuel Johnson, LL.D. With introductory remarks . . . Life of Johnson, and appendixes. By the Rev. John Hunter . . . London: Longman, Green, Longman and Roberts. 1860.

The History of Rasselas, Prince of Abyssinia. A Tale. By Samuel Johnson, LL.D. Masterpieces of Fiction by Eminent Authors. London: Charles Griffin & Co. [1867]. pp. 331–70.

Rasselas. A Tale. By Dr. Johnson. New York. 1869. 16°.

Rasselas. Prince of Abyssinia. By Samuel Johnson, LL.D. With an introduction by the Rev. William West, B.A.,

Incumbent of S. Columba's, Nairn. London: Sampson Low, Son, & Marston. 1869. 16°. Introduction, pp. v–xlv.

Rasselas. A Tale. By Dr. Johnson. London: Groombridge. 1870. 32°.

The History of Rasselas, Prince of Abyssinia. By Dr. Johnson. London: Whittaker & Co., Ave Maria Lane. [1879.] 16°. Reissued in 1880.

Clarendon Press Series. Johnson, Select Works. [Lives of Dryden and Pope and *History of Rasselas.*] Edited, with introduction and notes, by Alfred Milnes. Oxford. MDCCCLXXIX. 8°.

Classical Tales, comprising Johnson's *Rasselas*, Goldsmith's *Vicar of Wakefield*... London: George Bell and Sons, York Street, Covent Garden, 1882 (Bohn's Standard Library).

The Vicar of Wakefield, Rasselas, Paul and Virginia. George Routledge and Sons, London [1882].

The impression of *Rasselas* was also issued separately.

The History of the Caliph Vathek. By William Beckford. . . . Also Rasselas, Prince of Abyssinia. By Samuel Johnson, LL.D. London: J. C. Nimmo and Bain . . . 1883. 8°.

The History of Rasselas, Prince of Abyssinia. By Samuel Johnson, LL.D. London: T. Fisher Unwin, 17 Holborn Viaduct, E.C. 1883. 12°.

Voltaire's Candide or the Optimist; and Rasselas, Prince of Abyssinia, by Samuel Johnson. With an introduction by Henry Morley. London: George Routledge and Sons. ... 1884 (Morley's Universal Library, vol. xix).

Rasselas, Prince of Abyssinia. By Samuel Johnson, LL.D. Being a Facsimile Reproduction of the First Edition published in 1759. In two volumes. With an introduction by Dr. James Macaulay; and a bibliographical list of editions of *Rasselas* published in England and elsewhere. London: Elliot Stock, 62, Paternoster Row. 1884. 2 vols. 8°.

Ten copies were printed on large paper bound in wood from Dolly's Chop-house.

Johnson: History of Rasselas, Prince of Abyssinia. Edited, with introduction and notes, by George Birkbeck Hill, D.C.L. Oxford, At the Clarendon Press, 1887.

Rasselas, Prince of Abyssinia. By Samuel Johnson, LL.D. (Cassell's National Library). London. 1889. Also 1904.

Introduction, signed H. M. [Henry Morley], pp. 5–8.

The History of Rasselas. With an introduction and notes by Oliver Farrar Emerson. New York, Henry Holt and C°. 1895. 16°. Pp. lv, 179.

Rasselas, Prince of Abyssinia. A Romance, by Dr. Samuel Johnson. Edited with an Introduction by Justin Hannaford. Illustrated by W. S. Rogers. London. 1900.

Introduction, pp. xv–xxiv.

The History of Rasselas, Prince of Abissinia, by Samuel Johnson, LL.D. Van Vechten & Ellis, Wisconsin. September, 1902.

Rasselas, Prince of Abyssinia. By Samuel Johnson, LL.D. (Gibson's New Literary Reader, No. 5). Glasgow [1904].

Rasselas, Prince of Abyssinia. By Samuel Johnson, LL.D. With Biographical Introduction by Hannaford Bennett. London, John Long. 1905 (Carlton Classics).

Rasselas. By Dr. Samuel Johnson. London: George Routledge & Sons, Limited. New York: E. P. Dutton and Co. [1906.] (Vol. i of Dr. Johnson's Works in The New Universal Library.)

Rasselas, Prince of Abissinia: A Tale: By Dr. Samuel Johnson. In *Classic Tales*, with an introduction by C. S. Fearenside, M.A. London, 1906 (The York Library).

Rasselas, Prince of Abyssinia. By Samuel Johnson, LL.D. (Cassell's Little Classics, vol. 9). London, 1909.

Introduction, signed H. M. [Henry Morley], pp. 5–8.

An extravaganza, by William Brough, '*Founded on Dr. Johnson's well-known Tale, but at times getting very wide of its foundation*', and called 'Rasselas, prince of Abyssinia, or the Happy Valley', was performed on December 26, 1862, and published by T. H. Lacy (Lacy's Acting-edition of Plays, vol. 57, 1863).

Dinarbas, continuation of 'Rasselas'.

Sir John Hawkins, in his *Life of Johnson* (1787, p. 372), says that Johnson 'had meditated a second part, in which he meant to marry his hero, and place him in a state of permanent felicity'. This suggested:

1790 Dinarbas; A Tale: Being a continuation of Rasselas, Prince of Abissinia [by Ellis Cornelia Knight, then resident in Genoa]. London: Printed for C. Dilly. 1790.

It was passed through the press by John Hoole (*European Mag.*, xxi (1792), p. 165).

Dinarbas, 2nd ed. 1792.

Dinarbas, 3rd ed. 1793.

Dinarbas, 4th ed. 1800.

* Dinarbas, 5th ed. 1811.

Rasselas, and Dinarbas. London, 1817. Also 1823.

Dinarbas, a tale . . . mit Noten u. e. Wörterbuche von F. E. Feller: Leipzig, 1837.

Collection des meilleurs auteurs modernes. *The British Portfolio*, vols. iii and iv. Rasselas, and Dinarbas. 1846.

French Translations and Editions.

Quérard in his *La France littéraire* (vol. iv, 1830) specifies the following editions and translations of Rasselas:

The History of Rasselas, Prince of Abyssinia; Paris, 1818 —Engl. and French, Paris, 1818—Paris, 1821—Boulogne, 1822—Paris, 1825, or 1829.

Histoire de Rasselas, Prince d'Abyssinie, trad. . . . (par Mme Belot, depuis Mme Durey de Meynières). Paris, 1760, 1768, 1788.

La Vallée heureuse, ou le Prince mécontent de son sort, trad. par Louis (D. F. Donnant). Paris, 1803.

Le Vallon fortuné, ou Rasselas et Dinarbas; trad. par M. M.*** C*** (Mac-Carthy). Paris, 1817. 3 vols.

Rasselas, Prince d'Abyssinie, avec la vie de l'auteur, traduct. nouv. (par Fr. Louis). Paris, 1818.

Histoire de Rasselas, Prince d'Abyssinie, traduct. nouv. par M. G. (Gosselin). Paris, 1822. 2 vols.

In *Littérature française contemporaine* (vol. iv, 1852) Quérard adds:

The History of Rasselas, Prince of Abyssinia, a tale. Paris, 1831 and 1842; Lyon, 1834; Paris, 1835; Paris, 1842; Lyon and Paris, 1847; Paris, 1847.

Histoire de Rasselas, Prince d'Abyssinie. Paris, 1827. 2 vols. (coll. des meilleurs romans français et étrangers). —Traduction nouvelle . . . avec le texte en regard par Mme ***. Paris, 1832.

The following works have also appeared:

Rasselas, Prince d'Abissinie. Roman. Traduit . . . par le Comte de Fouchecour. Londres, 1798.

* Rasselas, Prince d'Abyssinie . . . traduit de l'anglais par Alexandre Notré. Londres, 1823.

Aventures de Rasselas, Prince d'Abyssinie (imitation du conte de S. Johnson), par J. J. M. C. de Bergues-la-Garde. Limoges, 1882.

Histoire de Rasselas, Prince d'Abyssinie, conte de Samuel Johnson, LL.D. Traduction littérale de l'anglais par J. Bérard, 2me édition, Paris, 1886.

[Baretti made a translation of *Rasselas* into French, but it was not printed. The opening sentence was dictated to him by Johnson. See Sir James Prior's *Life of Edmond Malone*, 1860, p. 161, and Lacy Collison-Morley's *Giuseppe Baretti*, 1909, pp. 360–1. Ed.]

Other Translations and Editions.

German.

Rasselas, trans. into German by J. F. Schiller. Mainz, 1785.

Rasselas, anonymous trans. into German. Meissen, 1786.

Rasselas, trans. into German by G. Smout. Hamburg, 1827. 2 vols.

The History of Rasselas, Prince of Abissinia. Mit grammatischen, synonymischen und erklärenden Noten und einem Wörterbuche. Leipzig, 1832. Also 1844.

Rasselas, a tale (Campe's edition). Nürnberg and New York, 1836.

Rasselas, Prinz von Habesch. Eine Erzählung von Sam. Johnson. Aus d. Engl. übers. von Georg Nicol. Bärmann. 2 Thle. (Miniaturbibliothek ausländ. Classiker. Vols. iv and v.) 1840. New issue. 185–.

Rasselas, Prince of Abyssinia. A Tale. Für Deutsche bearbeitet und mit einer einleit. Formenlehre, syntaktischen u. die Wortbildung betreff. Noten u. einem etymolog. Wörterbuche versehen von J. Wedewer. Münster, 1841.

The history of Rasselas, Prince of Abissinia. Schmidt's Edition. Nordhausen, 1842.

The history of Rasselas, prince of Abyssinia. With a complete vocabulary compiled by E. Amthor. Revised edition. Leipzig, 1846. Another revised ed., Berlin, 1862.

Die Geschichte v. Rasselas dem Prinzen v. Abessinien u. seinen Forschungen nach dem Glücke u. dem besten Lebensberufe. Eine moral. Erzählg. f. die reifere Jugend u. Jedermann. Aus dem Engl. übers. v. S. Gätschenberger. Würzburg, 1874.

History of Rasselas, prince of Abyssinia, by Samuel Johnson; Bibliothek gediegener und lehrreicher Werke der englischen Litteratur, vol. xiii. 1884.

Italian. Il Principe d'Abissinia, novella in due volumi tradotta per la prima volta dall' originale inglese in toscano da Mimiso Ceo; Padova, G. A. Volpi, 1764.

Mimiso Ceo is the pseudonym of the Cavalier Mei who anticipated Baretti's Italian translation. Cf. Lacy Collison-Morley in *N. & Q.*, 11th Ser., i. 404 (1910), who refers to an article, 'Per la fortuna del *Rasselas* di Samuele Johnson in Italia', by Luigi Piccioni in *Giorn. storico della letter. ital.*, vol. xv, 1910, p. 339.

Rasselas, Principe d'Abissinia: Tradotto dall' Inglese del Signor Dottor Johnson. Londra: Presso G. e W. B. Whittaker, 1823. 12°.

The following Italian translation is from the *Bibliography* of Dr. James Macaulay:

Storia di Rasselas, Principe d'Abissinia, di S. Johnson. Tradotta dall' Inglese da *******. Livorno, dalla Stamperia di G. P. Pozzolini. 1825. 8°.

Spanish.

Ráselas, Principe de Abisínia. Romance. Traducido del Ingles del Dóctor Johnson, por el Rev. Don Felipe Fernandez, A. M. y Fundadór de la Reál Sociedád Economica de Xeréz de la Frontera. Impreso en Londres, por Henrique Bryer, Bridge-Street, Blackfriars, á expensas de Francisco Wingrave, y de dicho Rev. Traductor, 1813, 12°, pp. xviii, 251. Errata on p. [252].

A Spanish translation, by Doña Ines Joyes y Blake, Madrid, 1798, 8°, is mentioned in Graesse's *Tresor de Livres rares*.

Dutch.

Rasselas, Prins van Abyssiniën. Eene Geschiedenis, Naar het Engelsch van Dr S. Johnson. Te Rotterdam, bij J. Immerzeel, Junior. MDCCCXXIV. 8°.

Hungarian.

Rasszelasznak, egy Abyssziniai Királyi herczegnek történetei. Regény Johnson Sámuel 'Angol munkájából. *In* Soproni Estvék. Literatúrai Egyveleg. Kiadja Kis János. Füzet 2. 1840. 8vo. Pp. 40–194.

Polish.

Historya Rasslasa Krolewicza Abissynii, z Angielskiego Przełożona. Juliana Niemcewicza, pism różnych wierszem i prozą. Tom. i, w Warszawie, 1803. 8vo. Pp. 1–208.

Modern Greek.

Ὁ Ῥασσέλας, πρίγγιψ τῆς Ἀββυσινίας, συγγραφ. παρὰ Σαμ. Γιονσονη, μεταφρασ. παρὰ Π.Π. Κερκυρα 1817. 12°.

Quaritch's Catalogue, No. 303, August 1876, p. 1113.

Bengalee.

The History of Rasselas, Prince of Abyssinia, a tale, by Samuel Johnson, LL.D. Translated into Bengalee by Maha-raja Kalee-Krishna Bahadur. Calcutta, 1833.

English and Bengalee on opposite pages.

Brumoy's 'Greek Theatre'.

1759
Boswell, i. 345.

The Greek Theatre of Father Brumoy. Translated By Mrs. Charlotte Lennox. In three volumes. London: Printed for Mess. Millar, Vaillant, *etc.* MDCCLIX.

The 'Dissertation upon the Greek Comedy', vol. iii, pp. 121–61, and 'The General Conclusion', vol. iii, pp. 428–40, are translated by Johnson.

The World Displayed.

1759
Boswell, i. 345.

The World displayed; or, a Curious Collection of Voyages and Travels, Selected from The Writers of all Nations.... London. Printed for J. Newbery, MDCCLIX(–LXI). 20 volumes. 18°. Third edition, 1767, &c. Fourth edition, 1774, &c.

The Introduction, vol. i, pp. iii–xxxii, is by Johnson.

The Daily Gazetteer.

1759
Boswell, i. 351–2.

Johnson contributed to the three numbers for December 1, 8, and 15, 1759, three letters on behalf of his friend John Gwynn, who was engaged in a competition for the erection of Blackfriars Bridge. They were reprinted, with additional information on the bridge, in *The Architect*, Jan. 7, 1887, pp. 13–15.

The Monthly Melody.

1760

The Monthly Melody: or polite amusement for gentlemen and ladies; being a Collection of vocal and instrumental music composed by Dr. Arne. London. Printed for G. Kearsly. MDCCLX.

The Dedication 'To his royal highness Prince Edward' [Duke of York], signed 'The Proprietors, March 30, 1760', pp. i–ii; Introduction, pp. iii–vi; text, pp. vii–47; then Music, 1–37, and 1–35 leaves. The advertisements of the parts in the *London Chronicle* set out that it 'was adapted to the Violin, German Flute, and Guittar'.

(Boswell, ii. 2, *sub* 1765.)

'Johnson told me, a great many years ago, *he believed he had dedicated to all the Royal Family round.* . . . He once dedicated some Musick for the German Flute to Edward, Duke of York.'

Baretti's Dictionary.

1760
Boswell, i. 353.

A Dictionary of the English and Italian Language by Joseph Baretti . . . to which is added an Italian and English grammar. London: 1760. 2 vols.

The dedication (vol. i) 'To his Excellency Don Felix, Marquis of Abren and Bertodano, ambassador extraordinary and plenipotentiary from his Catholic Majesty to the King of Great Britain' was written by Johnson. Baretti states in the Preface that in the composition of his grammars he had taken Johnson and Buonmattei as his guides. The dedication is in the edition of 1771, but the edition of 1778 does not contain it.

Baretti's *Grammar of the Italian Language* (1762) contained (pp. 153–288) a 'Praxis of sentences [entitled Thoughts on various subjects] collected from the works of my friend and instructor Mr. Samuel Johnson,' both in Johnson's English and Baretti's Italian version. These are reproduced in the 1778 ed., pp. 165–399.

Baretti's *Journey from London to Genoa* (1770, 2 vols.) was suggested by Johnson. 'It was he', says the preface, 'that exhorted me to write daily and with all possible minuteness: it was he that pointed out the topics which would most interest and most delight in a future publication. To his injunctions I have kept as close as I was able.'

Proceedings of Committee.

Proceedings of the Committee appointed to manage the contributions begun at London Dec. xviii, MDCCLVIIII, for cloathing French prisoners of war. . . . London, MDCCLX.

1760 Boswell, i. 353.

The introduction (2 pp.) was written by Johnson.

The Gentleman's Magazine.

Account of a Book, entitled, 'An historical and critical Enquiry into the Evidence produced by the Earls of Moray and Morton, against Mary Queen of Scots. With an Examination of the Rev. Dr. Robertson's Dissertation, and Mr. Hume's History, with respect to that Evidence.' [By William Tytler. Edinburgh, MDCCLX.] October 1760, pp. 453–6.

1760 Boswell, i. 354.

Address to the King.

Address of the Painters, Sculptors, and Architects to George III on his accession to the throne. *London Gazette*, Jan. 6–10, 1761, p. 1.

1761 Boswell, i. 352.

This address was drawn up by Johnson.

Gwynn's 'Thoughts on the Coronation'.

1761
Boswell, i. 361.

Thoughts on the Coronation of his present Majesty, King George the Third, or Reasons offered against confining the Procession to the usual Track and pointing out others more commodious and proper [by John Gwynn]. London: MDCCLXI. 1*s.* 6*d.*

Johnson 'lent his friendly assistance to correct and improve' this pamphlet.

Edition of Ascham.

1761
Boswell, i. 464,

The English works of Roger Ascham, Preceptor to Queen Elizabeth. . . . With Notes and Observations, and the Author's Life. By James Bennet, Master of the Boarding-School at Hoddesdon in Hertfordshire. London: MDCCLXI. —Another issue with undated title-page [1762].

The dedication 'To Anthony Ashley Cooper, Earl of Shaftesbury' and 'The Life of Roger Ascham' (pp. i–xvi) were written by Johnson. Tom Davies stated that Johnson was 'in reality' the editor and that he gave the work to Bennet for his advantage. The work was issued to the subscribers early in January 1762. The death on August 14, 1762, of Bennet's wife is given in the *London Chronicle*, Aug. 21–24, p. 191.

The English Works of Roger Ascham, *etc.* A new edition. London: MDCCCXV.

The Life by Johnson is reprinted in this edition (pp. xxviii).

The Gentleman's Magazine.

1762
Boswell, i. 406–8.

An Account of the Detection of the Imposture in Cock-Lane. February, 1762, p. 81.

This account, which was written by Johnson, is stated to have been 'drawn up by a gentleman of veracity and learning'. According to Boswell, it had been previously published in the newspapers.

Churchill introduced Johnson in the second book of his poem called *The Ghost,* which describes this imposture. He figures as '*Immane* Pompose' and as 'Pomposo (insolent and loud)', but justice is done to his strong sense.

The subject is treated in a chapter, pp. 161–79, in Andrew Lang's *Cock Lane and Common-sense,* 1894 and 1896.

Kennedy's Astronomical Chronology.

A Complete System of Astronomical Chronology unfolding the Scriptures. . . . By John Kennedy, rector of Bradley, in Derbyshire. London. MDCCLXII.

1762 Boswell, i. 366.

The dedication 'To the King' was written by Dr. Johnson. Boswell suggests that the concluding paragraph was also written by him.

Catalogue of Pictures, &c.

Catalogue of the Pictures, Sculptures, Models, Drawings, Prints, &c., exhibited by the Society of Artists of Great Britain at the great room in Spring Gardens, Charing Cross, May the 17th, anno 1762 (being the Third Year of their Exhibition).

1762 Boswell, i. 363.

The preface (pp. 3–vi) to this Exhibition was written by Johnson. It is reprinted in William Sandby's *History of the Royal Academy* (1862), pp. 37–8.

Hoole's Tasso.

Jerusalem Delivered; an heroic poem: translated from the Italian of Torquato Tasso, by John Hoole. London, printed for the Author. . . . MDCCLXIII. 2 vols. 8°.

1763 Boswell, i. 383.

The dedication 'To the Queen' was written by Johnson. The Preface (p. xiv) records that 'Mr. Samuel Johnson, whose judgment I am happy in being authorised to make use of on this occasion, has given me leave to publish it, as his opinion, that a modern translation of the *Jerusalem Delivered* is a work that may very justly merit the attention of the *English* reader'.

Johnson subscribed for a copy.

Fawkes and Woty's 'Poetical Calendar'.

The Poetical Calendar . . . Written and Selected by Francis Fawkes, M.A. and William Woty. Vol. XII. [For December.] London: MDCCLXIII.

1763 Boswell, i. 382–3.

The concluding pages (pp. 107–12) of this work are occupied by 'Some account of the life and writings of Mr. William Collins', and of these pp. 110–12 contain a character of Collins by Johnson, who is described as 'a gentleman deservedly eminent in the republic of letters, who knew him intimately well'.

The entire account, with Johnson's character, is included in the *Gent. Mag.* for 1764, pp. 23–4, and the character was inserted in the account of Collins in the *Lives of the Poets*.

[Some of the doubtful pieces in the collected editions of Johnson's poems (cf. above, p. 21) are also included, e.g. vol. i, pp. 3, 17; vol. iv, p. 3.

Johnson's name is in the list of subscribers to Fawkes's *Original Poems*, 1761, and Woty's *Poetical Works*, 1770. Ed.]

The Critical Review—1763.

1763
Boswell, i. 411.

Review of 'Telemachus, A Mask. By the Rev. George Graham, M.A., Fellow of King's-College, Cambridge.' April, 1763, pp. 314–18.

Johnson in this review commended 'the fertility of imagination, the depth of sentiment, and the knowledge of passion, which are occasionally displayed'.

An abbreviated version of *Telemachus* was set to music by Philip Hayes (1765). Genest (x. 181) says that Graham's mask 'is not badly written, but as a Drama it is very dull'.

A meagre biography of Graham is given in the *D. N. B.* Different versions of the incident when he, 'half drunk,' insulted Goldsmith by dubbing him 'Dr. Minor' in contrast with 'Dr. Major' (Johnson) will be found in Mrs. Piozzi's *Anecdotes of Johnson*, p. 180, and in Boswell's *Hebrides* (under date August 24). Johnson, who delighted in repeating the story, used to add that its effect on Goldsmith, who was as irritable as a hornet, may be imagined. Goldsmith's subsequent remark was, 'Graham is a fellow to make one commit suicide'.

Percy Fitzgerald says (*Life of Garrick*, i. 381–2) that David Garrick used in 1759 to meet Graham at Hampton, 'who was teaching his nephews'. They rode together and Garrick found him 'an agreeable companion'. Graham imparted to the manager that he was planning a tragedy on the Duke of Milan. Garrick encouraged him in his plans and Graham thereupon set to work in earnest. When the piece was finished and sent to Garrick, it was declined. The subsequent letters are set out in the *Private Correspondence of Garrick* (1831), i. 188–9, 193–5.

Johnson wrote to Boswell, on May 27, 1775, 'There are two little books, published by the Foulis, *Telemachus* and Collins's Poems, each a shilling: I would be glad to have them'; and repeated his request on February 18, 1777, 'I wish you would be diligent and get me Graham's *Telemachus*, that was printed at Glasgow, a very little book' (*Boswell*, iii. 104).

Telemachus was published by Robert and Andrew Foulis in 1767, 'a very prettily printed small octavo', an exact reprint of the original quarto.

Graham's nickname among the boys at Eton was Gronkey Graham (Maxwell-Lyte, *Eton College*, fourth ed., p. 317).

1764.

(1) Review of 'The Sugar-cane: A Poem . . . By James Grainger, M.D.' October, 1764, pp. 270–7.

1764
Boswell, i. 481-2.

This is attributed to Johnson. He also reviewed the poem in the *London Chronicle*, xvi (1764), pp. 12, 20, 28. See the *Gent. Mag.*, 1847, pt. ii. 251–2.

(2) Notice of 'The Traveller, or a Prospect of Society. . . . By Oliver Goldsmith, M.B.' December, 1764, pp. 458–62.

This concluded with the statement that it would not be easy to find any thing equal' since Pope's death.

Johnson's Shakespeare.

1765

Johnson's edition of Shakespeare dragged a slow course for many years. He had the scheme in contemplation in 1745, when he issued his pamphlet on the tragedy of *Macbeth*, and he announced his intention in 1756 by publishing proposals for a new edition. The work was promised by Christmas, 1757. When that date arrived, the publication was postponed to March 1758, and in that month was extended to before summer. Subscriptions were duly received, but the more astute among his friends paid him only in part or not at all. Dr. Grainger wrote to Percy (June 1758) that Johnson 'never thinks of working if he has a couple of guineas in his pocket', and next month stated to the same friend that he would 'feed him occasionally with guineas'. Some new particulars relating to the amounts paid him by Tonson are set out in the *Athenæum* for 1909, pt. ii, p. 298, and in the *Bi-Centenary Commemoration Festival Reports*, ed. J. T. Raby, 1909, pp. 29–32.

Many years were to pass away before the new edition came out. Year after year Boswell records the suggestion that Johnson was engaged on Shakespeare. His friends reminded him of his obligations, but procrastination prevailed over duty. A public taunt at his supineness was soon to be levelled at him. The first parts of Churchill's *Ghost* were issued in the spring of 1762, the third part somewhat later in the year. In this Johnson is lashed under the name of Pomposo, and his projected *Shakespeare* supplies the opportunity for a slashing attack. These satiric lines record how

> He for *subscribers* baits his hook
> And takes their cash—but where 's the book?
> No matter where—Wise fear, we know,
> Forbids the robbing of a foe;
> And what, to serve our private ends,
> Forbids the cheating of our friends?

At last—it was in October, 1765, twenty years after the original intention—the promised edition saw the light. The Preface attracted general admiration. Adam Smith is said to have called it 'the most manly piece of criticism that was ever published in any country'. In the Cambridge edition both Preface and notes are described as 'distinguished by clearness of thought and diction and by masterly common sense'. But, taken as a whole, the edition disappointed the expectations of the subscribers. Considerable improvements were made by George Steevens (a student of intelligence and industry, but a malicious opponent of Malone and several of his contemporaries), who co-operated in bringing out the edition of 1773, and reissued it in 1778. To this later edition, Malone added a Supplement of two volumes in 1780.

The third edition of this joint labour of Johnson and Steevens, 'revised and augmented by the Editor of Dodsley's Collection of Old Plays', i. e. by Isaac Reed, came out in 1785 (10 vols.), and the fourth edition in 1793 (15 vols.). To a reissue of this edition new title-pages were added, with the dates running from 1799 to 1802.

Reed produced in 1803 the fifth edition, to which was given the appellation of the 'first variorum', in 21 volumes. The 'second variorum' (1813: 21 vols.) differed but little from its predecessor, but the 'third variorum' (1821), the work of Edmund Malone and James Boswell, the son of Johnson's biographer, was of higher value. Other editions, based on Johnson's labours and making use of his name, are set out on p. 110.

Johnson was attacked at once by the notorious William Kenrick in 'A Review of Dr. Johnson's new edition of Shakespeare: In which the ignorance or inattention of that editor is exposed, and the poet defended from the persecution of his commentators.

London: MDCCLXV.' In the Preface to it he alludes to Johnson's pension, nicknames him 'his Majesty's pensioner,' and revives the story that he felled Tom Osborne to the ground with 'a thundering folio'. His work is called an outrage on Shakespeare.

Kenrick's work was hurried through the press and dealt with a part only of Johnson's volumes. At the end of the *Review* was an Advertisement, that the remainder, 'containing similar remarks on the other five volumes of Dr. Johnson's Commentary, together with a review of his *Preface*, will be published with all convenient speed'. A second Advertisement promised 'some time after Christmas' in one volume, octavo, 'A ramble through the Idler's Dictionary, in which are picked up several thousand etymological, orthographical and lexicographical blunders. By the author of this Review. *His work demands a volume and it shall have it.*'

These works never saw the light. The publisher probably lost money by the publication of the *Review*. Even if it sold sufficiently well to repay him its cost, the comments of his friends in the trade would have told him that the profit did not cover the shame of the publication.

'A young student at Oxford, of the name of Barclay, wrote an answer to Kenrick' which Johnson at first resented. But afterwards he recognized the youth's kindly attention and would have done more but for his early death (*Boswell*, sub 1765). During the tour to the Hebrides (Oct. 1, 1773), Johnson returned to the subject, adding that 'the boy made a good figure at Oxford'. From the language it would seem that the 'boy' was James Barclay, son of the Rev. James Barclay, of Middlesex, who matriculated from Balliol College on Oct. 11, 1764, aged 17, and took the degree of B.A. in 1768. Mr. Gordon Goodwin, in an excellent memoir of Kenrick (*D. N. B.*), mentions 'An Examination of Mr. Kenrick's Review' as the title of the youth's work, but I have not been able to find a copy of it. That 'examination' is briefly noticed in the *Monthly Review*, xxxiv. 316, with the statement that Kenrick had 'met with his match, in every respect'. The reviewer deprecated such abuse.

Kenrick promptly retaliated with 'A Defence of Dr. Kenrick's Review. By a Friend', disguising himself under the initials of R. R., and for long years afterwards lost no opportunity of attacking Johnson's reputation. He referred to the subject in the Preface, dated 1766, to his play of *Falstaff's Wedding*, which was published in January of that year, though the title-page bore the date of 1760.

He assailed him in 1768 in 'An epistle to James Boswell, Esq., occasioned by his having transmitted the Moral writings of Dr. Samuel Johnson to Pascal Paoli', which Boswell would have answered but for Johnson's interposition, and he is said to have addressed in after years another 'Letter to James Boswell, Esq., on the Moral System of the *Idler*'. [It would appear that the Monthly Reviewers regarded Kenrick's *Defence* as a rejoinder to them (xxxiv, p. 45). The *Defence* appeared in January, 1766 (cf. *Gent. Mag.*, 1766, p. 38), and was immediately noticed. Barclay's *Examination*, which is evidently later, was noticed in April. Ed.]

Johnson's Preface gave a great impetus to Shakespearian study. It attracted the admiration of the erudite as well as the vituperation of the libeller. The anonymous volume of 'Observations and conjectures upon some passages of Skakespeare. Oxford, At the Clarendon Press, MDCCLXVI', the work of Thomas Tyrwhitt, was elicited by Johnson's edition. Tyrwhitt was the student whose initials are appended to some notes in the subsequent edition of George Steevens. Ritson pointed out the defects of Johnson and Steevens in an anonymous volume of *Remarks, critical and illustrative, on the text and notes of the last edition of Shakspeare* (1783), and supplemented that treatise with another diatribe which he christened *The Quip Modest* (1788), and in which he attacked Isaac Reed's edition of 1785.

E. H. Seymour was the author of *Remarks, critical, conjectural, and explanatory, upon the plays of Shakspeare* (1805, 2 vols.), which resulted from a collation of the early copies with that of Johnson and Steevens, as edited by Isaac Reed.

Stephen Weston brought out in 1808 a small pamphlet of 18 pages entitled 'Short Notes on Shakespeare by way of supplement to Johnson, Steevens', &c., in the edition of 1793.

John Poole, best known as the author of *Paul Pry*, was the author in 1810 of 'Hamlet travestie . . . with annotations by Dr. Johnson', &c. It was very popular. A sixth edition appeared in 1817, and so late as 1853 it was in the tenth volume of Lacy's acting-edition of plays. There also appeared travesties of *Romeo and Juliet* (1812) and of *Macbeth* (fourth edition, 1813) with burlesque annotations.

Lastly, [Sir] Walter Raleigh gratified the literary world in 1908 by a volume of *Johnson on Shakespeare*, in which he reprinted Johnson's Proposals (1756), the Preface, and some of the Notes on the Plays, and to which he prefixed an introduction of twenty-five

Mr. JOHNSON's

PREFACE

To his EDITION of

Shakespear's Plays.

LONDON:
Printed for J. and R. TONSON, H. WOODFALL, J. RIVINGTON,
R. BALDWIN, L. HAWES, CLARK and COLLINS, T. LONGMAN,
W. JOHNSTON, T. CASLON, C. CORBET, T. LOWNDS,
and the Executors of B. DODD.
M,DCC,LXV.

THE PLAYS OF WILLIAM SHAKESPEARE,

IN EIGHT VOLUMES,

WITH THE

CORRECTIONS and ILLUSTRATIONS

OF

Various COMMENTATORS;

To which are added

NOTES by SAM. JOHNSON.

LONDON:
Printed for J. and R. TONSON, C. CORBET, H. WOODFALL, J. RIVINGTON, R. BALDWIN, L. HAWES, CLARK and COLLINS, W. JOHNSTON, T. CASLON, T. LOWNDS, and the Executors of B. DODD.
M,DCC,LXV.

pages. The Essay in *Johnson on Shakespeare* is reproduced in his *Six Essays on Johnson* (1910), pp. 75–97.

EDITIONS.

The Plays of William Shakespeare, in Eight Volumes, with the Corrections and Illustrations of Various Commentators; To which are added Notes by Sam. Johnson. London: Printed for J. and R. Tonson [*and others*]. MDCCLXV. 8 vols. 8°.

1765 Boswell, i. 318–23, 327–30, 496.

Collation:—Vol. i. Portrait of Shakespeare; general title-page to eight volumes (as above), p. [i]; title-page to vol. i, p. [iii]; Johnson's Preface, pp. v–lxxii; other introductory matter (see below), pp. [lxxiii]–clv (= clxxv).

[Published October 1765; the notice in the *Gentleman's Magazine* for October 1765, p. 479, says that 'the rapid sale of the impression has already made a second necessary, though it has not been published a month'. Ed.]

The Preface by Johnson is followed by the dedication of John Heminge and Henry Condell to the Earl of Pembroke and Montgomery, and by their 'Preface of the Players'. Then come—Pope's preface, Theobald's preface, Sir T. Hanmer's preface, Dr. Warburton's preface, Rowe's Life of Shakespeare, Shakespeare's will, a note to the Life, and the poem of Ben Jonson to Shakespeare. These are succeeded by the plays and an Appendix (vol. viii) of additional notes. In this Appendix are incorporated the observations of many of his friends—Thomas Warton, Sir John Hawkins, George Steevens, Langton, Chamier, Goldsmith, Reynolds, Percy, J. Simpson, Esq. (probably Joseph Simpson), and Holt (John Holt, of Gray's Inn, who published in 1749 a pamphlet on *The Tempest*, and issued 'Proposals for publishing by subscription, Shakespear's Plays'). Last of all is an Appendix, giving a list by Steevens of the editions of Shakespeare's Plays.

The preface was issued separately as 'Mr. Johnson's Preface to his Edition of Shakespear's Plays. London: MDCCLXV.' 8°. 1*s*.

The first forty-two pages of it, translated into Italian, are printed in the first volume (pp. 31–74) of 'Tragedie di Shakspeare tradotte da Michele Leoni. Verona 1819.' A translation into German of some part of it occupies pp. 381–94 of 'G. G. Bredow's nachgelassene Schriften, ed. J. G. Kunisch: Breslau, 1816.'

A considerable portion of the preface was appropriated by

Stendhal (i. e. Marie Henri Beyle). See *Stendhal et l'Angleterre*, by Doris Gunnell, 1909, pp. 249–59.

It is reprinted from the 1778 edition in *Eighteenth Century Essays on Shakespeare*, ed. by D. Nichol Smith, M.A., 1903, pp. 112–61. Cf. introduction, pp. lix–lx, and notes, pp. 321–6.

The views on Shakespeare's Declamations and Narrations are combated in *Hood's Magazine* (vi. 1846) in three articles (pp. 113–23, 209–23, 317–36) entitled 'A Word with Dr. Johnson'.

Johnson's edition formed the subject of two articles (vol. xxxiii, pp. 285–301, 374–89) in the *Monthly Review*, and Kenrick's attack on him was noticed at length (pp. 457–67) in the same volume. An article by J. Parker Norris on Johnson, as editor of Shakespeare, appeared in *Shakespeariana* (Phila., vol. iii, 1886), pp. 25–30. Many of Johnson's notes are printed in the Edinburgh (1768) edition of Shakespeare's Works in ten volumes.

The Plays of Shakespeare, with the corrections and illustrations of various commentators. To which are added notes by Samuel Johnson. Dublin, 1766. 10 vols. 8°.

1768 The Plays of William Shakespeare, in eight volumes, *etc.* [2nd edition]. London: 1768.

The Plays of Shakespeare from the Text of Dr. S. Johnson, with the Prefaces, Notes, etc., of Rowe, Pope . . . Johnson. Dublin, 1771, 7 vols. (vols. 1–6 each in two parts).

1773 The Plays of William Shakespeare. In ten volumes. With the Corrections and Illustrations of Various Commentators; To which are added Notes by Samuel Johnson and George Steevens. With an Appendix. London: MDCCLXXIII.

Johnson added to his Preface the following paragraph: 'Of what has been performed in this revisal, an account is given in the following pages [Advertisement to the Reader, 11 pages] by Mr. Steevens, who might have spoken both of his own diligence and sagacity, in terms of greater self-approbation, without deviating from modesty or truth.'

The list of 'ancient translations from classic authors' (14 pages in vol. i) was corrected and amplified by Richard Farmer. At the end of the last volume is 'a letter from the Rev. Mr. Farmer . . . to Mr. Steevens' containing additional notes (Appendix II, 41 pages).

[The introduction to Appendix I is by Johnson. Ed.]

The Plays of William Shakespeare. In ten volumes, *etc.* The second edition, revised and augmented. MDCCLXXVIII. **1778**

The chief additions in this issue consisted of a 'List of detached pieces of criticism on Shakespeare, his Editors, &c.', vol. i, pp. 248–52; Extracts from the books of the Stationers' Company, pp. 253–68; [Edmond Malone's] Attempt to ascertain the order in which the Plays were written, pp. 269–346.

An imperfect copy of this edition, with copious manuscript notes by Isaac Reed, is in the British Museum. Edmond Malone produced in 1780, in two volumes, a 'Supplement to the edition of 1778'. This was the edition of Shakespeare which John Monck Mason criticized in his *Comments on the last edition of Shakespeare's Plays* (1785), and from it are taken the references to Shakespeare throughout the *Elements of Orthoepy* (1784) by Robert Nares. Edward Capell, in his *Notes and various readings of Shakespeare*, accused Steevens of wholesale plagiarism from his edition of 1768. Cf. the *Critical Review*, Dec. 1783, pp. 403–4.

Johnson and Steevens were satirized in 'The Etymologist, a comedy of three acts, most humbly dedicated to the late Doctor Samuel Johnson's negro servant; to the august and learned body of reviewers; to all the commentators that ever wrote, are writing, or will write, on Shakespear; and particularly to that commentator of commentators, the conjectural, inventive and collatitious, G. S. Esq. [Mottoes]. London. Printed for J. Jarvis, opposite Norfolk-Street, Strand. 1785.'

The Plays of William Shakespeare. In ten volumes, *etc.* The third edition, revised and augmented by the Editor of Dodsley's Collection of Old Plays [Isaac Reed]. 1785. —— 4th ed. . . . by the editor of Dodsley's Collection, etc. 1793, 15 vols. —— New ed. [a reissue of the 1793 with new title-pages]. 1799–1802. —— 5th ed. revised and augmented by I. Reed. 1803. 21 vols. [known as the First variorum edition]. —— 6th ed. 1813. 21 vols. [the Second variorum ed.] —— another ed. 1821. 21 vols. [under editorial care of James Boswell, the Younger. This is the Third variorum ed.]. **1785** and later.

The edition printed by J. Bell in 1788 (20 vols.) and that by W. Gordon at Edinburgh in 1792 (8 vols.) are both said to be 'printed complete from the best editions of Samuel Johnson' and others.

Editions of the Plays and Poems of Shakespeare with the Notes of Johnson and others appeared at Leipzig in 1833 and 1840.

Editions of Shakespeare's Plays partly based on that of Johnson appeared in 1803–5 (10 vols.); 1807 (6 vols.); 1809 (12 vols.); 1823 (1 vol.); 1824 (1 vol.); 1824–6 (Leipzig, 2 vols.); 1825 (1 vol.); 1827 (ed. C. H. Wheeler, 1 vol.); 1841 (1 vol.); 1851 (Hazlitt's ed., in 4 vols.); 1851 (Maunder's ed., 1 vol.); 1864 (M. Cowden Clarke, 1 vol.).; 1868 (M. Cowden Clarke, 1 vol.). Six volumes of 'Shakspeare's Selected Plays from the last edition of Johnson and Steevens' were printed at Avignon by Séguin frères in 1809. Many editions of single plays of Shakespeare, from the text of Johnson, were published at home and abroad, one of the earliest being '*Macbeth*, a tragedy by Shakespear, with explanatory notes selected from Dr. Johnson's and Mr. Steevens's Commentaries. Goettingen, 1778.' For further information about them consult the lists in William Jaggard's exhaustive *Shakespeare Bibliography*, pp. 175–6.

The Preface of Johnson was generally reproduced in the editions based upon his text and containing his Notes, and may be found in the following editions: 1771, Dublin; 1798–1800, 12 vols. (vol. i, pp. xxvii–lxxxii); 1802–4 (Boston, U. S., 8 vols.); 1803 (Johnson, Baldwin and others, 10 vols.); 1803–5 (T. Bensley [for Wynne & Scholey], ix. 92–155); 1806 (ed. Manley Wood); 1815 (7 vols.); 1818 (Whittingham's ed.); 1823 (Bumpus's ed., 9 vols.; Rivington's ed., 10 vols.; Pickering's ed., 9 vols.); 1824 (Otridge & Rackham, 10 vols.); 1825, 1830, 1833, and 1836 (ed. Harness); 1832 (published at Halifax); 1832–4 (Valpy's ed., 15 vols.); 1836, 1838, 1839, and 1840 (Scott, Webster & Geary); 1840 and 1849 (Bohn's ed.); 1841, 1843, 1845, and 1847 (published by Chidley); 1842 (New York ed.); 1855 (T. Nelson & Sons); 1858, 1860, 1862, 1863, and 1875 (published at Halifax).

Two volumes of 'Annotations illustrative of the Plays of Shakespeare by Johnson', and a score of other commentators, were published in 1819. A little pamphlet of fifty-two pages, with the title of *Doctor Johnson's 'Short Strictures' of the Plays of Shakespeare*, was published at 32 Hanway Street, in 1900, and a work by F. B. Ribbans, entitled *Instructive copies selected from Dr. Johnson's criticisms on Shakespeare's Plays*, is said to have been issued about 1873.

Percy's 'Reliques'.

Reliques of Ancient English Poetry. . . . London: Printed for J. Dodsley in Pall-Mall. MDCCLXV. 3 vols. 8°. 1765

The dedication to Elizabeth, Countess of Northumberland (pp. v–viii), is signed Thomas Percy. It 'owed its finest strokes to the superior pen of Dr. Johnson' (letter of Bishop Percy in Robert Anderson's *Life of Johnson* (1815 ed.), p. 309). The Preface (p. ix) states that the ancient folio manuscript containing most of these poems was shown to his friends, who importuned him to publish. 'He could refuse nothing to such judges as the author of the RAMBLER, and the late Mr. SHENSTONE.' Percy adds, on p. xiii, that to Johnson he 'owes many valuable hints for the conduct of the work'. [See G. B. Hill's paper on 'Boswell's Proof-sheets' in *Johnson Club Papers*, 1899, p. 69. Ed.]

Gwynn's 'London Improved'.

London and Westminster improved, illustrated by Plans. To which is prefixed a Discourse on Publick Magnificence; with Observations on the State of Arts and Artists in this Kingdom, *etc.* By John Gwynn. London: Printed for the Author. Sold by Mr. Dodsley, &c. MDCCLXVI. 4°. 1766 Boswell, ii. 25.

Johnson wrote the Dedication 'To The King' (pp. iii–iv).

Considerations on the Corn Laws.

Parliamentary Logick . . . by the right honourable William Gerard Hamilton. With an appendix, containing Considerations on the Corn Laws, by Samuel Johnson, LL.D., never before printed. London: Printed by C. and R. Baldwin, for Thomas Payne, Pall-Mall. MDCCCVIII. 8°. 1766 Boswell, i. 518.

Johnson's tract is printed in an appendix, pp. 239–53. It was written in Nov. 1766, a time when corn was very dear and riots had occurred. He was in favour of continuing the bounty on the exportation of corn. See the Preface, pp. viii–xi. [The volume was edited by Malone. Ed.]

Johnson and Miss Williams.

Miscellanies in Prose and Verse. By Anna Williams. London: Printed for T. Davies, in Great Russel-Street, Covent-Garden. MDCCLXVI. 4°. 1766 Boswell, ii. 25–26.

These pieces were published for the benefit of Miss Anna

Williams, the blind lady who lived with Johnson. He furnished, according to Boswell—

1. The Advertisement. 2 pp.

2. The Ant, from Proverbs, chap. vii [= vi], ver. 6. pp. 1–2.

3. To Miss —— On her giving the Author a Gold and Silk net-work Purse of her own weaving. p. 10.

4. The Happy Life. pp. 18–19.

5. An Epitaph on Claudy Phillips, a Musician. p. 23.

6. An Ode on Friendship. pp. 90–1.

7. A Translation of the Latin Epitaph on Sir Thomas Hanmer, written by Doctor Friend. pp. 94–6.

8. The Fountains: a fairy tale [in prose]. pp. 111–41.

He is said by Boswell to have revised—

1. Verses addressed to Mr. Richardson, on his History of Sir Charles Grandison. pp. 31–4.

2. The Excursion. pp. 49–58.

3. Reflections on a Grave digging in Westminster Abbey. pp. 68–70.

Johnson told Boswell that he had written all but two lines of—

4. On the Death of Stephen Grey (*sic*), F.R.S., the Author of the Present Doctrine of Electricity. pp. 42–3. For this distinguished man of Science, see my Memoir in *N. and Q.*, 10th S., vi. 161, 354 (1906).

[To Miss * * *. On her playing upon the harpsichord. pp. 104–6. This, which Boswell does not mention, has been included among Johnson's poems since 1785. Ed.]

Mrs. Piozzi's copy of this work, presented to Sir James Fellowes 'as the *last* Testimony of true Regard and Esteem', is in the Johnson Museum at Lichfield.

[Johnson had written in 1750 the Proposals for Miss Williams's 'Essays in Prose and Verse',—*Gent. Mag.*, Sept. 1750, p. 423. They were included by Chalmers among Johnson's works in 1823. Ed.]

Adams's Celestial and Terrestrial Globes.

1766
Boswell, ii. 44.

A Treatise describing and explaining the Construction and Use of New Celestial and Terrestrial Globes. . . . By George Adams, Mathematical Instrument-Maker to His Majesty. MDCCLXVI. 8°. —— 2nd ed. MDCCLXIX. 8°.

The dedication 'To The King' (pp. iii–vi) was by Johnson.

Johnson and Goldsmith.

The Good-Natur'd Man: A Comedy. By Mr. Goldsmith. London: Printed for W. Griffin. MDCCLXVIII. 8°.

1768
Boswell, ii. 45.

This piece was produced at Covent Garden on January 29, 1768. The Prologue was written by Johnson and spoken by H. Bensley. It is printed in the *Gentleman's Mag.*, Feb. 1768, pp. 86–7. John Taylor of the *Sun* (*Records of my Life*, 1832, vol. i, p. 109) says that 'our anxious Bard' was originally 'our little Bard', and that the Prologue as published in the *Public Advertiser* in 1769 contained this additional couplet:

> Amidst the toils of this returning year,
> When Senators and Nobles learn to fear.

[The two versions are printed in the *London Magazine* for February 1768, pp. 61 and 98–9. Ed.]

The rest of the Prologue was in keeping with the gloom of its first two lines:

> Prest by the load of life, the weary mind
> Surveys the general toil of human kind.

Johnson contributed to Goldsmith's poem *The Traveller* (1765), line 420, and the last ten lines except the last couplet but one. The last four lines in Goldsmith's *Deserted Village* (1770) were by Johnson (*Boswell*, ii. 5–7).

Goldsmith dedicated his play *She Stoops to Conquer* to Johnson.

See also above, p. 103, *The Critical Review*, 1764.

The London Chronicle.

Character of the Rev. Zachariah Mudge, prebendary of Exeter and Vicar of St. Andrew's, Plymouth. April 29 to May 2, 1769, p. 410, col. 3.

1769
Boswell, iv. 76–7.

Reprinted in *Boswell*, ed. Hill, iv. 77, and in *Mudge Memoirs* (1883), by S. R. Flint, pp. 21–2. Mudge died at Coffleet, Brixton, near Plymouth, the seat of Thomas Veale, on April 2, 1763. Mr. Flint says in the memoir that Mudge died on April 2; in the pedigree at the end of the volume, on April 3.

The False Alarm.

The False Alarm. London: Printed for T. Cadell in the Strand. MDCCLXX. 8°.

1770
Boswell, ii. 111–13.

Half-title:—'The False Alarm. [Price One Shilling.]'

Collation :—Half-title ; title ; text, pp. [3]–53.

[Published January 1770 : see the *Gent. Mag.*, 1770, pp. 32–6, where there is a notice consisting 'chiefly of extracts from the pamphlet itself'. Ed.]

—— The second edition. MDCCLXX.

This, the first of Johnson's series of political pamphlets, all of which were anonymous, though their authorship was generally known, was composed at the request of the Ministry. It was written in Thrale's house 'between eight o'clock on Wednesday night and twelve o'clock on Thursday night'. It supported the action of the Ministerial majority in the House of Commons in assuming that the expulsion of a member of Parliament was equivalent to exclusion, and in asserting that Col. Luttrell (not John Wilkes, who had a great majority of votes) was the duly-elected representative of Middlesex.

The pamphlet, which was at once known to be by Johnson, was fiercely attacked, both in the newspapers and in separate productions. The latter class included—(1) 'A Letter to Samuel Johnson, L.L.D. [Anon. by John Wilkes.] 1770, 1*s*.', which began with the words, 'Sir, Without hesitation or Apology, I address myself to YOU, as the undoubted author of the ministerial rhapsody that has been so industriously circulated under the titled (*sic*) of THE FALSE ALARM. You have ambitiously declared yourself the spitter forth of that effusion of servility and bombast. You *could not* have been concealed.' (2) 'The Constitution defended, and Pensioner exposed ; in Remarks on The False Alarm. [Anon. by John Scott of Amwell.] London : MDCCLXX.' Each tract has on the title-page the six lines from Johnson's *London* on the part played by a pensioner. The note of Wilkes was savage abuse ; that of Scott was respectful regret. (3) 'The Crisis. In answer to The False Alarm. 1770.' The 'very angry answer' of Wilkes is referred to in Langton's notes of Johnson's conversations (*Boswell*, iv. 30).

Johnson was defended in an anonymous poem entitled 'The Remonstrance. MDCCLXX'.

The title of Johnson's tract suggested that of 'The True Alarm. London : MDCCLXX' on the government of Bengal.

Thomas Townshend, Jun., afterwards the first Viscount Sydney, referred to *The False Alarm* in the House of Commons on March 14, 1770, and was answered by William Fitzherbert

(Cavendish, *Debates*, pp. 515–16). A foot-note by John Wright stated that the first edition of this pamphlet came out on Jan. 16, 1770, the second on Feb. 16, and the third on March 12.

Thoughts on Falkland's Islands.

Thoughts on the Late Transactions respecting Falkland's Islands. London: Printed for T. Cadell, in the Strand. MDCCLXXI. 8°.

1771
Boswell, ii. 134–6.

Half-title :—'Falkland's Islands. [Price 1*s.* 6*d.*]'
Collation :—Half-title; title; text, pp. [1]–75.

—— The second edition. London; MDCCLXXI.

This pamphlet was written in answer to Letter 42 (Jan. 30, 1771) of Junius. It contained a history of the Islands from the earliest times to their seizure by the Spaniards and their restoration to the English, without prejudice to the question whether the Spaniards possessed 'the prior right of sovereignty', with a long dissertation on the evils of warfare and the reasons why war against Spain should not be declared. At p. 37 is a paragraph attacking the 'feudal gabble of a man of lessening character' [Lord Chatham]. Two pages later is a reference to Junius, 'one of the few writers of his despicable faction whose name does not disgrace the page of an opponent', and pp. 54 to 58 are occupied with a criticism of his style and opinions. The celebrated sarcasm on George Grenville will be found on p. 68: 'Let him not, however, be depreciated in his grave; he had powers not universally possessed; if he could have got the money, he could have counted it.'

Johnson wrote on March 20, 1771, to Bennet Langton: 'After much lingering of my own and much of the ministry, I have at length got out my paper. But delay is not yet at an end; not many had been dispersed before Lord North ordered the sale to stop. His reasons I do not distinctly know. You may try to find them in the perusal. Before his order a sufficient number were dispersed to do all the mischief, though perhaps not to make all the sport that might be expected from it.'

In the revised issue of the remaining copies of the first edition this stroke on Grenville was robbed of its point. It was reduced (p. 68) to the flat level of 'he had powers not universally possessed; and if he sometimes erred he was likewise sometimes right.' A sarcastic letter (dated April 2, 1771) to the *Public*

Advertiser comments on this alteration. It can be seen in the 1812 edition of Junius, ii. 199–200.

Thoughts on the late transactions, *etc.* [Anon.] Dublin: Printed for J. Williams at N° 5 in Skinner-Row. MDCCLXXI.

This was an Irish piracy of the revised issue.

Johnson was answered in 'A Refutation of a Pamphlet called *Thoughts on the Late Transactions respecting Falkland's Islands.* In a letter addressed to the author and dedicated to Dr. Samuel Johnson.' 1771.

Thomas Townshend, Jun., brought this pamphlet also before the House of Commons, and commented on the fact that Johnson was a pensioner of the Crown. Wedderburn protested that the pension was given for Services in letters, and Townshend then gave some explanation of his action (Cavendish, *Debates,* ii. 456–7).

1772
Boswell, ii. 144.

In 1772 Johnson had been 'altogether quiescent as an authour' (Boswell, ii. 143). In this year he wrote the two lines of Latin verse which were afterwards published with the title 'Facsimile inscription for the collar of Sir Joseph Banks's Goat; designed in 1772 by Dr. Samuel Johnson'. Norwich, [? 18..]. 4°.

Macbean's Geography.

1773
Boswell, ii. 204.

A Dictionary of Ancient Geography. . . . By Alexander Macbean, M.A. London, 1773. 8°.

The preface (pp. iii–iv) was written by Johnson. Macbean had been one of his old amanuenses, but Johnson lost faith in him when as much space was devoted in this work to Capua as to Rome.

Miscellaneous and Fugitive Pieces.

1773
Boswell, ii. 270–1.

Miscellaneous and Fugitive Pieces. London: Printed for T. Davies, in Russell-Street, Covent-Garden, Bookseller to the Royal Academy. [1773]. 2 Vols. 8°.

All the pieces in the first volume were by Johnson, and most of those in the second. Boswell says that these volumes were published during Johnson's absence and advertised by Davies as 'by the Authour of the Rambler'. But the second volume contained several pieces which were not by Johnson, who was at first very angry with the liberty which Davies had taken. A third volume, dated MDCCLXXIV and containing more pieces by

MISCELLANEOUS

AND

FUGITIVE PIECES.

VOLUME THE FIRST.

LONDON:

Printed for T. Davies, in *Ruſſel-Street*, *Covent-Garden*, Bookſeller to the Royal Academy.

Johnson, was issued as the property of 'T. Davies . . . and Carnan and Newbery, St. Paul's Church Yard'. A 'second edition, corrected' of the first two volumes was published in 1774, but the title-page was the only novelty.

The Patriot.

1774 Boswell, ii. 285–8.

The Patriot. Addressed to the Electors of Great Britain. They bawl for Freedom . . . must first be wise and good. Milton. London: Printed for T. Cadell, in the Strand. MDCCLXXIV. [Price *6d.*] 8°.

Collation :—Title ; text, pp. [1]–33.

'The *Patriot* was called for by my political friends on Friday, was written on Saturday' (Johnson to Boswell, Nov. 26, 1774). Its object was to defend the Ministry and to support his friend Thrale, the Ministerial candidate for Southwark. The best part of the pamphlet is in vindication of the Quebec Act.

The Patriot. The second edition. MDCCLXXIV. 8°.

The Patriot. The third edition. MDCCLXXV. 8°.

The Patriot. Dublin: Printed for E. Lynch. MDCCLXXV.

It was answered in 'Remarks on the Patriot. Including some hints respecting the Americans: with an address to the electors of Great Britain. [Anon.; by John Scott of Amwell.] 1775.' 1*s.*

The Rev. Joseph Towers, LL.D., published 'A Letter to Dr. Samuel Johnson: occasioned by his late political publications. With an Appendix, containing some observations on a pamphlet lately published by Dr. Shebbeare. [Anon.] London: MDCCLXXV.' 1*s.* 6*d.* This was reprinted in 'Tracts on political and other subjects. By Joseph Towers, LL.D. London: MDCCXCVI,' vol. i, pp. 145–232.

1775 Boswell, ii. 289–90.

Proposals for publishing the Works of Mrs. Charlotte Lennox.

Boswell found in Johnson's Diary, January 2, 1775, the entry: 'Wrote Charlotte's Proposals'.

Journey to the Western Islands.

This journey was long in Johnson's contemplation. It was mooted by him in July 1763, when he was nearly 54 years old, at a supper with Boswell 'in a private room at the Turk's Head coffee-house in the Strand', and the possibility of its accomplishment was often dwelt upon in their subsequent intercourse. Boswell did not forget it, and Johnson's courage did not fail. In 1773, when 54 years of age had ripened into 64, the journey was made.

The wish for this expedition had a strange origin. When Johnson was very young, a copy of Martin Martin's *Description of the Western Islands of Scotland* (1703) was put into his hands by his father. His attention was drawn to the anecdote of the man of St. Kilda, who thought that the high church of Glasgow had been carved out of a high rock, and remarked that there were some in that island 'much higher' (p. 297). This fascinated him and remained, while life lasted, in his mind. The question of *Second-sight* may also have attracted him. Eight pages of Johnson's volume (pp. 248–56) are given to this subject, and Martin had devoted to it much more of his space (pp. 300–35). The copy of Martin's work (1703 edition) which the travellers took with them in their travels is in the Advocates' Library in Edinburgh. A manuscript note by Boswell, dated April 16, 1774, and written on the back of the title-page, says: 'His book is a very imperfect performance, and is erroneous as to many particulars, even some concerning his own Island. . . . I cannot but have a kindness for him notwithstanding his defects.'

Johnson arrived at Edinburgh on August 14, and left it, on his return to London, on November 22, a period of one hundred days. He started on his journey from Edinburgh on August 18, passing through St. Andrews and Aberdeen, where he received the freedom of the city, and reached Inverness on the 28th. There they mounted horses and proceeded to Glenelg, where they took boat on Sept. 2 for Skye. They remained in these islands of the West, 'placed far amid the melancholy main', until Friday, October 22, when they crossed from Mull to the mainland at Oban. This period of their travels occupies Johnson's volume to p. 369. The rest of it (to p. 384) very briefly dismisses his stay at Glasgow, his visit to Boswell's father at Auchinleck, and his sojourn at Edinburgh.

During this stay in Edinburgh Johnson was 'at great pains to obtain information concerning Scotland', and in writing to Boswell, on the day after his arrival in London, urged him to 'quicken' Dr. Alexander Webster, a laborious collector of statistics, who had 'promised him information concerning the Highlands and Islands of Scotland'. It was some time before he received Dr. Webster's 'informations', and when he did, they were 'much less exact and much less determinate' than he expected.

Meantime, Johnson proceeded vigorously with his book. The first sheets went to the press on June 20, 1774, and all but two were written before his visit to Wales with the Thrales. Owing to the dissolution of Parliament and the dilatoriness of the printer, progress was but slow. However, by October 27 he had printed 240 pages, and on the night of November 25 he corrected the last page. A copy of it reached Boswell on January 18, 1775. He stayed up the greatest part of the night to read it, and next day wrote to Johnson to correct a brace of errors: 'In page 106, for Gordon read Murchison; and in page 357, for Maclean read Macleod'. But the second edition of the *Journey* did not come out until the year after Johnson's death, and these, like other mistakes, have not been corrected. The correspondence on the blunder relating to the Macleods of Rasay is printed in Boswell's *Journal of a Tour to the Hebrides* (Hill's edition, pp. 410–13). An advertisement of this error was inserted by Johnson in the Edinburgh newspapers in May 1775, and prefixed to the second edition of his *Journey* (1785).

Four thousand copies of his work, priced at 5*s.* apiece, were sold very quickly, but the demand then ceased. Its subsequent sale in England was probably stimulated by the appearance in 1785 of Boswell's popular volume.

These travels of Johnson were no inconsiderable feat for a man of his age and size. They were not free from danger or discomfort. But he went through the troubles which attended his wanderings without flinching. His narrative of the journey was written in a more homely style than many of his previous publications, and it was not meant unkindly. He commented on the paucity of trees of any age, and on the abundance of beggars. He protested against the lack of fresh air in the rooms, and he dwelt on the increase of rents. He clamoured for evidence on the authenticity of the poems attributed to Ossian. But he paid compliments when he could, even praising 'the melody of the bagpipe'. The social life of the inhabitants was scrutinized closely. 'A man of the Hebrides, . . . as soon as he appears in the morning, swallows a glass of whisky' was one of his dicta. Another observation of the old man was that, 'if an epicure could remove by a wish, in quest of sensual gratifications, wherever he had supped he would breakfast in Scotland'. I always feel pleasure in the confession: 'I sat down on a bank, such as a writer of Romance might have delighted to feign. I had indeed no trees to whisper over my head, but a clear rivulet streamed at my feet. The day was calm, the air soft, and all was rudeness, silence, and solitude. Before me, and on either side, were high hills, which by hindering the eye from ranging, forced the mind to find entertainment for itself. Whether I spent the hour well I know not; for here I first conceived the thought of this narration.' But his most eloquent passage, perhaps the best-known prose sentence of any writer in the English language, records the opinion: 'That man is little to be envied, whose patriotism would not gain force upon the plain of *Marathon*, or whose piety would not grow warmer among the ruins of *Iona*' (p. 347). A handsome volume entitled *Footsteps of Dr. Johnson* (Scotland) was published by Dr. Birkbeck Hill in 1890. It was illustrated by Lancelot Speed, who had visited many of the scenes in Hill's company.

The best among the Scotch read his disquisitions on the raising of rents and the numbers of emigrants with keen interest and treated his prejudices in a spirit of forgiveness. But a crowd of scribblers buzzed around him, both in separate publications and in paragraphs in the Edinburgh papers, which James Macpherson, the Court-superintendent of the newspapers, could order for insertion.

The separate answers to Johnson were:

(1) Remarks on a Voyage to the Hebrides, in a Letter to Samuel Johnson, LL.D. [Anon.] London: Printed for George Kearsly, No. 46 Fleet-street. MDCCLXXV.

(2) A Letter to Dr. Samuel Johnson, on his Journey to the Western Isles. By Andrew Henderson. [London. 1775.]

(3) A Second Letter to Dr. Samuel Johnson. In which his wicked and opprobious (*sic*) Invectives are shewn; the Conspiracy against Mr. Macklin clear'd up; an Anecdote submitted to David Garrick Esq; With An impartial Character of Doctor Smollet; and a Method laid down for adding to the British Revenue 1,000,000 Sterling. By Andrew Henderson. London. [1775.]

(4) A Journey to the Highlands of Scotland. With Occasional Remarks on Dr. Johnson's Tour: By a Lady [i. e. Mary Ann Hanway]. London. [1776?]

(5) Remarks on Dr. Samuel Johnson's Journey to the Hebrides; in which are contained, Observations on the Antiquities, Language,

Genius, and Manners of the Highlanders of Scotland. By The Rev. Donald McNicol, A.M. Minister of Lismore in Argyleshire. *Old Men* and *Travellers* LIE by Authority. Ray's Proverbs. London: Printed for T. Cadell, in the Strand. M.DCC.LXXIX.

Boswell refers (ii. 308) to this as 'a scurrilous volume, larger than Johnson's own, filled with malignant abuse, under a name, real or fictitious, of some low man in an obscure corner of Scotland, though supposed to be the work of another Scotchman [Macpherson], who has found means to make himself well known both in Scotland and England'. It was reprinted, together with Johnson's *Journey*, at the Stanhope Press in Glasgow in 1817, in one volume, 'in a fine large type', and was reproduced in Glasgow in 1852, and in London by Tegg in 1875.

McNicol was a real person, the minister of Lismore. He died on March 28, 1802, in his sixty-seventh year. He is mentioned by A. C. Fraser in *Biographia Philosophica* (second edition, MCMV, p. 33) as 'a Celtic poet' and a 'caustic critic'. This work is described in the Rev. William Shaw's *Enquiry* as having 'been many years in composing. It underwent a vast variety of editions in manuscript, and has been corrected, amended, and improved by many hands in Scotland; and, finding its way to London, was prepared for the press by a friendly embellisher. These amendments and additions are ascribed by many to Mr. Macpherson himself.' A favourable notice of it is in the *Critical Review*, 1780, pt. i, 241–8. The draft of the *Remarks* belongs to the Rev. George Henderson. See *A descriptive Catalogue of Gaelic MSS. in the Advocates' Library, Edinburgh*, by Donald Mackinnon, 1912, p. 320.

Johnson was severely attacked also by Captain Edward Topham in Letter xvii ('On the Reception of Dr. Johnson's Tour at Edinburgh') of his popular *Letters from Edinburgh* (Anon. 1776), pp. 137–43, and in a whimsical book by A. G. Sinclair, M.D., which was entitled *The Critic Philosopher* (1789), pp. 86–91; fifth edition (1791), pp. 156–62. James Macpherson threatened him with personal violence, and Johnson retorted by the purchase of a cudgel six feet long and by the sending to Macpherson of a sharp letter (T. Bailey Saunders, *Life of Macpherson*, 1894, pp. 233–57). Robert Fergusson addressed a poem 'To the Principal and Professors of the University of St. Andrews on their Superb Treat to Dr. Samuel Johnson' (Poems, ed. Robert Ford, 1905, pp. 60–3). John Knox, bookseller, published in 1787 *A Tour through the Highlands of Scotland and the Hebride Isles.* This contained (pp. lxvi–lxix) a courteous account of Johnson's book and (Appendix, pp. 1–7) his description of Icolmkill. Peter Buchan, in his *Annals of Peterhead* (1819), pp. 32–7, included an account of an excursion to the Bullers of Buchan, Slains Castle, etc., with remarks on Dr. Johnson's *Tour to the Hebrides.* There was inserted in *All the Year Round*, May 14, 1870, pp. 561–5, an article on Dr. Johnson—'from a Scottish point of view'; and even so late as 1905 an article by J. Cuthbert Haddon on 'Johnson and Boswell in Scotland' came out in the *Gentleman's Magazine*, vol. ccxcviii, pp. 597–605.

There appeared in May 1787 a volume of 'Extracts from the publications of Mr. Knox, Dr. Anderson, Mr. Pennant and Dr. Johnson; relative to the northern and north-western Coasts of Great Britain. London: Printed by C. Macrae, Orange-Street, Leicester-Square.' One extract only (pp. 11–12) was given from Johnson. An abridgement of Johnson's volume appeared in *The Modern Traveller* (1777), 6 vols. It is slightly shortened in William Mavor's *British Tourists*, vol. ii, 1798. Several extracts from it are given in 'The Flowers of Modern Travels. By the Rev. John Adams. Boston, U.S., 1797,' vol. ii, pp. 262–312.

Johnson's Latin ode on Insula Sancti Kennethi [Inchkenneth] was translated into English verse by Sir Daniel K. Sandford. It will be found in *The Book of Highland Verse*, ed. Dugald Mitchell (1912), p. 204.

EDITIONS.

1775
Boswell, ii. 288, etc.

A Journey to the Western Islands of Scotland. London: Printed for W. Strahan; and T. Cadell in the Strand. MDCCLXXV. 8°.

Collation:—Title-page; the journey, pp. [1]–384; errata, p. [385].

A presentation copy, marked 'Pemb: Coll: Library, from the Author', but not in Johnson's handwriting, is in Pembroke College, Oxford. [In this copy the page of errata is inserted between the title-page and the text. Ed.]

Although there is no mention on the title-page of Johnson as the author, the opening sentence must have indicated the writer to every one.

There is a curious misprint on p. 60, *sub* Lough Ness, where Johnson says: 'we mounted our steeds on the thirteenth of

A JOURNEY TO THE WESTERN ISLANDS OF SCOTLAND.

LONDON:
Printed for W. STRAHAN; and T. CADELL in the Strand.
MDCCLXXV.

away, and converted into money for the ſupport of the army. A Scotch army was in thoſe times very cheaply kept; yet the lead of two churches muſt have born ſo ſmall a proportion to any military expence, that it is hard not to believe the reaſon alleged to be merely popular, and the money intended for ſome private purſe. The order however was obeyed; the two churches were ſtripped, and the lead was ſhipped to be ſold in Holland. I hope every reader will rejoice that this cargo of ſacrilege was loſt at ſea.

Let us not however make too much haſte to deſpiſe our neighbours. There is now, as I have heard, a body of men, not leſs decent or virtuous than the Scotiſh council, longing to melt the lead of an Engliſh cathedral. What they ſhall melt, it were juſt that they ſhould ſwallow.

Thoſe

This Leaf was cancelled by the Author & is reckoned uncommon on account of this last Paragraph. Litchfield is the Cathedral alluded to

ERRATA.

Page 102 line 6, for *Mull Buy* read *Mull Roy*.
—— 110 —- 6, for *ſkin* read *hair*.
—— 147 —- 7, for *Iſland* read *Iſlands*.
—— 173 —- 9, for *ſecond* read *third*.
—— 180 line laſt, for *food* read *ſeed*.
—— 182 —- 3, for *parched* read *not parched*.
—— 199 —- 13, for *afford* read *affording*.
—— 207 —- 15, for *treaſon* read *weapon*.
—— 222 —- 12, for *their* read *his*.
—— 231 — 13, for *ſtoves* read *ſtores*.
—— 278 —- 3, for *in* a very active and ſkilful *manner*, read *is* a very active and ſkilful *mariner*.

ERRATA.

Page 102 line 6, for *Mull Buy* read *Mull Roy*.
—— 110 —- 6, for *ſkin* read *hair*.
—— 147 —- 7, for *Iſland* read *Iſlands*.
—— 173 —- 9, for *ſecond* read *third*.
—— 180 line laſt, for *food* read *ſeed*.
—— 182 —- 3, for *parched* read *not parched*.

August'. This should have been printed 'the thirtieth'. A second and equally curious misprint occurs on p. 107, where they are said to have crossed to Skye on 'September the twentieth' instead of September 2. The first of these misprints has been noticed, but the second has never been corrected.

Archdeacon Wrangham says (*Catal. of my English Lib.*, p. 302) that 'in a Copy sold at Dr. Lort's sale for 15*s.* were preserved the cancelled parts of p. 84 relative to Lichfield Cathedral, and of p. 296 respecting the Cave of Egg and the transaction at that place'.

A translation into German was published at Leipzig in this year (1775).

A French translation is in *Nouveau recueil de voyages au nord de l'Europe et de l'Asie*, Genève, 1785–6, 3 vols. 4°, or 6 vols. 8°. Quérard (*La France littéraire*, vol. iv) mentions a translation by H. de Labédoyère, Paris, 1804.

A Journey to the Western Islands of Scotland. By Dr. Samuel Johnson. Dublin: MDCCLXXV.

1785

A Journey to the Western Islands of Scotland. A new edition. London: Printed for A. Strahan; and T. Cadell, in the Strand. MDCCLXXXV.

Prefixed to the narrative, p. [iii], is the following notice: 'Strand, Oct. 26, 1785. SINCE this Work was printed off, the Publisher having been informed that the Author, some years ago, had promised the Laird of Rasay, to correct, in a future edition, a passage concerning him, p. 133, thinks it a justice due to that Gentleman to insert here the Advertisement relative to this matter, which was published, by Dr. Johnson's desire, in the Edinburgh Newspapers in the year 1775, and which has been lately reprinted in Mr. Boswell's *Tour to the Hebrides:*

'*The Authour of the* Journey to the Western Islands, *having related that the* Macleods *of* Rasay *acknowledge the chieftainship, or superiority, of the* Macleods *of* Sky, *finds that he has been misinformed or mistaken. He means in a future edition to correct his errour, and wishes to be told of more, if more have been discovered.*'

A Journey to the Western Islands of Scotland. A new edition. London: Printed for A. Strahan; and T. Cadell, in the Strand. MDCCXCI.

The notice prefixed to the 1785 edition is repeated in this.

A Journey to the Western Islands of Scotland. A new edition. Edinburgh, 1792.

The passage about the Macleods of Rasay remains unaltered.

A Journey to the Western Islands of Scotland. A new edition. Edinburgh, 1798.

The passage about the Macleods of Rasay remains unaltered, but the above notice is prefixed to the narrative.

Journey to the Western Islands of Scotland, by Samuel Johnson, LL.D. 1773. The British Tourists, ed. William Mavor, LL.D., vol. ii, 1798; vol. ii (third ed.), 1809.

The passage relating to the Macleods of Rasay remains unaltered.

A Journey to the Western Islands of Scotland. A new edition. Alnwick: printed by J. Catnach for J. Wallis, 46 Paternoster-Row, London, 1800. Price 3*s.* in boards.

This is the first edition in which I have noticed that the misprint (*sub* Lough Ness) has been altered to 'thirtieth of August'. The passage on the Macleods of Rasay has not been altered.

Journey to the Western Islands of Scotland. By Samuel Johnson, LL.D. Philadelphia, 1810.

A Journey to the Western Islands of Scotland. By Samuel Johnson, LL.D. A new edition. Edinburgh, 1811.

The word 'thirteenth' of August still remains, nor has the sentence about the Macleods of Rasay been corrected.

Tour to the Western Islands of Scotland; with essays on a variety of subjects. By Samuel Johnson, LL.D. New York, 1812.

A Journey to the Western Islands of Scotland; by Samuel Johnson, LL.D. A new edition. London: printed by *Luke Hansard and Sons, near Lincoln's-Inn Fields,* for T. Cadell And W. Davies, In The Strand. 1816.

The date (*sub* Lough Ness) has been mistakenly corrected to 'the twenty-eighth of August', and the erroneous sentence on the Macleods of Rasay has been omitted.

Taxation no Tyranny;

AN

ANSWER

TO THE

RESOLUTIONS AND ADDRESS

OF THE

AMERICAN CONGRESS.

LONDON,

PRINTED FOR T. CADELL, IN THE STRAND.

MDCCLXXV.

A Journey to the Western Islands of Scotland. By Samuel Johnson, LL.D. A new edition. Edinburgh, 1819.

In this edition the misprint 'thirteenth' and the mistake concerning the Macleods of Rasay are retained.

Journey to the Western Islands of Scotland and political tracts. By Samuel Johnson, LL.D. 1824.

A Journey to the Western Islands of Scotland in 1773. By Samuel Johnson, LL.D. Glasgow, 1876.

In this edition the two misprints and the error concerning the Macleods of Rasay are retained.

A Journey to the Western Islands of Scotland. By Samuel Johnson, LL.D. Cassell & Company, Limited. [Vol. 51 of Cassell's National Library.] London. . . . 1886.

The introduction is signed H. M. [Henry Morley]. The misprint *sub* Loch Ness is altered, but erroneously, to 'the 28th of August', and the error concerning the Macleods of Rasay has been omitted. The mistake of 'September the twentieth' is uncorrected.

A Journey to the Western Islands of Scotland. Leipzig, 1889.

A Journey to the Western Islands of Scotland in 1773. By Samuel Johnson, LL.D. With a preface by D. T. Holmes. Paisley [1906].

In this edition the two misprints and the error relating to the Macleods of Rasay are all retained.

Taxation no Tyranny.

1775 Boswell, ii. 312–15.

Taxation no Tyranny; an Answer to the Resolutions and Address of the American Congress. London, Printed for T. Cadell, in the Strand. MDCCLXXV. 8°.

Half-title:—'Taxation no Tyranny. [Price 1*s*. 6*d*.]'

Collation:—Half-title; title; text, pp. [1]–91.

[Published March, 1775; see *Gent. Mag.*, 1775, pp. 134–6. Ed.]

Four editions came out in 1775. Boswell gives several passages which had been struck out as too violent by the ministers.

Johnson's pamphlet was answered in:

(1) The Pamphlet, entitled, 'Taxation no Tyranny' candidly

considered, and it's arguments, and pernicious doctrines, exposed and refuted. [Anon.] London. [1775].

The copy in the Bodleian Library is that of Jonathan Boucher, Ex Dono Auctoris.

(2) An Answer to a Pamphlet entitled Taxation no Tyranny. Addressed to the Author, and to Persons in Power. [Anon.] London: MDCCLXXV.

(3) A Defence of the Resolutions and Address of the American Congress, in reply to Taxation no Tyranny. By the Author of Regulus. To which are added, General remarks on the leading principles of that work, as Published in *The London Evening Post* of the 2d and 4th of May . . . London. [1775] 2*s*.

(4) Taxation, Tyranny. Addressed to Samuel Johnson, L.L.D. (*sic*). [Anon.] London: MDCCLXXV.

(5) Tyranny Unmasked. An answer to a late pamphlet, entitled Taxation no Tyranny. [Anon.] London: MDCCLXXV.

(6) An Appendix to a letter to Dr. Shebbeare. To which are added Some observations on a pamphlet, entitled, Taxation no Tyranny; in which the Sophistry of that Author's reasoning is detected. By a Doctor of Laws [i. e. Hugh Baillie]. London: MDCCLXXV.

(7) Resistance no Rebellion; in answer to Doctor Johnson's Taxation no Tyranny. [Anon.] London: MDCCLXXV. 1*s*.

The aim of 'Resistance no Rebellion' was to prove that John Wesley's *Calm Address to the American Colonies* was 'pirated, almost verbatim, from Johnson's Pamphlet, called *Taxation no Tyranny*', p. 2.

Johnson's Tory predilections were satirized in:

(1) An Essay upon the KING'S FRIENDS; with an account of some discoveries made in Italy and found in a Virgil, concerning the Tories, to Dr. S—— J——n. London: J. Almon, MDCCLXXVI.

This is by John Hall Stevenson. See his works, vol. i (1795), pp. 249–85.

(2) The sixteenth ode of the Third book of Horace imitated. With a dedication [signed S——l J——n] to . . . the Lord N——h. Printed for J. Almon in Piccadilly . . . MDCCLXXVII.

(3) Tyranny the worst taxation; a poetical epistle to the Right Honourable Lord N——, ostensible Prime M——R. By the author of *Royal Perseverance*. London, Printed for J. Bew in Pater-Noster-Row. MDCCLXXVIII.

POLITICAL

TRACTS.

CONTAINING,

THE FALSE ALARM.
FALKLAND'S ISLANDS.
THE PATRIOT; and,
TAXATION NO TYRANNY.

Fallitur, egregio quisquis sub principe credit
Servitium, nunquam Libertas gratior extat
Quam sub Rege pio. CLAUDIANUS.

LONDON:
Printed for W. STRAHAN; and T. CADELL in the Strand.
MDCCLXXVI.

Portions of a projected answer by R. B. Sheridan will be found in the lives of that politician, notably in that of Walter Sichel (1909), i. 472–4.

Baretti's 'Easy Phraseology'.

EASY PHRASEOLOGY, for the use of Young Ladies, who intend to learn the colloquial part of the Italian Language. By Joseph Baretti. . . . London, MDCCLXXV. 8°.

1775 Boswell, ii. 290.

The Preface (pp. iii–iv) was written by Johnson.

[The book concludes with the Italian verses beginning 'Viva! viva la padrona!' of which Johnson made an impromptu translation for Mrs. Thrale (*Anecdotes*, 1786, pp. 68, 69). Ed.]

Political Tracts.

Political Tracts. Containing, The False Alarm. Falkland's Islands. The Patriot; and, Taxation No Tyranny. Fallitur, egregio quisquis sub principe credit Servitium, nunquam Libertas gratior extat Quam sub Rege pio. Claudianus. London: Printed for W. Strahan; and T. Cadell in the Strand. MDCCLXXVI. 8°.

1776 Boswell, ii. 315.

Collation:—Title; text, pp. [1]-264.

The copy in the library of Pembroke College, Oxford, bears the inscription in Johnson's hand: 'To Sir Joshua Reynolds from the Authour.' [Thomas Warton's copy, with the inscription 'From the Author' in Warton's hand, is in the library of the Taylor Institution, Oxford. Ed.]

Boswell says that these effusions were collected into a volume, with the title of 'Political Tracts, by the Authour of the Rambler', but I have not met with any copy bearing the last six words.

Mickle's 'Lusiad'.

The Lusiad; or the discovery of India, an Epic Poem, translated from the original Portuguese of Luis de Camoëns, by William Julius Mickle. Oxford, MDCCLXXVI. 4°.

1776 Boswell, iv. 250–51.

Johnson hated a sea-life, and held the view that it would have been happy for the world had the schemes of the explorers not been carried into effect. This sentiment he expressed to Mickle in conversation and set out in his *Introduction* to *The World Displayed.* Mickle combated this opinion in the introduction to his translation. Johnson subscribed for a copy of Mickle's work, and dictated the acknowledgement of his good wishes which is printed on p. cliii.

Pearce's 'Four Evangelists'.

1777
Boswell, iii. 112–13.

A Commentary, with notes, on the Four Evangelists and the Acts of the Apostles . . . by Zachary Pearce, D.D., late Lord Bishop of Rochester. Published by John Derby, A.M. London: MDCCLXXVII. 2 Vols.

Johnson wrote the dedication (I, pp. v–vi) 'To the King', and made some additions to the Life of the Bishop.

Kelly's 'A Word to the Wise'.

1777
Boswell, iii. 113–14.

A Word to the Wise, a comedy by Mr. Hugh Kelly.

Revived at Covent Garden, May 13 and 29, 1777. The second performance was for the benefit of Kelly's wife and children. The Prologue was written by Johnson and spoken by Thomas Hall. Eight lines from it are quoted in Genest, *Some Account of the English Stage*, v. 569–70. It is given in full in the *Works of Hugh Kelly* (1778), pp. x–xi, and in *Westminster Mag.*, May 1777, p. 273; *Gent. Mag.*, June 1777, p. 286; [*London Mag.*, July 1777, p. 375; *Annual Register*, 1777, p. 198. Ed.].

Johnson and Dr. Dodd.

1777
Boswell, iii. 120–2, 141–8.

The Convict's address to his unhappy Brethren, delivered in the Chapel of Newgate on Friday, June 6, 1777. By William Dodd, LL.D. [but mostly by Dr. Johnson].

—— A Sermon preached by the Rev. Dr. Dodd . . . in the Chapel of Newgate on Friday, June 6, 1777. Salisbury: 1777.

This address was many times reprinted, in London and in the country, along with 'Thoughts in Prison. By the Rev. William Dodd, LL.D.'

Boswell says that Johnson also wrote for Dodd his—

(1) Speech to the Recorder of London.
(2) Letter to Lord Chancellor Bathurst.
(3) Letter to Lord Mansfield.
(4) A petition from Dr. Dodd to the King.
(5) A petition from Mrs. Dodd to the Queen.
(6) Observations in the newspapers.

(7) A petition from the City of London.

(8) Dr. Dodd's last solemn Declaration.

Other letters by Johnson are inserted in Boswell.

Most of these papers were reproduced with a preliminary note in *The Life of Samuel Johnson, LL.D.* (London: G. Kearsley, 1785), pp. 128–40. Mr. Percy Fitzgerald published in 1865 a life of Dodd. Mr. H. C. Biron contributed to the *National Review* for Nov. 1911, pp. 455–63, an article on 'Dr. Johnson and Dr. Dodd'.

Shaw's 'Galic Language'.

An Analysis of the Galic Language. By William Shaw, A.M. London, MDCCLXXVIII.

1778 Boswell, iii. 107.

'To the advice and encouragement of Dr. Johnson, the friend of letters and humanity, the Public is indebted for these sheets' (Introduction, p. xxiii). Johnson contributed to Shaw's proposals for publication two paragraphs, which are quoted by Boswell.

See also below, p. 153.

Reynolds's 'Discourses'.

Seven Discourses delivered in the Royal Academy by the President [i. e. Sir Joshua Reynolds]. MDCCLXXVIII.

1778 Boswell, ii. 2.

The dedication 'To the King' was written by Johnson.

[See *Johnson Club Papers*, 1899, p. 69. Ed.]

Maurice's 'Free Translation of Sophocles'.

Poems and Miscellaneous Pieces, with a free translation of the *Oedipus Tyrannus* of Sophocles. By the Rev. Thomas Maurice. 1779.

1779 Boswell, iii. 370.

The Preface (pp. 149–52) to this 'free translation' was written by Johnson. The Preface was reprinted, with a preliminary advertisement, in Maurice's volume of poems, entitled *Westminster Abbey* (1813), pp. 122–9, and in his separate issue of 'A free translation of the *Oedipus Tyrannus* of Sophocles' (1822), pp. i–v.

The Lives of the Poets.

1779–81 Boswell, iii. 108–11; iv. 34–65, 153, 157.

The second great work with which Johnson's name is now generally associated is *The Lives of the Poets*. It was the simplest in style and expression of all his literary labours, the subject appealed to every man of letters in the three kingdoms, and it abounded in anecdote and in criticism.

The origin of the undertaking is told by Edward Dilly, the publisher, in a letter to Boswell (Sept. 26, 1777). A 'little trifling edition' of the Poets was being printed by the Martins at Edinburgh for sale by Bell in London. The type was 'extremely small' and 'the inaccuracy of the press was very conspicuous'. These were two of the objections which the booksellers in London put forward to the scheme; but still more important in their eyes was the fact that the proposed edition involved 'an invasion of their Literary Property'.

They met in solemn conclave and determined 'to print an elegant and accurate edition of all the English Poets of reputation from Chaucer to the present time'. It was their wish that 'a concise account of the life of each authour' should be supplied by Dr. Johnson, and three of their number waited on him on March 29, 1777, 'to solicit him to undertake the lives'. The proposal was congenial to him; he 'very politely' accepted it, and when asked his terms suggested two hundred guineas. The booksellers spontaneously added a third hundred, and at a later date (1783) a further sum of one hundred pounds was paid to him. The reward for his toil was not excessive, but the completed lives were very different in substance from the original scheme. The 'concise account' often expanded into an elaborate memoir, accompanied by a detailed criticism of the poet's works.

The first conception of the booksellers was to begin with the works of Chaucer, but that project was too vast for them, and the first author in their edition was Cowley. The diminution of the scheme is not greatly to be regretted. The poets before Cowley were not so well known to Johnson, and he had no special information on their lives. Much of the charm of his undertaking lay in the anecdotes which he stored in his memory. Goldsmith's poems were not included, owing to a difficulty about copyright, and probably the same explanation could be given for the omission of Churchill. Five authors—Sir Richard Blackmore, Isaac Watts, John Pomfret, and Thomas Yalden, and, it would seem from his letter to Boswell of May 3, 1777, James Thomson—were included on Johnson's suggestion, but the stock of national poetry would not have been impaired had the first four been excluded. Johnson remarked, May 19, 1778, 'I shall do what I can for Dr. Watts, but my materials are very scanty. His poems are by no means his best works.

I cannot praise his poetry itself highly, but I can praise its design,' and he applied to William Sharp, Junior, the possessor of the correspondence of Watts, for some information about him. Boswell (iii. 150–1) was clearly desirous that the pieces of Hamilton of Bangour should be inserted in this collection, but Johnson was obdurate, and would not accept the proposition. One of the poets included in the collection, William Walsh, is ironically dubbed by Johnson with the epithets 'the sublime and pathetic Mr. Walsh' (*Letters*, ed. Hill, ii. 178).

The life of Waller was in print in the middle of April, 1778. That of Cowley was in the printer's hands on July 27, 1778. Johnson considered it his best production, and it contained a dissertation on the Metaphysical poets. His admiration for Cowley was such that he once contemplated an edition of his works. Milton's was begun in January 1779, and finished in six weeks. It gave the 'hounds of Whiggism' many an opening.

Dryden was always a favourite with Johnson. To write that poet's life was one of the dreams of his youth. An opinion by Johnson is quoted in Derrick's edition of Dryden's *Miscellaneous Works* (1760, notes, p. lxxxiv). Lord Marchmont, in an interview of two hours, communicated his anecdotes of Pope, and this life had the benefit of *Spence's Anecdotes*, which were then in manuscript and remained so until 1820, when two rival editions appeared on the same day. 'Johnson's hints for the life of Pope' are printed in Isaac Disraeli's *Curiosities of Literature*, 1858 ed., ii. 380–2. This was the last to be written, and it is the longest of all the Lives. It ended with a reprint of Johnson's dissertation on Pope's epitaphs, which had appeared in 1756 in the *Universal Visiter*. [The Cole collection of manuscripts in the British Museum contains Johnson's 'Memoranda for Life of Pope': Add. MS. 5994. 2. Ed.]

The life of Congreve was written in the Borough during the contested election of 1780. It is 'one of the best of the little lives', wrote Johnson to Mrs. Thrale, 'but then I had your conversation'. Johnson disliked Swift, Lord Lyttelton, and Gray; all three of whom suffered for this antipathy. His dislike of Swift was severely reprobated in the life published by Thomas Sheridan in 1784 (Introduction and elsewhere). Nor did Johnson neglect to expose the faults of Mallet, both in the memoir of him and in that of Thomson. The life of Edmund Smith was mainly taken from the previous memoir by William

Oldisworth; that of Young was written by Sir Herbert Croft (cf. above, p. 69), a poor imitator of Johnson, but the criticism of Young's poems was by Johnson.

The writing of these lives occupied Johnson for four years. The first four volumes, with twenty-two lives, came out in 1779; the remaining six, containing thirty lives, in 1781. The first set, 'put neatly together', was sent to the King in March 1779. The memoirs were written in his usual way, 'dilatorily and hastily, unwilling to work and working with vigour and haste'. Johnson's communications to John Nichols, the printer, on the *Lives* are incorporated in Hill's edition of the *Letters*, ii. 68 et seq.

Boswell asked for the proofs of the *Lives* and was thus able to furnish many interesting notes of 'various readings'. Some of the proof-sheets with corrections in the Doctor's handwriting are in the Forster Collection at the South Kensington Museum. They were purchased from the library of James Boswell, the younger, by William Upcott in 1825. The proofs in sheet-form of pp. 1–16 and 65–80 of the life of Dryden, with Johnson's manuscript corrections, are in the library of the British Museum. Those of the life of Pope were kept for Miss Burney. They were sold at Sotheby's in August 1890, and are now the property of R. B. Adam, of Buffalo, who allowed Dr. Hill to examine them. [Cf. his paper on 'Boswell's Proof-Sheets' in the *Atlantic Monthly*, lxxiv, 1894, and in *Johnson Club Papers*, 1899, p. 54. Ed.]

Much of the charm of *The Lives of the Poets* lies in the anecdotes and reminiscences which Johnson has embodied in them. He had passed many years of life in the company of men of letters, and his retentive memory preserved the criticisms and the facts which had fallen from their lips. Moreover, he was helped by many of his literary friends, especially Malone, Steevens, and Isaac Reed. There was one exception. He applied to Dr. Farmer for information from the University registers of Cambridge on many of the poets, but Farmer neglected to answer his letter. William Cole, the Cambridge antiquary, sent several anecdotes on Gray, a life-long friend, but Johnson was then weary of his labours and anxious to complete his task. They were omitted from the life.

Johnson's life of Cowley records that Sir Joshua Reynolds 'had the first fondness for his art excited by the perusal of Richardson's treatise'. He repeats the statement of Mr. Hampton, the translator of Polybius, 'that Milton was the first Englishman who, after the revival of letters, wrote Latin verses with classick elegance', and echoes the expression of Dr. Gregory that he had seen erected in Westminster Abbey 'a statue of that man, whose name I once knew considered as a pollution of its walls'. Cradock lent him a copy of Euripides which contained the manuscript notes of Milton. The life of the Earl of Dorset was enriched by an anecdote which Johnson had heard from the late Earl of Orrery, 'who was likely to have good hereditary intelligence'.

Johnson's father, who was a bookseller, had told him that the sale of Dryden's *Absalom and Achitophel* was never 'equalled but by Sacheverell's trial', and from the same authority, 'an old man, who had been no careless observer of the passages of those times', he had heard how the Whigs and Tories delighted to hum, both loud and long, at the best passages in the sermons of their respective champions, Burnet and Sprat. Lord Hailes sent him communications on Dryden and Thomson, and through Percy he obtained Clifford's remarks on Dryden.

By 'discoursing with the late amiable Mr. Tonson', Johnson obtained some particulars of the sums which Dryden received from Jacob Tonson in 1698, and Dr. King, of Oxford, gave him a story about that publisher and Dryden which Lord Bolingbroke had remembered. Cibber told him that Dryden was 'the arbiter of critical disputes at Will's' coffee-house, and MacSwinny, 'the director of the play-house', fixed the positions of 'his winter and his summer seat' in that gathering. Garrick allowed Johnson to print the observations which Dryden had written on the blank leaves of a copy of Rymer's *Remarks on the Tragedies of the last Age*; and at the close of the life was inserted the letter in the Lambeth Library which Dryden had sent to his sons at Rome in 1697, and Vyse had 'kindly imparted to the publick'.

An amusing story narrated in Johnson's life of Edmund Smith, familiarly known as Captain Rag, was repeated to him by 'the late Mr. Clark of Lincoln's Inn'. This was the barrister described in Johnson's *Shakespeare*, viii. 337, as 'the late learned and ingenious Mr. Thomas Clark of Lincoln's Inn', whom I identify with 'Thomas Clarke, son and heir-apparent of John Clarke of Mellis, Suff., arm.', admitted at Lincoln's Inn on Jan. 21, 171$\frac{5}{6}$. He died on Jan. 9, 1761 (*Gentleman's Mag.*, 1761, p. 44).

In the same life is embalmed the account of Gilbert Walmsley with the tributes of affection to the memory of Dr. James and

David Garrick. No less expressive of the old man's feelings are the references under Parnell to the talents of Goldsmith.

From Andrew Corbet, of Shropshire, there came to Johnson the details of the barring-out at Lichfield Grammar-school, which 'was planned and conducted by Addison'. Mrs. Porter, the actress, related how Addison, during the representation of his play of *Cato*, wandered behind the scenes 'with restless and unappeasable solicitude'; and Mr. Locker, clerk of the Leather-sellers' Company (John Locker, *d.* May 1760: see *My Confidences*, by F. Locker-Sampson, 1896, pp. 12–13), 'who was eminent for curiosity and literature,' sent Johnson a collection of examples of words drawn by Addison from the works of Tillotson. The Irish Dr. Madden gave Johnson the opinion, not one I think readily to be adopted, that if he had set ten school-boys to write on the battle of Blenheim, and eight had brought him the simile of the Angel, he 'should not have been surprised'.

'Mr. Draper, an eminent bookseller', related to Johnson the account by Ambrose Philips, which is inserted in the life of Sir Richard Blackmore, of the composition of *Creation, a Philosophical Poem*. 'A conversation, which I once heard between the Earl of Orrery and old Mr. Lewis', gave Johnson different notions of Swift's *History of the Four last Years of Queen Anne* from those which he experienced on its publication by Dr. Lucas; and Lord Orrery told him of Swift's irritation at the conduct of a servant waiting at the earl's table who had 'committed fifteen faults'. Dr. Madden imparted to him that Swift was in 1716 'privately married to Mrs. Johnson by Dr. Ashe, Bishop of Clogher'; and on Dr. Madden's authority, he adds that Stella told 'her melancholy story to Dr. Sheridan, when he attended her as a clergyman to prepare her for death'.

'The well-known Ford', Johnson's cousin, gave his recollection of Broome's character at St. John's College, Cambridge; and Warburton, 'in his warm language', blurted out to Johnson that the statement of the shares of Pope and his assistants in the *Odyssey*, as given in the note at the end of the translation, was in his opinion 'a lie'. A reference in the life of Pope to a niece of Mrs. Arabella Fermor, whom Johnson had talked to in the English convent of the Austin nuns at Paris, furnishes the opinion of that family on the poem which has immortalized the name of Fermor. The details of the life of the Man of Ross were communicated to Johnson by Benjamin Victor. Osborne, the bookseller, expressed to Johnson his opinion of the resentment of Pope; the younger Richardson told him how the features of the satirist were 'writhen with anguish' by a pamphlet of Cibber; and Richard Paul Jodrell supplied Pope's letter of 1708 to the Rev. Ralph Bridges on translating Homer.

Savage told Johnson that the first part of the prologue of Thomson's *Sophonisba* was written by Pope, and Johnson himself remembered to have seen Thomson sitting in the upper gallery of the theatre and accompanying the performance of his drama of *Agamemnon* 'by audible recitation'. Through Boswell's 'friendly assistance' a letter from Thomson to his sister was inserted in the life, but some corrections of statements in the life which Boswell supplied were never made.

The excellence of Isaac Watts in the 'art of pronunciation' was an observation derived from Hawkesworth; and from another friend, Samuel Dyer, was borrowed a criticism of Watts's 'metaphysical disquisitions'. 'Mr. Ing, a gentleman of great eminence in Staffordshire', had 'long ago' related to Johnson the story of the discomfiture of Ambrose Philips at a dinner table; and a 'critical visitor' in Dodsley's shop was the father of the jest that John Dyer, the author of the *Fleece*, would be 'buried in woollen'. Joseph Warton gave information about Fenton, Collins, and Pitt; George Steevens pointed out that Young's three plays all ended 'with lavish suicide'; and the unrevealed lady, of whose praise Young 'would have been justly proud', was Mrs. Thrale.

Johnson's *Lives of the Poets* were read by J. B. Trotter to C. J. Fox in his last illness, and were often at midnight heard with eager delight. 'You may go a little more,' was the sick man's frequent exclamation. Dryden was much admired by Fox, who conversed about him a great deal (Trotter's *Fox*, p. 446).

Sir James Mackintosh was invited about 1801, 'by a body of London booksellers, to superintend a new edition of Johnson's Poets', which was intended to run from Chaucer to Cowper. A long character of Johnson, dealing especially with his *Lives of the Poets*, was drawn up by Mackintosh (*Life*, 2nd ed. 1836, i. 168, ii. 71–7).

The Lives of the Poets gave rise to much controversy and produced several diatribes from other writers. The memoir of Lord Lyttelton was censured by many, notably in the drawing-rooms of Mrs. Montagu and her friends. The strictures in the notice of Hammond produced in 1782 a slight pamphlet of thirty-five pages, entitled 'Observations on Johnson's Life of Hammond'. It is attributed by Dr. Robert Anderson, in his *Life of Dr. Johnson*, 1815 ed., p. 401, to Mr. Beville (*sic*), a misspelling for William Bevil, of Peterhouse, Cambridge, B.A. 1778, M.A. 1781, and Fellow of his College in 1781 (*d.* July 16, 1822). He is lauded in the obituary columns of the *Gentleman's Magazine* for that year as a popular preacher and as the anonymous author of this defence of Hammond.

Johnson's criticism in the life of Waller on religious poetry induced the Rev. Daniel Turner, minister of the Baptist Church at Abingdon, to compose his little volume of *Devotional Poetry vindicated* (1783). His severe or inadequate remarks on the writings of some of these poets drew out the 'Critical Essays on some of the poems of several English Poets by John Scott, Esq.' of Amwell, which were edited by John Hoole in 1785. Two anonymous attacks on the *Lives of the Poets* and on the *Dictionary* are attributed in the Catalogue of the British Museum Library to John Callander, of Craigforth, but strangely enough no mention of them is made by Robert Chambers in his memoir of Callander (*Biog. Dict. of Eminent Scotchmen*, vol. i) or by the writer of the memoir in the *D. N. B.* They are:

(1) Deformities of Dr. Samuel Johnson. Selected from his works. [Anon.] Edinburgh: Printed for the Author; and sold by W. Creech. And T. Longman, and J. Stockdale, London. MDCCLXXXII. ——— Second edition. London: Printed for the Author; and sold by J. Stockdale; and W. Creech, Edinburgh. MDCCLXXXII. (Preface to the Second Edition dated 'Edinburgh, Nov. 21, 1782'.)

(2) A Critical Review of the Works of Dr. Samuel Johnson, containing a particular Vindication of several eminent Characters. [Anon.] Edinburgh: MDCCLXXXIII. —— 2nd ed.; London: MDCCLXXXIII. —— Another issue. London: MDCCLXXXVII.

I saw, in September 1912, in the Signet Library, Edinburgh, a pamphlet entitled 'Remarks on Dr. Johnson's Lives of the most eminent English Poets. By a Yorkshire Freeholder. York: Printed by A. Ward in Coney-Street . . . MDCCLXXXII'. No copy of it is in the British Museum Library, nor is it referred to in the *Memoirs of the York Press*, by Robert Davies, F.S.A. The writer was a Whig, and he was goaded into the publication of this tract (pp. vi and 25) by the account, in the life of Edmund Smith, of Gilbert Walmsley as 'a Whig with all the virulence and malevolence of his party'. He picks out for special condemnation the following passage in the life of Cowley: 'A memory admitting some things and rejecting others, an intellectual digestion that concocted the pulp of learning, but refused the husks, had the appearance of an instinctive elegance, of a particular provision made by Nature for literary politeness.'

These effusions showed the widespread interest and general importance attaching to the last labour of Dr. Johnson. But it was over his reflections on Milton and Gray that the full storm of indignation raged in frenzy. The political side of Milton's life aroused the antipathy of Johnson; the ways and habits of the shrinking recluse at Cambridge did not attract the sympathy of a man who had battled with poverty for many a year and had passed his days amid the turmoil of Fleet Street. References to Johnson, and especially to his *Lives of the Poets*, will be found in the *Correspondence of William Cowper*, ed. Thomas Wright (1904, 4 vols.), i. 154, 164–5, 355, 362, 421, 427–8; ii. 2, 167, 177–9, 205–6, 213, 290–2, 348–54; iii. 295, 379, 386–7. The treatment of Milton inspired Cowper with fierce resentment. 'Oh! I could thresh his old jacket till I made his pension jingle in his pocket,' was the poet's bitter phrase. The manuscript notes of Cowper on Johnson's life of Milton are inserted by Mitford in the *Gentleman's Magazine* for October, 1835, pp. 343–5.

There was printed at London, for private circulation, in 1780, a volume of 'Remarks on Johnson's Life of Milton. To which are added, Milton's Tractate of Education and Areopagitica.' It was written by Francis Blackburne, the Archdeacon of Cleveland, and was probably printed at the expense of Brand Hollis. One of the copies at the British Museum contains a letter from Hollis to the Rev. John Bowle, forwarding a copy for his acceptance as the first discoverer of 'the infamous and false attack on the fame and character of the Divine Milton'. These Remarks had previously appeared in Blackburne's *Memoirs of Thomas Hollis* (1780), ii, pp. 533*–84*.

'A dialogue between Dr. Johnson and Dr. Goldsmith in the Shades', on Johnson's strictures on the English Poets, particularly on Pope, Milton, and Gray, was published in 1785. It is noticed in the *Monthly Review*, lxxiii (1785), pp. 232–3.

Thomas Holt White (*d.* November 1841) was the author in

1818 of 'A review of Johnson's criticism of the style of Milton's English prose'.

The 'malignant' censures of Johnson were partly responsible for the publication of the lives of Milton by William Hayley, Charles Symmons, D.D., and Joseph Ivimey. The last work contains an appendix (pp. 349–82) of 'Animadversions on Dr. Johnson's life of Milton'. The expressions on Johnson which are used by the author of the life of Milton in *Lardner's Cabinet Encyclopaedia* are quoted and condemned in the *Gentleman's Magazine* for 1839, pt. ii, pp. 257–9. Many writers on Milton contrast the severity of the remarks on Milton in *The Lives of the Poets* with Johnson's temperate criticisms on his works in *The Rambler*, Nos. 86, 88, 90, 94, 139, and 140.

De Quincey contributed to *Distinguished Men of Modern Times*, published by Charles Knight for the Society for the Diffusion of Useful Knowledge (1838, 4 vols.), a memoir of Milton. This was included in his *Works* (1859, vol. xi, and 1897, vol. iv), with a prefatory memorandum in reply to Johnson's criticisms.

The defenders of Gray were soon on the alert. An anonymous brochure of twenty-two pages came out in 1781, at the price of one shilling, with the title 'A Cursory Examination of Dr. Johnson's strictures on the lyric performances of Gray'. It was followed in the next year by 'Remarks on Dr. Johnson's life and critical observations on the works of Mr. Gray', which was also anonymous, but was the work of William Tindal. Hurd pronounced it 'the best defence' of Gray 'against the Goliath of literature' (John Chambers, *Biog. Illustrations of Worcestershire*, p. 572). The writer of the second pamphlet, 'living in a deep and distant retirement', asserts in a postscript that he had not seen its predecessor 'till my own was written'.

'A Criticism on the Elegy written in a Country Church-yard, being a continuation of Dr. J——n's Criticism on the Poems of Gray', was published in London in 1783. The editor's advertisement, dated from Lincoln's Inn, Jan. 15, 1783, professed that the criticism was written by Johnson, printed off for publication, and then withdrawn. But it was soon known to be written by John Young, the Professor of Greek at Glasgow. Boswell called it 'the most perfect imitation of Johnson', and Sir Walter Scott praised it as 'the cleverest parody of the Doctor's style of criticism' and 'very capital'. A second edition of it appeared at Edinburgh in 1810.

Sir Walter Raleigh, in the introduction to his reprint of *The Heroine*, by Eaton Stannard Barrett, 1909, supports these praises of Young's imitation of the Doctor's critical manner, and adds that Johnson's 'biographical style and his light occasional verse have never been so happily mimicked' as by Eaton Stannard Barrett in the *Memoirs of James Higginson by Himself* (in Letter X of *The Heroine*).

The best imitator of Johnson's style in his lifetime was, in his own opinion, Miss Aikin, afterwards Mrs. Barbauld (*Boswell*, Sept. 19, 1777, vol. iii, p. 172). Her composition was an essay 'On Romances, an imitation'. It originally appeared in *Miscellaneous Pieces* by J. and A. L. Aikin (1773), pp. 30–49, and was afterwards included in her *Works* (1825, vol. ii, pp. 171–5).

Johnson's censures on Gray elicited from Gilbert Wakefield his edition of 'The Poems of Mr. Gray, 1786'. Gray was also defended by A. J. Wright in the Preface to *Elegia scripta in sepulchreto rustico latine reddita* (1786). See *Monthly Review*, lxxiv (1786), pp. 231–2.

The Rev. Robert Potter, afterwards Canon of Norwich Cathedral and Vicar of Lowestoft, published in 1783 'An Inquiry into some passages in Dr. Johnson's Lives of the Poets, particularly his observations on Lyric Poetry and the Odes of Gray'. It is referred to in *Beattie and his Friends*, by Margaret Forbes, 1904, p. 195.

Potter was also the author of the anonymous 'Art of Criticism, as exemplified in Dr. Johnson's Lives of the most eminent English Poets, MDCCLXXXIX', to which was appended 'A Dream' recording the observations of the two illustrious critics, Dr. Warton and Dr. Johnson, when they met after the publication of the *Lives of the Poets*. Potter's copy, with his notes for a new edition (Dec. 1789), is in the British Museum.

A letter (July 9, 1788) from Anna Seward to the Rev. Mr. FitzThomas 'On his vindication of Gray from the envious strictures of Johnson' is in her *Letters*, ii. 146–8. The 'vindication' is there said to have been earlier than Potter's *Inquiry*, and to be then out of print. The author was probably William Windsor FitzThomas, of Trinity Hall, Cambridge, who graduated LL.B. in 1774. After his death there was published, in 1807, a volume containing his translations into English verse, with introduction and notes to 'Ten epistles of Ovid'. He was Rector of Arrow and Beaudesert, Warwickshire, and is recorded in the

Gentleman's Magazine for 1806, pt. ii, p. 875, as having died in August.

The anonymous volume by the Rev. Richard Graves of *Recollections of some particulars in the life of the late William Shenstone*, was drawn from him by 'some particulars published by Dr. Johnson and others'.

EDITIONS.

1779 Prefaces, Biographical and Critical, to the Works of the English Poets. By Samuel Johnson. Volume the First (–Tenth). London: Printed by J. Nichols; for C. Bathurst, J. Buckland, W. Strahan, J. Rivington and Sons, T. Davies, T. Payne, L. Davis, W. Owen, B. White, S. Crowder, T. Caslon, T. Longman, B. Law, E. and C. Dilly, J. Dodsley, H. Baldwin, J. Wilkie, J. Robson, J. Johnson, T. Lowndes, T. Becket, G. Robinson, T. Cadell, W. Davis, J. Nichols, F. Newbery, T. Evans, J. Ridley, R. Baldwin, G. Nicol, Leigh and Sotheby, J. Bew, N. Conant, J. Murray, W. Fox, J. Bowen. MDCCLXXIX(–MDCCLXXXI). 10 vols. sm. 8°.

Collation:—Vol. I. Title, p. [i]; 'Prefaces to Cowley and Waller', p. [iii]; Advertisement, pp. v–vii, dated March 15, 1779; Directions to the binder, pp. ix, x; Errata, p. xi. Cowley, 1–165, three blank pages. Waller, 1–128. (MDCCLXXIX.) In some issues a portrait of Johnson, engraved by T. Trotter after Reynolds, faces the title-page (cf. vol. v).

Vol. II. Title, p. [i]; 'Prefaces to Milton and Butler,' p. [iii]. Milton, 1–223. Butler, 1–39. (MDCCLXXIX.)

Vol. III. Title, p. [i]; 'Preface to Dryden,' p. [iii]. Dryden, 1–349, three blank pages. (MDCCLXXIX.)

Vol. IV. Title, p. [i]; 'Prefaces to Denham, Sprat, Roscommon, Rochester, Yalden, Otway, Duke, Dorset, Halifax, Stepney, Walsh, Garth, King, J. Philips, Smith, Pomfret, Hughes,' p. [iii]. Denham, 1–31. Sprat, 1–15. Roscommon, 1–27. Rochester, 1–20. Yalden, 1–12. Otway, 1–12. Duke, 1–4. Dorset, 1–9. Halifax, 1–12. Stepney, 1–6. Walsh, 1–5, three blank pages. Garth, 1–13, three blank pages. King, 1–11. J. Philips, 1–42, two blank pages. Smith, 1–64. Pomfret, 1–4. Hughes, 1–13, three blank pages. (MDCCLXXIX.)

PREFACES,

BIOGRAPHICAL AND CRITICAL,

TO THE

WORKS

OF THE

ENGLISH POETS.

BY SAMUEL JOHNSON.

VOLUME THE FIRST.

LONDON:

PRINTED BY J. NICHOLS;

FOR C. BATHURST, J. BUCKLAND, W. STRAHAN, J. RIVINGTON AND SONS, T. DAVIES, T. PAYNE, L. DAVIS, W. OWEN, B. WHITE, S. CROWDER, T. CASLON, T. LONGMAN, B. LAW, E. AND C. DILLY, J. DODSLEY, H. BALDWIN, J. WILKIE, J. ROBSON, J. JOHNSON, T. LOWNDES, T. BECKET, G. ROBINSON, T. CADELL, W. DAVIS, J. NICHOLS, F. NEWBERY, T. EVANS, J. RIDLEY, R. BALDWIN, G. NICOL, LEIGH AND SOTHEBY, J. BEW, N. CONANT, J. MURRAY, W. FOX, J. BOWEN.

M DCC LXXIX.

THE
LIVES
OF THE
ENGLISH POETS;
AND A
CRITICISM
ON THEIR
WORKS.

BY SAMUEL JOHNSON.

DUBLIN:

Printed for Meſſrs. WHITESTONE, WILLIAMS, COLLES, WILSON,
LYNCH, JENKIN, WALKER, BURNET, HALLHEAD,
FLIN, EXSHAW, BEATTY, and WHITE.

M,DCC,LXXIX.

Vol. V. Title, p. [i]; 'Prefaces to Addison, Blackmore, and Sheffield,' p. [iii]. Addison, 1–162. Blackmore, 1–53, three blank pages. Sheffield, 1–20. (MDCCLXXXI.) In some issues the portrait of Johnson faces the title-page of this volume (cf. vol. i).

Vol. VI. Title, p. [i]; 'Prefaces to Granville, Rowe, Tickell, Congreve, Fenton, and Prior,' p. [iii]. Granville, 1–56. Rowe, 1–30, two blank pages. Tickell, 1–43. Congreve, 1–38, two blank pages. Fenton, 1–19. Prior, 1–63. (MDCCLXXXI.)

Vol. VII. Title, p. [i]; 'Preface to Pope,' p. [iii]. Pope, 1–373, three blank pages. (MDCCLXXXI.)

Vol. VIII. Title, p. [i]; 'Prefaces to Swift, Gay, Broome, Pitt, Parnell, A. Philips, and Watts,' p. [iii]. Swift, 1–112. Gay, 1–30, two blank pages. Broome, 1–12. Pitt, 1–7. Parnell, 1–11. A. Philips, 1–23. Watts, 1–24. (MDCCLXXXI.)

Vol. IX. Title, p. [i]; 'Prefaces to Savage, Somervile, Thomson, Hammond, and Collins,' p. [iii]. Savage, 1–147 (printed in smaller type than the other lives). Somervile, 1–7. Thomson, 1–40. Hammond, 1–11. Collins, 1–14, two blank pages. (MDCCLXXXI.)

Vol. X. Title, p. [i]; 'Prefaces to Young, Dyer, Mallet, Shenstone, Akenside, Lyttelton, West, and Gray,' p. [iii]. Young, 1–113. Dyer, 1–8. Mallet, 1–16. Shenstone, 1–20. Akenside, 1–18. Lyttelton, 1–22. West, 1–15. Gray, 1–56. (MDCCLXXXI.)

These volumes were the first publication of the work now known as Johnson's *Lives of the Poets*. The whole set consisted of 68 volumes, viz. Works, 56 vols.; Prefaces, 10 vols.; Index, 2 vols. Another edition, comprising 75 volumes in all, appeared in this form, dated 1790, and the Prefaces appeared in the first six volumes ('Printed by John Nichols'). Fourteen brief new lives, including those of Churchill, Matthew Green, Goldsmith, Johnson, and Soame Jenyns, were added.

The Lives of the English Poets, and a criticism of their works. By Samuel Johnson. Vol. I, Dublin, MDCCLXXIX. Vols. II & III, Dublin, MDCCLXXXI. 8°.

At the end of the memoir of Gray are printed *A Long Story* and his *Ode for Musick* on the installation of the Duke of Grafton as Chancellor of the University of Cambridge.

The Lives of the most eminent English Poets; with 1781

Critical Observations on their Works. By Samuel Johnson. In Four Volumes. Volume I (–IV). London: Printed for C. Bathurst, *etc.* MDCCLXXXI. 8°.

[The Advertisement in vol. i, pp. iii–v, reproduces with slight alterations the advertisement in the edition of 1779, and contains an additional paragraph. The sequence of the *Lives* is altered. Ed.]

A translation into German (2 vols. 8°), edited by C. F. von Blankenburg, was published at Altenburg, in 1781–83. The *Lives* also appeared in English at Göttingen in 1783.

1783 The Lives of the most eminent English Poets; By Samuel Johnson. In Four Volumes. A new edition, corrected. The First (–Fourth) Volume. London: Printed for C. Bathurst, *etc.* MDCCLXXXIII. 8°.

[The Advertisement in the edition of 1781 is reproduced with the omission of the paragraph on Dryden's funeral, and with the alteration of 'my friends' to 'Mr. Steevens and other friends'. Ed.]

The alterations and corrections in this issue were printed separately and offered gratis to the purchasers of the former editions, but scarcely a single copy was demanded. Nearly all them were printed in the *London Magazine* for Sept. 1783, pp. 248–53. An interleaved copy, with some manuscript notes by Sir Egerton Brydges, is in the British Museum. At the end of vol. i is an inserted sheet of paper containing 'Notes by Cowper written on the margin of a copy of Johnson's Lives of the Poets (art. "Milton", edition 1781, 8vo, 4 vols.) presented by Hayley to Mr. William Mason, Booksr, Chichester'.

Another copy in the British Museum belonged to Sir Herbert Croft and has a few manuscript notes by him, with an autograph letter to him from Dr. Johnson and one from Mrs. Montagu. At the end of vol. iv is bound up a copy of the *Deformities of Dr. Samuel Johnson* (1782), which Croft preserved 'that future times may know what was the perfection of abuse in 1782'.

The Lives of the most eminent English Poets, *etc.* By Samuel Johnson. London: Printed for J. Rivington & Sons, *etc.* 1790 (Vols. I & II)–1791 (Vols. III & IV). 8°.

The Lives of the most eminent English Poets, *etc.* By Samuel Johnson. London: Printed for J. Buckland, C. Bathurst and T. Davies. MDCCXCIII. 4 vols. 8°.

The Lives of the most eminent English Poets, *etc.*

THE
LIVES
OF THE MOST EMINENT
ENGLISH POETS;
WITH
CRITICAL OBSERVATIONS
ON THEIR
WORKS.

By SAMUEL JOHNSON.

IN FOUR VOLUMES.

VOLUME I.

LONDON:

PRINTED FOR C. BATHURST, J. BUCKLAND, W. STRAHAN, J. RIVINGTON AND SONS, T. DAVIES, T. PAYNE, L. DAVIS, W. OWEN, B. WHITE, S. CROWDER, T. CASLON, T. LONGMAN, B. LAW, C. DILLY, J. DODSLEY, J. WILKIE, J. ROBSON, J. JOHNSON, T. LOWNDES, G. ROBINSON, T. CADELL, J. NICHOLS, E. NEWBERY, T. EVANS, P. ELMSLY, J. RIDLEY, R. BALDWIN, G. NICOL, LEIGH AND SOTHEBY, J. BEW, N. CONANT, W. NICOLL, J. MURRAY, S. HAYES, W. FOX, AND J. BOWEN.

M DCC LXXXI.

THE PRINCIPAL

ADDITIONS and CORRECTIONS

IN THE THIRD EDITION OF

Dr. JOHNSON's

LIVES OF THE POETS;

COLLECTED TO COMPLETE

THE SECOND EDITION.

By Samuel Johnson. London: Printed for T. Longman, *etc.* 1794. 4 vols. 8°.

This edition contained notes signed (1) R. [i. e. Isaac Reed], (2) N. [i. e. John Nichols], (3) H. [i. e. Sir John Hawkins].

The Lives of the most eminent English Poets, *etc.* By Samuel Johnson, LL.D. Dublin, 1795. 8 vols.

1797 Johnson's Lives of the English Poets abridged; with Notes and illustrations by the Editor . . . to which is prefixed some account of the Life of Dr. Johnson. London: Printed for E. Newbery. 1797. 12°.

The Lives of the most eminent English Poets, *etc.* By Samuel Johnson. Montrose: MDCCC. 4 vols. 8°.

The Lives of the most eminent English Poets, *etc.* By Samuel Johnson, LL.D. A new edition, corrected. London: Printed by Nichols and Son, Red-Lion-Passage, Fleet-Street, For H. Baldwin, *etc.* 1801. 3 vols. 8°.

Contained the notes of (1) R., (2) N., (3) H. The copy in the British Museum belonged to Philip Bliss, the antiquary, who inserted some cuttings and notes.

*The Lives of the Poets of Great Britain and Ireland; and a Criticism on their Works. By Dr. Samuel Johnson. Dublin: Printed by Pat. Wogan, Old-Bridge. 1804.

[This is the first volume of a Dublin edition of the Poets. It gives in one volume Johnson's *Lives* and the fourteen additional Lives in Nichols's edition, 1790. Ed.]

The Lives of the most eminent English Poets, *etc.* By Samuel Johnson, LL.D. London: Printed at the Stanhope Press by Charles Whittingham . . . for John Sharpe, 1805–6. 7 Vols. 16°.

The Lives of the most eminent English Poets, *etc.* By Samuel Johnson, LL.D. London: Printed by J. Nichols and Son, Red-Lion-Passage, Fleet Street, for J. Johnson, *etc.* 1806. 3 Vols. 8°. —— 1810. 3 vols. 8°.

These editions are in substance the same as that of 1801, but further notes, signed C. [Alexander Chalmers], are added.

The Lives of the English Poets, by Samuel Johnson,

LL.D. [Small woodcuts by Bewick.] Alston, 1810. 2 vols. 8°.

The Lives of the most eminent English Poets. With life of the author and his poetical works. By Samuel Johnson, LL.D. 1815. 4 vols. 12°.

The Lives of the most eminent English Poets. By Samuel Johnson, LL.D. 1816. 3 vols. 8°.

The Lives of the most eminent English Poets, *etc.* By Samuel Johnson, LL.D. London: Stereotyped and Printed by and for J. Fergusson, 42 Newman Street, Oxford Street; and sold by all booksellers. 1819. 2 vols. (*Encyclopaedia of British Literature. Biography*, Vols. I & II.)

The Lives of the English Poets. By Samuel Johnson, LL.D. 1820. 2 vols. 24°.

The Lives of the most eminent English Poets. By Samuel Johnson, LL.D. 1821. 3 vols. 8°.

The Lives of the most eminent English Poets. By Samuel Johnson, LL.D. 1822. 2 vols. 8°.

Dove's English Classics. The Lives of the English Poets: by Samuel Johnson, LL.D. London: printed by J. F. Dove . . . 1826. 2 vols. 9*s*.

Contains the notes of (1) R., (2) N., (3) H., (4) C. Others are added with the initials of J. B. [James Boswell the younger]. There are also some notes by Malone.

Lives of the English Poets. By Samuel Johnson, LL.D. Chiswick, 1831.

The Lives of the most eminent English Poets, *etc.* By Samuel Johnson, LL.D. Halifax. 1835. Reissued, Halifax, 1836. 2 vols.

The Lives of the English Poets . . . and Lives of Sundry Eminent Persons. By Samuel Johnson, LL.D. London: Charles Tilt, Fleet Street. MDCCCXL. 8°.

The 'eminent persons' comprised Ascham, Barretier, Blake, Boerhaave, Browne, Burman, Cave, Cheynel, Sir Francis Drake, Morin, King of Prussia, Father Paul Sarpi, and Sydenham.

The Lives of the most eminent English Poets. . . . By Samuel Johnson, LL.D. A new and complete edition. Four volumes in one. Aberdeen: Published by George

Clark and Son. Ipswich: J. M. Burton. MDCCCXLVII. 12°.

The copy in the British Museum has copious manuscript notes by John Dingwall Williams.

Johnson's Lives of the British Poets completed by William Hazlitt. London: Nathaniel Cooke, Milford House, Strand. MDCCCLIV. 4 Vols. 8°.

In *The National Illustrated Library*. Dedicated to Richard Monckton Milnes, M.P. Preface dated 'Chelsea, Feb. 1854'. Hazlitt asserted that the lives in this collection were in number 'ten times greater than those given by Dr. Johnson'. Johnson's were included entire; the others were very concise, being limited to a mention of the 'chief incidents of each person's life and literary progress, with . . . cursory notices of the nature and character of his principal productions'.

LIVES of the most eminent ENGLISH POETS. . . . By Samuel Johnson. With notes corrective and explanatory, By Peter Cunningham, F.S.A. London: John Murray, Albemarle Street. 1854. 3 vols. 8°.

By far the best edition which had yet appeared, and it held the field for fifty-one years.

Cunningham contributed to this edition (vol. i, pp. v–xxvii) an interesting preface in which he pointed out many of the errors into which Johnson had fallen, and enumerated the many friends in youth and in advanced years, from whom he had derived information. Strangely enough, for a man at this date, both industrious and knowledgeable, Cunningham confesses that he had 'learnt nothing of Mr. Locker, of the Leather-sellers' Company'.

Cunningham 'silently corrected' many of the errors in the dates, and 'added to the text [in square brackets] other dates, likely to prove of use to the reader'. The new matter provided by Cunningham is—*Cowley*, his parentage and his will; *Milton*, his nuncupative will; *Dryden*, letters to and from the Earl of Chesterfield; *Edmund Smith*, will of Garrick's father; *Addison*, memorial to George I; *Swift*, letters to Lord Halifax and Arbuthnot; *Broome*, his will; *Akenside*, three unpublished letters; *Gray*, case in Doctors' Commons.

Additional notes (including four letters from Prior) are printed in vol. iii, pp. 423–31. The 'strictly new information' in this edition is described at length in the preface to that volume (pp. v–vii).

The Lives of the English Poets. By Samuel Johnson. Collection of British Authors, Tauchnitz edition, Vols. 418 & 419. 1858. 2 vols. 8°.

The Lives of the most eminent English Poets, *etc.* By Samuel Johnson. Oxford and London: John Henry & James Parker. 1864–5. 3 vols. 18°.

Part of the Oxford English Classics. Mainly a reprint of the third edition (1783), with a very few notes, 'for the most part relating to dates'.

Lives of the Most Eminent English Poets, *etc.* By Samuel Johnson, LL.D. Carefully collated with the best editions. London: Alfred Thomas Crocker, 303 & 304 Strand. 1868. 8°.

Preliminary notice (pp. iv–v), signed F. C.

Lives of the English Poets: Waller, Milton, Cowley. By Samuel Johnson, LL.D. Cassell's National Library. Vol. 17. 1886. 8°. —— Butler, Denham, Dryden, Roscommon, Sprat, Dorset, Rochester, Otway. Vol. 37. 1886. 8°. —— Addison, Savage, Swift. Vol. 131. 1888. 8°. —— Prior, Congreve, Blackmore, Pope. Vol. 159. 1889. 8°. —— King, Halifax, Parnell, Garth, Rowe, Gay, Tickell, Somervile, Thomson, Watts, A. Philips, West, Collins, Dyer, Shenstone, Young, Mallet, Akenside, Gray, Lyttelton. Vol. 166. 1889. 8°.

Johnson's Lives of the Poets. Edited, with notes, by Mrs. Alexander Napier. And an introduction by J. W. Hales. London: George Bell & Sons, York Street, Covent Garden. 1890. 3 Vols. 8°. (Bohn's Standard Library.)

The text is that of the 1783 edition and the volumes are well annotated. Appendix C to the first volume relates to 'The Scots in Poland during the fifteenth, sixteenth, and seventeenth centuries'. The Appendix in the second volume contains a note by Mr. Austin Dobson on 'Prior's early years'.

The Lives of the most eminent English Poets, by Samuel Johnson, LL.D. Methuen and Co., 36 Essex Street,

Strand, London, 1896. 3 vols. 8°. (English Classics, ed. W. E. Henley.)

The text only, without notes. The introduction (vol. i, pp. vii–xxxi) is by John Hepburn Millar.

Johnson's Lives of the Poets, a new edition, with notes and introduction, by Arthur Waugh. London: Kegan Paul, Trench, Trübner and Co., Ltd. MDCCCXCVI. 6 vols. 8°.

A well-annotated edition. The portraits inserted in it are described in vol. vi, pp. 211–13.

LIVES OF THE ENGLISH POETS. By Samuel Johnson, LL.D. Edited by George Birkbeck Hill, D.C.L. With brief memoir of Dr. Birkbeck Hill, by his nephew, Harold Spencer Scott. Oxford: at the Clarendon Press. MDCCCCV. 3 vols. 8°.

The definitive edition, with ample notes, appendixes, and index. The Prefatory Note is signed by Harold Spencer Scott, who saw the edition through the press.

Lives of the ENGLISH POETS, by Samuel Johnson. With an introduction by Arthur Waugh. Henry Frowde, Oxford University Press, London, New York, and Toronto [1906]. 2 vols. 8°. (The World's Classics, vols. LXXXIII and LXXXIV.)

Without any annotations; the introduction is condensed from that in the 1896 edition.

Johnson's *Lives* were incorporated in John Bell's *Poets of Great Britain*, 109 vols.; the *Works of the English Poets, Chaucer to Cowper*, by Alexander Chalmers (1810; 21 vols.); in the Chiswick edition of the *British Poets* (1822; 100 vols.); and in William Hazlitt's *Lives of the British Poets* (1854; 4 vols.). The Rev. H. F. Cary contributed to the *London Magazine*, between 1821 and 1824, the 'Lives of English Poets, from Johnson to Kirke White, designed as a continuation of Johnson's Lives'. They were published in a volume in 1846.

Articles on Johnson's *Lives* and on the collection of poetry appeared in the *Gentleman's Magazine* for 1779, pp. 312, 362, 453, 505, 549, 593; 1781, pp. 224, 271, 358, 420, 432, 463, 506, 561; 1782, pp. 17, 19, 24, 116. The lengthy notices of Johnson's *Lives* in the *Monthly Review*, lxi (1779), pp. 1–10, 81–92, 186–91; lxv (1781), pp. 100–12, 353–62, 408–11; lxvi, pp. 113–27 (1782), were the work of the Rev. Edmund Cartwright. A long letter from Griffiths, its proprietor, in correction of Johnson's statement in the memoir of Hammond on the share of Theophilus Cibber in the *Lives of the Poets* (1753) bearing Cibber's name, is in the memoir of Cartwright (1843), pp. 34–7. The question is elucidated in Sir Walter Raleigh's *Six Essays*, pp. 120–6.

Peter Cunningham's edition of the *Poets* was noticed in the *Athenæum*, vol. i, Oct. 28, 1854, pp. 1297–8; vol. ii, Nov. 25, 1854, p. 1430; and vol. iii, April 14, 1855, pp. 424–5. The last of these articles was by Mr. Charles Wentworth Dilke, and it is reproduced in his *Papers of a Critic*, i. 160–4.

'Dr. Johnson's *Lives of the Poets*' was the title of an article contributed by J. Churton Collins to the *Quarterly Review*, vol. 208 (January 1908), pp. 72–97. 'Dr. Birkbeck Hill and his edition of Johnson's *Lives of the Poets*' formed the substance of a review by Professor W. P. Trent in *The Forum*, xxxvii (1906), pp. 540–51.

SEPARATE ISSUES.

Milton, Dryden, Swift, Addison, Pope, Gray.

The Six Chief Lives from Johnson's 'Lives of the Poets', with Macaulay's 'Life of Johnson'. Edited with a preface by Matthew Arnold. London: Macmillan & Co., 1878. 8°.

The life was that contributed to the *Encyclopaedia Britannica*. The only note was from Macaulay, showing that Johnson was wrong in identifying Addison's 'little Dicky' with Steele.

The Six Chief Lives, *etc.* [School edition]. 1886. 8°.

A few passages were excised or condensed in this edition. Some notes are contained on pp. 457–63, in the compilation of which Arnold received much assistance.

The lives of Milton and Addison (in French) were published at Strassburg in 1805.

Addison.

Johnson's Life of Addison, with introduction and notes, by F. Ryland. London: George Bell & Sons, 1893. 8°.

Dryden.

Johnson's Life of Dryden, with introduction and notes, by F. Ryland. London: George Bell & Sons, 1895. 8°.

Johnson's Life of Dryden [with summary and notes] by Peter Peterson [and C. D. Punchard]. London: Macmillan & Co. 1899. 8°.

Dryden and Pope.

The Lives of Dryden and Pope . . . By Samuel Johnson. Oxford: James Parker & Co. 1876.

Clarendon Press Series. Johnson, Select Works. [Lives of Dryden and Pope, and *Rasselas.*] Edited with introduction and notes, by Alfred Milnes. Oxford, MDCCCLXXIX. 8°. —— Clarendon Press Series. Johnson, Lives of Dryden and Pope. Edited, with introduction and notes, by Alfred Milnes. Oxford, MDCCCLXXXV. 8°. (Same introduction and notes. *Rasselas* is omitted.)

Dryden and Pope.

The Lives of Dryden, Pope, and Addison . . . By Samuel Johnson. Oxford: James Parker & Co. 1877. 12°.

Dryden, Pope, and Addison.

Clarendon Press Series. Johnson's Lives of the Poets; Milton. Edited with notes, by C. H. Firth. Oxford, 1888. 8°. (Later editions in 1891 and 1907.)

Milton.

Johnson's Lives of the Poets. Milton. With an introduction and notes, by K. Deighton. London, Macmillan & Co. 1892. 8°.

Johnson's Life of Milton. With introduction and notes, by F. Ryland. London, George Bell & Sons, 1894. 8°.

Johnson. Lives of Milton and Addison. By J. Wight Duff. Edinburgh, William Blackwood & Sons, 1900. 8°.

Milton and Addison.

Johnson's Life of Pope. By Peter Peterson [and C. D. Punchard]. London, Macmillan & Co. 1899. 8°. —— With introduction and notes, by F. Ryland. London, George Bell & Sons, 1900. 8°.

Pope.

Johnson's Lives of Prior and Congreve. With introduction and notes, by F. Ryland. London, George Bell & Sons, 1897. 8°.

Prior and Congreve.

Johnson's Life of Swift. With introduction and notes, by F. Ryland. London, George Bell & Sons, 1894. 8°.

Swift.

The Life of the Rev. Isaac Watts, DD. By Samuel Johnson, LL.D. With notes containing animadversions and additions. [By Samuel Palmer.] London: Printed for J. F. and C. Rivington. MDCCLXXXV.

Watts.

The second edition of this tract was published with additions, and with the author's name on the title-page, in 1791. The Rev. William Hawkins, in his Bampton Lecture, and the Bishop of St. Davids, in his *Review of the case of the Protestant Dissenters*, animadverted severely on Dr. Watts and on Palmer. The latter thereupon retorted with 'A vindication of the modern Dissenters

. . . intended as a supplement to Dr. Johnson's life of Dr. Watts, with notes, MDCCXC'.

LIVES OF THE POETS IN OTHER WORKS.

Akenside. Included in editions of his *Poetical Works*, 1823, pp. iii–xii, and 1855, pp. iii–xii.

Broome. Prefixed to Broome's *Poetical Works*, 1807, pp. 7–12. It had previously been adopted, but without Johnson's name and with some insignificant alterations, in Cooke's edition [1796], pp. 5–10.

Butler. Included in Cooke's edition of Butler's *Poetical Works* [1803, 2 vols.], i, pp. 7–18; Aikin's *English Poets*, vol. x; and in Aikin's edition of Butler's *Works* (1806, 2 vols.), vol. i, pp. 1–xxvi.

Collins. Prefixed to Collins's *Poetical Works*,—(1798), pp. iii–xiv; (1800), pp. iii–xiii; (1804), pp. 3–11; (1808), with Johnson, Pomfret, Hammond, and Lord Hervey, pp. 5–10; (1827), ed. Rev. Alexander Dyce, pp. 1–8, notes on the life by Dyce, pp. 9–38, by Rev. John Mitford, pp. 39*–40*; (1821), ed. Rev. William Crowe, pp. i–xvi (the life being corrected and enlarged); and (1848), pp. iii–vii. It also appeared in the *European Mag.*, lx. 208–10 (1811).

Cowley. Included in Aikin's *English Poets*, vol. vii (1805); and in Sharpe's edition of his *Works* (1809), vol. i, pp. i–xcix. It was issued at Berlin in 1879, under the editorship of Carl Böddeker, as pt. i of the *Lives of the English Poets*, and at Leipzig, with the lives of Milton and Waller, in 1884.

Dorset. Included in Cooke's edition of his *Works*.

Dryden. Prefixed to the edition of his *Poetical Works*, which appeared in 1807, 10 vols., and 1811, 4 vols. Johnson's estimate of Dryden's critical essays is reprinted in Edmond Malone's *Prose Works of Dryden*, vol. i, pt. i (1800), pp. viii–xix.

Dyer. Included in Sanford [and Walsh], *British Poets*, vol. xix (1819), pp. 251–61. Some further information about Dyer is in the *Westminster Mag.*, xi (1783), pp. 127–8.

Gay. Prefixed to *The Poetical, Dramatic, and Miscellaneous Works of John Gay* (1795, 6 vols.), vol. i, pp. v–xxiv; to editions of the *Poems or Fables of Gay* (1811), pp. iii–xvii; (1812), pp. v–xx; (1820), pp. v–xii; (1824), pp. xii–xxi; (1828), pp. v–xii; (Boston, 1854, 2 vols.), vol. i, pp. ix–xxiii, (1855) pp. vii–xxi.

Gray. Included in the *Select British Poets*, 1808, and in editions of Gray's *Poems* edited by Francis Storr (1879, and later issues 1882 and 1886), pp. 1–15.

Lyttelton. Included (in substance) in an edition of Lyttelton's *Poetical Works* (1801), pp. iii–x.

Mallet. Included in an edition of Mallet's *Select Poems*, in Sanford's *British Poets*, vol. xxvi.

Milton. Included in an edition of *Paradise Lost* (1796, 2 vols.), vol. i, pp. i-xxxviii (condensed); his 'Dissertation on the poetical works of Milton, with observations on his language and versification', occupied pp. xxxix–lxxv of the same volume. His 'criticism on *Paradise Lost*' was contained in vol. i, pp. xvii–xli, of an edition of Milton's *Poems* (1795-6, 2 vols.); in the edition of *Paradise Lost*, with a life by the Rev. John Evans (1799), pp. xxxiii–xlix; in an edition of 1802, pp. xix–xliii; in an edition of 1808, pp. xix–xlii; in an edition of 1817, pp. xix–xliii; in an edition of 1821, pp. xix–xlviii. Addison's criticism on *Paradise Lost* and Johnson's remarks on Milton's versification were published by Sharpe in one volume in 1805. His 'Remarks on the versification of Milton' are printed (i. 195–241) in the Rev. H. J. Todd's edition of Milton's *Poetical Works* (1801, 6 vols.) and in Park's *Works of the British Poets, Milton*, vol. iii (1808), pp. 135–66.

The complete life of Milton was inserted by Aikin in his *Works of the English Poets, Milton*, vol. xii (1805), pp. i–cliii, and in his edition of *The Poetical Works of John Milton* (1806, 3 vols.), vol. i, pp. i–cliii. It also appeared in an edition of Milton's *Poetical Works* in 1809 (3 vols.), occupying vol. i, pp. 3–102, and in the *Select British Poets*, 1810. It was reprinted at Berlin, under the editorship of Carl Böddeker, in 1884. In the Dyce collection in South Kensington Museum is a copy of the life of Milton with the autograph and manuscript notes of Isaac Reed and J. Mitford.

Otway. Included (in an enlarged form) in an edition of Otway's *Works* (1812, 2 vols.), vol. i, pp. 3–13.

Pitt. Inserted in Sanford's *British Poets* (xxi), pp. 337–9.

Pope. Included in an edition of Pope's *Works* in Sanford [and Walsh], *British Poets*, xx, pp. 1–69, and in editions of his *Poetical Works*, 1824, 1827, and (Philadelphia) 1830.

Rochester. Reprinted (with Bishop Burnet's account of Rochester and the funeral sermon by Robert Parsons) by T. Davies,

Russel-Street, Covent-Garden in 1782; by W. Lowndes, No. 77 Fleet-Street, 1787; by W. Baynes, 54 Paternoster-Row, 1805 and 1810; by Ogle, Duncan, & Co., 37 Paternoster Row, and 295 Holborn, 1819; and by W. Baynes & Son, 23 and 54 Paternoster Row, 1820.

Rowe. Included in Rowe's *Works*, 1792, vol. i, pp. 1–11.

Shenstone. Included in *Essays on Men and Manners*, by W. Shenstone, Cooke's ed., *n.d.*

Swift. The life in Sanford's *British Poets* (xviii, pp. 36 et seq.) was based on Johnson and Scott.

Thomson. Included in McKenzie's edition, *The Seasons*, Dublin, 1793, pp. iii–xxi; in the *Select British Poets, Thomson*, 1808; in Thomson's *Poetical Works*, Gloucester, 1809; in an edition of *The Seasons* printed by Ballantyne & Co., Edinburgh, 1809 (but without acknowledgement); in an edition of *The Seasons*, ed. Percival Stockdale, 1793 (substantially); in *The Seasons* and *Castle of Indolence*, 1837; in *The Seasons* and *Castle of Indolence* (London: Charles Daly, *n.d.* [1849]); and in *The Seasons* and *Castle of Indolence*, 1852, pp. v–xvi.

Tickell. Included in an edition of his *Poems* (Boston, U.S.A., 1854), pp. 5–11.

Watts. Included in Sanford's *British Poets*, xxiii, pp. 3–11, and in the *Biographia Evangelica* of the Rev. Erasmus Middleton, iv (1786), pp. 265–72.

Young. Included in the *Select British Poets*, 1809. That in Sanford's *British Poets*, vol. xxv, was 'from Johnson and other authorities'.

[For French translations see Quérard, *La France littéraire*, vol. iv, p. 230. Ed.]

Davies' 'Memoirs of Garrick'.

1780
Boswell, iii. 434.

Memoirs of the Life of David Garrick . . . by Thomas Davies. MDCCLXXX. 2 vols. 8°.

The first paragraph of this book was composed by Johnson. He prompted Davies to write this biography, and supplied 'the early part of Garrick's life' and 'several diverting anecdotes'.

Thrale's Election Address.

1780
Boswell, iii. 440.

Address by Henry Thrale 'To the worthy Electors of the Borough of Southwark', *dated* 'Southwark, Sept. 5, 1780'.

Boswell inserts this as a specimen of the 'advertisements and letters' which Johnson wrote for Thrale.

Johnson and 'Ossian'.

An Enquiry into the Authenticity of the Poems ascribed to Ossian. With a Reply to Mr. Clark's Answer. The Second Edition corrected. By W. Shaw, A.M. F.S.A. . . . London. M.DCC.LXXXII. 8°.

1782
Boswell, iv. 252–3.

The first edition of William Shaw's 'Enquiry' had been published in London in 1781 (reprinted Dublin, 1782), and had been attacked by John Clark, translator of the *Caledonian Bards* (1778 and 1783) and member of the Society of Scots Antiquaries, in 'An Answer to Mr. Shaw's Inquiry, &c. Edinburgh: MDCCLXXXI.'

In the composition of the Reply, which is given as an Appendix, pp. 51–80, to the second edition, Shaw was assisted by Johnson, who furnished several complete paragraphs. This was followed by 'A Rejoinder to an Answer from Mr. Clark on the subject of Ossian's poems', by W. Shaw, 1784.

Shaw was also the author of *An Analysis of the Galic Language*, 1778, see above, p. 129; *A Galic and English Dictionary*, 1780, 2 vols. (in which he was encouraged and helped by Johnson); *Memoirs of the Life and Writings of the late Dr. Samuel Johnson* [Anon.], 1785; and later works. [An account of Shaw's relations with Johnson is given in the *Memoirs*, pp. 148 *et seq.* The long and disproportionate section on the Ossianic controversy supplies evidence of Shaw's authorship of this anonymous work. Ed.]

A memoir of Shaw (by Mr. Thompson Cooper) is in the *D. N. B.* This may be supplemented by reference to the Scottish *N. and Q.*, vol. vi (Dec. 1892), p. 110; Alexander Campbell's *Hist. of Poetry in Scotland*, 1798, p. 131; *Hist. MSS. Commission*, Report on the MSS. of the Marquess of Lothian, 1905, p. 338.

The views of Dr. Johnson on the poems of Ossian were keenly attacked in 'The Fingal of Ossian . . . translated from the original Galic language by Mr. James Macpherson and now rendered into heroic verse by Ewen Cameron. Warrington: MDCCLXXVI', Preface, pp. 19–90.

Some slight references to Dr. Johnson are printed in *A Descriptive Catalogue of Gaelic MSS. in the Advocates' Library, Edinburgh*, by Donald MacKinnon, 1912.

Johnson's estimate of Macpherson is discussed by T. Bailey Saunders in his life of Macpherson (1894), pp. 191–7, 201–2, 241–57.

Burney's 'History of Musick'.

1782

A General History of MUSIC. . . . By Charles Burney, Mus.D., F.R.S. Vol. II. MDCCLXXXII.

Dr. Johnson is said by John Dingwall Williams, in one of the prefatory sheets to his copy (1847) of *The Lives of the Poets*, which is now in the British Museum, to have been the 'learned friend' who translated for Dr. Burney the lines from the *Medea* of Euripides v. 190 (*History of Music*, vol. ii, p. 340).

[In the Oxford edition of Johnson's works, 1825, vol. i, p. 142, there is the following foot-note, signed 'J. B.' (i. e. James Boswell, the younger): 'This translation was written for his friend, Dr. Burney. . . . It has always been ascribed to Johnson; but, to put the matter beyond a doubt, Mr. Malone ascertained the fact by applying to Dr. Burney himself.' This note had appeared in Chalmers's edition of 1816, vol. i, p. 411; cf. ed. 1823, vol. i, p. 354. A facsimile of Porson's transcript of the verses, which Porson definitely assigns to Johnson, had been given in James Savage's *Librarian*, No. 6, December 1808. The transcript is dated '7 Julii 1806'. Ed.]

'The Beauties of Johnson.'

1782
Boswell, i. 214; iv. 148–51.

The Beauties of Johnson: Consisting of Maxims and Observations. . . . Accurately extracted from the Works of Dr. Samuel Johnson, And arranged in Alphabetical Order, after the manner of the Duke de la Roche-Foucault's Maxims. Third Edition, Enlarged and corrected, and the References added. London: Printed for G. Kearsly (*sic*), at No. 46, in Fleet-street. M.DCC.LXXXII. 12mo.

The preface to the first edition, dated November 24, 1781, is reproduced on pp. iii–vii. It is followed by an 'Advertisement to the third edition' and an alphabetical 'table of the subjects', pp. viii–xii. Beauties, pp. 1–209. An announcement on p. 209 says that there is 'In the Press, and speedily will be published, A Second Volume of The Beauties of Johnson, With the References'.

A fourth edition was published in 1782. [An edition in two volumes, probably the fourth, is noticed in the *Monthly Review* for March 1782, p. 237. Ed.]

Many extracts from this work are inserted in the *Westminster Mag.*, xii (1784), 659–60, 691–5.

A New Edition, being the Seventh. Wherein the two volumes are comprised in one, and arranged under one alphabet, with considerable additions. The Beauties of Samuel Johnson, LL.D. . . . To which are now added, Biographical Anecdotes of the Doctor . . . also, His Will, and the Sermon he wrote for the late Doctor Dodd. London. Printed for G. Kearsley, . . . MDCCLXXXVII. 3*s.* 6*d.* sewed.

Portrait, etched by T. Trotter after Harding, prefixed. The Advertisement to this edition, dated November 6, 1786, says that the contents of the two volumes are 'now brought into one volume', as the selection has been 'introduced into several of the most reputable Schools, for both Sexes' (p. v). Preface (abridged) to the first ed., pp. vi–viii; Contents, ix–xiv; facsimile of Johnson's handwriting, 1 leaf; biographical anecdotes, &c., pp. xv–lxxx; Beauties, &c., pp. 1–297.

A New Edition, being the Eighth. . . . The Beauties of Samuel Johnson, LL.D. . . . London: Printed for C. and G. Kearsley. . . . M,DCC,XCII.

The biographical section was augmented from Boswell, and now ran from p. xv to p. cxv; Beauties, &c., pp. 1–297.

The Beauties of Samuel Johnson, LL.D. Ninth edition. 1797.

The Beauties of Samuel Johnson, LL.D. . . . 1804.

The Beauties of Samuel Johnson, LL.D. . . . Glasgow, 1819.

The Beauties of Samuel Johnson, LL.D. . . . A new edition. London: Printed and Published by J. Kay, 95 Wood Street, Cheapside, 1828.

The Beauties of Johnson, consisting of selections from his works. By Alfred Howard, Esq. London: Printed by T. Davison for Thomas Tegg. . . . [1834?].

A different compilation from the previous volumes of *Beauties*.

Crabbe's 'Village'.

1783

Boswell, iv. 175–6.

The Village: a poem in two books. By the Rev. George Crabbe. London, MDCCLXXXIII.

Lines 15–18, beginning with 'On Mincio's banks' and ending with 'Mantuan Song', and line 20 'When Virgil', *etc.*, were written by Johnson, who is said by Boswell to have revised the whole poem.

'A System of Vegetables.'

1783 — A System of Vegetables . . . translated from the thirteenth edition . . . of the Systema Vegetabilium of the late professor Linneus, and from the Supplementum Plantarum of the present professor Linneus. By a Botanical Society at Lichfield. Lichfield: Printed by John Jackson, for Leigh and Sotheby. . . . London. MDCCLXXXIII. 2 vols. 8°.

Most grateful acknowledgements are paid (p. xi) 'to that great Master of the English tongue, Dr. Samuel Johnson, for his advice in the formation of the botanic language'.

Lines on Dr. Levet.

1783 — On the Death of Dr. Robert Levet.

Boswell, iv. 137–9.

Printed in the *Gentleman's Magazine*, August 1783, p. 695; *London Mag.*, Sept. 1783, pp. 232–3.

[For a reference to Miss Reynolds's manuscript version, see *Johnsonian Miscellanies*, ed. Hill, ii. 250. Ed.]

The 'Gentleman's Magazine'.

1784 — Letter, dated Dec. 6, 1784, to John Nichols, assigning the parts of the first seven volumes of the *Ancient Universal History* to their respective authors. p. 892.

Boswell, iv. 382–3.

[Nichols says that he printed this letter not only with Johnson's permission, 'but by his express desire'. It was 'perhaps the last scrap he ever dictated for the press'. Ed.]

1785 — *A Speech* dictated *by Dr. Johnson, without premeditation or hesitation, on the subject of an Address to the Throne, after the Expedition to Rochfort, in September, 1757, at the desire of a friend, who delivered it the next day, at a certain respectable* talking *Society*. pp. 764–5.

Boswell, i. 321.

'The Patriot' (spurious).

1785 — The Patriot, a tragedy. From a manuscript of the late Dr. Samuel Johnson, corrected by himself [a fraudulent title-page. The play was by Joseph Simpson]. London. MDCCLXXXV.

Poems of Johnson.

The Poetical Works of Samuel Johnson, LL.D. now first collected in one volume. London. Printed for the Editor, and sold by G. Kearsley, No. 46, Fleet Street, 1785. [Price Two Shillings and Six Pence.] 8°. **1785**

Title-page, advertisement, and contents, pp. viii; poems pp. 196. The volume includes Johnson's *Irene*. Articles on this and other editions of Johnson's poems are in the *Athenæum* for 1909, pt. ii, 239, 267, 298, 329.

The Poetical Works of Samuel Johnson, LL.D. now first collected in one volume. Dublin: Printed for L. White, P. Byrne, and R. Marchbank. MDCCLXXXV. 8°.

The Poetical Works of Samuel Johnson, L.L.D. (*sic*) complete in one volume. A new edition. London: Printed for W. Osborne and T. Griffin, in St. Paul's Churchyard; and J. Mozley, Gainsbrough. M.DCC.LXXXV. 8°.

The same contents as in Kearsley's 1785 edition, but *Irene* is printed at the end of the volume.

The Poetical Works of Samuel Johnson, LL.D. A new edition considerably enlarged. London: Printed for George Kearsley, Johnson's Head, Fleet-Street, 1789. 8°. **1789**

Half-title; title; advertisement, and contents, pp. xv; poems pp. 212.

Advertisement signed G. K. The new pieces are marked in the table of contents by an asterisk.

The Poetical Works of S. Johnson, LL.D., with the life of the author. Cooke's edition . . . London: Printed for C. Cooke, No. 17 Paternoster-Row [1797?]. 12°.

The Poetical Works of Samuel Johnson, LL.D. With his life. Philadelphia, 1805.

The Poems of Dr. Samuel Johnson. To which is prefixed a life of the author. London: Published by Suttaby, Evance and Fox, Stationers'-court; and Baldwin, Cradock and Joy, Paternoster-row. 1820.

The poems of Johnson were included in:

(1) *The Works of the English Poets. With Prefaces*, . . . by Samuel Johnson, vol. lxxii (1790).

(2) *The Works of the British Poets*, ed. Robert Anderson, vol. xi (1794).

(3) *The Works of the British Poets*, ed. Thomas Park, vol. xxxvii (1805), and Supplement, vol. vi (1809). The elegy, signed 'T. H. 1785', preceding the poems in vol. xxxvii, is by Thomas Hobhouse. It was published with his name in full in 1785.

[There was another edition by Park,—'The Poetical Works of Samuel Johnson. Collated with the best editions: by Thomas Park, F.S.A. 1811.' This edition incorporates the poems in the supplementary volume of 1809. Ed.]

(4) *The Laurel* (1808). Prefixed is a life of Johnson, by F. W. Blagdon.

(5) *The Works of the English Poets*, vol. xvi (1810). With life by Alexander Chalmers.

(6) *The British Poets* (Chiswick ed.), vol. lxvii (1822). With life by S. W. Singer. Hobhouse's elegy is reprinted in this edition as the first of the preliminary encomiums.

(7) *Poetical Works of Goldsmith, Smollett, Johnson, and Shenstone*; George Routledge & Co., 1853,—and in Routledge's *Excelsior* series [1880].

(8) *Poetical Works of Johnson, Parnell, Gray, and Smollett.* MDCCCLV. With life, &c. by the Rev. George Gilfillan.

(9) *Cassell's Library edition of British Poets*, pt. 95 (poems of Johnson and Parnell (1878). Gilfillan's memoir is reproduced in this edition.

(10) *The Poems of Johnson, Goldsmith, Gray, and Collins*, ed. Colonel T. Methuen Ward (1905).

Some of his poems are given in George Pearch's *Collection of Poems*, vols. i and iii; J. Roach's *Beauties of the Poets* (1794); S. J. Pratt's *Cabinet of Poetry*, vol. vi, 1808; Sanford and Walsh, *British Poets*, vol. xxxi, 1822; and in *Rasselas and Select Poems* (1849).

Prayers and Meditations.

1785

Prayers and Meditations, composed by Samuel Johnson, LL.D. and published from his manuscripts, By George Strahan, A.M. Vicar of Islington, Middlesex; and Rector of Little Thurrock, in Essex. London: Printed for T. Cadell, in the Strand. MDCCLXXXV. 8º.

Collation:—Title, p. [i]; Preface (dated Islington, August 6, 1785), pp. [iii]–xvi; Prayers *etc.*, pp. [1]–227.

The original manuscript of this work is in the library of Pembroke College, Oxford (Macleane, *Pembroke College*, 1897, pp. 394-6), but it does not contain all his extant prayers. In MS. 25447, fol. 149, = MS. Montagu, d. 17, in the Bodleian Library, Oxford, is preserved Johnson's diary for Good Friday, March 28, 1766, and two following days, and for May 4. It was lot 586 of the Valentine sale, Nov. 19, 1842, and is described as 'from J. Boswell's Library'. This diary is printed by Hill, *Boswell*, vol. ii, pp. 476-8, and *Johnsonian Miscellanies*, vol. i, pp. 38-42. Johnson's prayer, dated Ashbourne, August 1, 1784, which also is not published in Strahan's volume, is in manuscript in the Johnson Museum, Lichfield.

An edition was printed at Dublin in 1785. Mitford's copy, with his manuscript notes and cuttings, is in the Dyce Collection, South Kensington Museum.

The profits of the first edition 'by the author's appointment' went to Dr. Bray's associates.

Prayers and Meditations, composed by Samuel Johnson, LL.D. and published from his manuscripts, By George Strahan, A.M. *etc.* The Second Edition. London: Printed for T. Cadell, in the Strand. MDCCLXXXV. 8°.

[Title-page and preface to first edition, pp. i–xvi; Prayers *etc.*, pp. 1–233. This edition prints for the first time (pp. 10–15) the three prayers of April 24, 25, and May 6, 1752, 'composed by me on the death of my Wife, and reposited among her Memorials, May 8, 1752'. Ed.]

Prayers and Meditations, composed by Samuel Johnson, LL.D. and published from his manuscripts, By George Strahan, A.M. Vicar of Islington, Middlesex; and Rector of Cranham, in Essex. The Third Edition. London: Printed for T. Cadell, Jun., and W. Davies . . . in the Strand. MDCCXCVI. 8°.

Title-page and preface to first edition, pp. i–xvi; 'advertisement to this third edition', dated Islington, May 2, 1796, pp. xvii–xxxii; Prayers *etc.*, pp. 1–230.

An additional prayer, April 26, 1752, was added at p. 15.

A letter (June 13, 1796) from Strahan to William Windham, sent with a copy of this edition, is in the *Windham Papers*, 1913, vol. ii, pp. 12–13.

Prayers and Meditations, composed by Samuel Johnson, LL.D., and published from his manuscripts, By George Strahan, A.M., Vicar of Islington, Middlesex, and Rector of Cranham in Essex. A new edition. London: Printed for Vernor, Hood and Sharpe in the Poultry. 1806.

Title-page, *etc.*, pp. 6, text pp. 192, index to prayers, pp. 4.

Prayers and Meditations, composed by Samuel Johnson, LL.D., and published from his manuscripts, By George Strahan, D.D., Prebendary of Rochester and Vicar of Islington in Middlesex. The Fourth Edition. London: Printed for T. Cadell and W Davies, in the Strand. MDCCCVII.

Prayers and Meditations, composed by Samuel Johnson, LL.D., and published from his manuscripts, By George Strahan, A.M., *etc.* A new edition. London: 1813.

Prayers and Meditations, composed by Samuel Johnson, LL.D. and published from his manuscripts, By George Strahan, D.D. Prebendary of Rochester, and Vicar of Islington in Middlesex. The fifth edition. London: Printed for T. Cadell and W. Davies, in the Strand. 1817.

Title-page and preface to first edition, pp. i–xvi; advertisement to the fourth edition, pp. xvii–xxxii.

It is stated at p. vii that the profits of the second edition were 'distributed among Dr. Johnson's poor relations and connections, all of whom are since dead, except Humphrey Hely (*sic*), who married [*for his first wife*] — Ford, sister to the Rev. Cornelius Ford, and first cousin to our Author. This poor man, who has seen better days, is now a tenant of [*George*] Whicher's Alms-houses, Chapel-street, Westminster. [It is now, April 1817, about twenty years since he died in these Alms-houses, and was buried in the adjoining burial-ground belonging to St. Margaret's Chapel.]'

Prayers, on several occasions. By Samuel Johnson, LL.D. A new edition. Dorchester: Printed by G. Clark, High-Street, 1821.

All the personal details were omitted in this issue.

Prayers and Meditations, composed by Samuel Johnson, LL.D., and published from his manuscripts, By George Strahan, A.M., Vicar of Islington in Middlesex, and Rector of Cranham, in Essex. Printed for Richard Griffin and Co.,

Glasgow; and Thomas Tegg, London. 1823. —— Reissue, 1826.

Reprints of the edition of 1813.

The Prayers of Samuel Johnson, LL.D. London: Henry Washbourne, Salisbury Square, Fleet Street, Bowdery & Kerby, Oxford Street, 1836.

Prayers and Meditations, composed by Samuel Johnson, LL.D. With a preface by the Rev. William Gresley, M.A., Prebendary of Lichfield. Lichfield: Printed and published by T. G. Lomax, at the Johnson's head. . . . MDCCCLX.

Title-page, dedication, and preface to first edition, pp. i–xvi; preface to this edition, pp. xvii–xxiv; Prayers, pp. 1–148. Another line, 'scrupulis obsistendum', is added to the four Latin lines contained in the meditation for April 6, 1777.

Prayers and Meditations, by Samuel Johnson, LL.D. A new edition, with notes and an introduction by the Rev. Hinchcliffe Higgins and a preface by Augustine Birrell, K.C. Also some opinions of Dr. Johnson on The Christian Religion. London: Elliot Stock [1904].

Prayers and Meditations, composed by Samuel Johnson, LL.D. New and revised edition, with additional matter. London: H. R. Allenson, Limited, Racquet Court, Fleet Street, 1906.

The *Prayers and Meditations*, with corrections, additions, and copious notes, were included by George Birkbeck Hill in his *Johnsonian Miscellanies* (1897), i, pp. 1–124.

*** Mrs. Piozzi's 'Anecdotes'.**

Anecdotes of the late Samuel Johnson, LL.D. during the last twenty years of his life. By Hesther Lynch Piozzi. London. MDCCLXXXVI.

Several of Johnson's verses were first printed in this volume.

Editions of Johnson's Works.

1787

The Works of Samuel Johnson, LL.D. Together with His Life, and Notes on his Lives of the Poets. By Sir John Hawkins, Knt. In eleven volumes. London: Printed for J. Buckland, J. Rivington and Sons, *etc.* MDCCLXXXVII. 8°.

Vol. I. Short title, portrait, title-page; dedication to George the

Third, p. [v]; advertisement, pp. vii-x, signed J. H.; *Life of Johnson*, pp. 1–602: index and errata, pp. 16. The life has in some copies a separate title-page. A second edition of the *Life*, 'revised and corrected', pp. 1–605, index, pp. 15, appeared separately in the same year, and it was reprinted at Dublin.

Vol. II. *Lives of the Poets* (to Duke).

Vol. III. *Lives of the Poets* (to Broome).

Vol. IV. *Lives of the Poets* concluded, and *Miscellaneous Lives.*

Vol. V. *The Rambler* (to No. 70).

Vol. VI. *The Rambler* (to No. 140).

Vol. VII. *The Rambler* concluded.

Vol. VIII. *The Idler.*

Vol. IX. *The Adventurer* and *Philological Tracts.*

Vol. X. *Political Tracts. Political Essays. Miscellaneous Essays. A Journey to the Western Islands of Scotland.* (Misprints (*sub* Lough Ness) of *thirteenth* of August and (*sub* Skye) of September the *twentieth* are retained. The error about the Macleods is corrected.)

Vol. XI. *Rasselas. The Vision of Theodore. The Apotheosis of Milton. Prayers and Devotional Exercises. Apophthegms, &c. Irene. London. The Vanity of Human Wishes. Miscellaneous Poems.*

The Works of Samuel Johnson, LL.D. In thirteen volumes. Vol. xii (xiii). London: Printed for John Stockdale, Opposite Burlington House, Piccadilly. M,DCC,LXXXVII.

Additional title-page: 'Debates in Parliament. By Samuel Johnson, LL.D. In two volumes. Vol. i (ii). London: Printed for John Stockdale . . . M,DCC,LXXXVII.'

The *Debates* were issued by Stockdale as two supplementary volumes to Hawkins's edition. They were also issued separately. See above, p. 5.

* The Works of Samuel Johnson, LL.D. In Fourteen Volumes. Vol. xiv. London: Printed for John Stockdale, Piccadilly; and G. G. J. and J. Robinson, Pater-noster-Row. M.DCC.LXXXVIII.

[Title; Preface (unsigned), pp. [iii–vi]; Contents, pp. [vii–xi]. Text, pp. [1]–556. Miscellaneous writings, pp. [1]–475, consisting of *Marmor Norfolciense, Vindication of the Licencers of the Stage, Observations on Macbeth, The Longitude at Sea, Idler No. 22, The Fountains*, and over thirty other articles, prefaces, *etc.* Dedications, pp. 475–89. Letters (41 in number), pp. 490–539. Epitaphs, pp. 539–45. Poems, pp. 545–7, including the 'Ode to Friendship' (see above, pp. 14, 112). *Scheme for the Classes of a Grammar School*, pp. 548–9 (cf. *Gent. Mag.*, 1785, p. 266). *Rules of the Essex-Head Club*, pp. 550–1 (cf. *Gent. Mag.*, 1785, p. 99). *Letter on Du Halde's History of China*, pp. 552–6.

'The performances contained in the present Volume', says the Preface, 'are such as it is presumed ought to have made a part of the Edition of Dr. Johnson's Works lately published.'... 'Recourse has been had to the friends of Dr. Johnson now living, and from them the chief authorities for ascribing the several pieces to him have been derived.'

This volume appears to be very rare. Not the least point of interest is that it reprints in part the Proposals for the edition of Shakespeare which were issued with the *Miscellaneous Observations on Macbeth* in 1745, and have recently been rediscovered. See above, pp. 17, 18. Ed.]

A short notice of vol. xiv is in the *Monthly Review*, vol. lxxix (1788), p. 380.

[For the supplementary volume edited by George Gleig, sometimes called vol. xv, see above, pp. 3, 4. Ed.]

The Works of Samuel Johnson, LL.D. A new edition, in twelve volumes. With An Essay on his Life and Genius, By Arthur Murphy, Esq. London: Printed for T. Longman, *etc.* MDCCXCII. 8°. **1792**

Vol. I. Portrait, general title, and contents, pp. iv; Murphy's *Essay*, pp. 187; *Poems*, including *Irene*, pp. 1–215.

The *Essay on the Life* was published by itself in 1792, and again in 1793.

Vol. II. *Philological Tracts. Political Essays. Miscellaneous Essays.*

Vol. III. *Dissertation upon the Greek Comedy, translated from Brumoy. General Conclusion thereto. Observations on Macbeth. Essays in The Adventurer. Rasselas.*

Vol. IV. *The Rambler* (to No. 70).

Vol. V. *The Rambler* (to No. 140).

Vol. VI. *The Rambler* concluded.

Vol. VII. *The Idler.* (No. 22 omitted.)

Vol. VIII. *Miscellaneous Essays. Political Tracts. A Journey to the Western Islands of Scotland.* (The misprint *thirteenth* of August has been altered, but erroneously, to *twenty-eight.* That of *twentieth* of September is uncorrected.)

Vol. IX. *Lives of the Poets* (to Dryden).

Vol. X. *Lives of the Poets* (to Savage).

Vol. XI. *Lives of the Poets* concluded.

Vol. XII. *Lives of Eminent Persons. Selected Letters. Prayers.* Index.

1796 The Works of Samuel Johnson, LL.D. To which is prefixed An Essay on his Life and Genius, By Arthur Murphy, Esq. A new edition, in twelve volumes. MDCCXCVI.

The special title-page of vol. i reads 'An essay on the life and genius of Samuel Johnson, LL.D. By Arthur Murphy, Esq.' Same arrangement of works as in 1792 edition, and misprints stand as in 1792 edition.

1801 The Works of Samuel Johnson, LL.D. A new edition, in twelve volumes. With An Essay on his Life and Genius, By Arthur Murphy. 1801. 8°.

Same arrangement, and same errors in dates, as in 1792 edition.

['Miscellaneous and Fugitive Pieces: consisting of Essays, Dissertations, Prefaces, Reviews, Lives, &c. &c. By Samuel Johnson, L.L.D. (*sic*). To which is prefixed, The Life of the Author. In two volumes. Sheffield: Printed by and for Slater, Bacon and Co. 1804.' This collection is made up of pieces in the second, eighth, and twelfth volumes of Murphy's edition. The Life, vol. i, pp. ix–xliii, is based on Murphy's *Essay*. Ed.]

1806 The Works of Samuel Johnson, LL.D. A new edition, in twelve volumes. With An Essay on his Life and Genius, By Arthur Murphy, Esq. 1806. 8°. [Also 12°. Ed.]

The advertisement (vol. i, pp. iii–v) is signed Alex. Chalmers and dated London, January 1806. 'The Picture of Human Life' is omitted from vol. ii, being the translation of Joseph Spence [see above, p. 22]. Five papers in *The Adventurer* have been added, and the dedication to 'The evangelical history of Jesus Christ'; see above, p. 78. A few notes have also been added, but the errors in the *Journey to the Western Islands* stand as in the edition of 1792.

1810 The Works of Samuel Johnson, LL.D. A new edition, in twelve volumes. With An Essay *etc.* 1810. 8°.

Two supplementary volumes, 'Volume the Thirteenth (Fourteenth)', were added, containing the *Debates*, and dated 1811.

The Works of Samuel Johnson, LL.D. A new edition, in twelve volumes. With An Essay *etc.* 1816. 8°. **1816**

[This edition is described, in a supplementary note to the preface of 1806, as the 'sixth'. It incorporates a few notes by Malone on *The Lives of the Poets*, taken from Malone's interleaved copy. It also adds three pieces which are said to 'have not hitherto been printed' among his works—'An Ode to Friendship' (vol. i, p. 409), the translation of a chorus in the *Medea* of Euripides (vol. i, p. 411), and 'The Fountains, a Fairy Tale' (vol. iii, p. 445 et seq.). The 'Ode to Friendship' and 'The Fountains' had, however, been included in Stockdale's supplementary volume to Hawkins's edition, vol. xiv, 1788 (see above); and the 'Ode to Friendship' had been included also in Boswell's *Life*, with the remark that it 'has not been inserted in any of the collections of Johnson's poetry'. The introductory notes to the two poems are signed 'J. B.', i. e. James Boswell the younger. Ed.]

Same arrangement as in earlier editions. The date (August 13) *sub* Lough Ness has been erroneously altered to August 28; that of September 20, instead of September 2, has been retained, but the error about the Macleods of Rasay has been corrected.

The Works of Samuel Johnson, LL.D. A new edition. In ten volumes. London: Printed for G. Offor, Tower-Hill [and for six booksellers in North of England]. 1818.

Vol. I. *Poems* and *Philological Tracts.*

Vol. II. *The Rambler* (to No. 77).

Vol. III. *The Rambler* (to No. 154).

Vol. IV. *The Rambler* concluded. *The Adventurer.*

Vol. V. *The Idler. Rasselas.*

Vol. VI. *Lives of the Poets* (to Rowe).

Vol VII. *Lives of the Poets* (to Pope).

Vol. VIII. *Lives of the Poets* concluded. *Lives of Eminent Persons.*

Vol. IX. *A Journey to the Western Islands of Scotland. Political Essays. Miscellanies.* In the *Journey*, the date (August 13) has been erroneously altered to August 28; that of September 20 has been retained, but the error about the Macleods of Rasay has been corrected.

Vol. X. *Miscellanies* (including the *Evangelical History*), *Letters* (*selectea*). *Prayers*. Index.

1823 *The Works of Samuel Johnson, LL.D. A new edition in twelve volumes. With An Essay on his Life and Genius, By Arthur Murphy, Esq. London: Printed for F. C. and J. Rivington, *etc.* 1823. 8°.

Vol. I. *Essay on the Life. Poems.*

Vols. II–IV. *The Rambler.*

Vol. V. *The Idler. Rasselas.*

Vols. VI–VIII. *Lives of the Poets.*

Vol. IX. *Lives of Eminent Persons. Letters. Prayers and Meditations.*

Vol. X. *Philological Tracts, &c.*

Vol. XI. *Miscellaneous Tracts. Dedications. Reviews and Criticisms. Tales of Imagination* (*The Vision of Theodore, The Fountains*). *The Adventurers.*

Vol. XII. *Political Tracts. A Journey to the Western Islands of Scotland. Sermons* (*Nos. X and XXV*). *Index.*

The advertisement (vol. i, pp. iii–v) is signed Alex. Chalmers and dated London, Feb. 1823. The edition is described therein as the 'seventh'. 'More than thirty articles, none of which have hitherto appeared in any edition' are said to be added. But some of these, which are distinguished by asterisks in the tables of contents, had been included in the edition of 1816, and others had been given in the two supplementary volumes, 1788 and 1789, to Hawkins's edition; see above, pp. 162 and 8. 'The whole of the *Prayers and Meditations* are now added'; but only two sermons are given, by way of specimen. Ed.

*The Works of Samuel Johnson, LL.D. With an essay *etc.* 1824. 12 vols. 12°.

1825 The Works of Samuel Johnson, LL.D. In nine volumes. Oxford. Printed for William Pickering, London; and Talboys and Wheeler, Oxford. MDCCCXXV. 8°. (Oxford English Classics.)

Vol. I. Half-title; title-page; contents, pp. v–vi; Murphy's Essay, pp. i–lxxxvi. Prefatory observations to the imitations of the third and tenth *Satires* of Juvenal, pp. i–iv. Poems (including *Irene*), pp. 1–194. *Rasselas*, pp. 195–310. *Letters*, pp. 311–94. A portrait of Johnson, engraved by W. H. Worthington after Reynolds, is the frontispiece in some issues of vol. i, in others of vol. iii.

Vol. II. *The Rambler* (to No. 105).

Vol. III. *The Rambler* concluded.

Vol. IV. *The Adventurer. The Idler* (with No. 22).

Vol. V. *Miscellaneous Pieces.*

Vol. VI. *Reviews. Political Tracts. Lives of Eminent Persons.*

Vol. VII. *Lives of the Poets* (to Sheffield).

Vol. VIII. *Lives of the Poets* concluded.

Vol. IX. *A Journey to the Western Islands of Scotland* (dates of August 13 and September 20 have been retained, but the error about the Macleods has been corrected). *Vision of Theodore. The Fountains. Prayers and Meditations. Sermons.* Index.

Supplementary volumes (X and XI) contain the *Debates.*

[This edition was superintended by Francis Pearson Walesby (1798–1858), Fellow of Lincoln College 1824–37, Professor of Anglo-Saxon in the University of Oxford 1829–34. See *Notes and Queries*, 2nd S., xi (1861), pp. 269, 335. There was a large paper issue. Ed.]

The Works of Samuel Johnson, LL.D. With Murphy's essay. Edited by the Rev. Robert Lynam. . . . In six volumes. London: Printed for George Cowie and Co. in the Poultry, 1825. 8°.

Vol. I. Portrait, title-page, advertisement, and contents of first volume, pp. viii; Essay, pp. i–cii; details of statue in St. Paul's, p. ciii. *The Rambler* (to No. 120) pp. 1–567.

Vol. II. *The Rambler* concluded. *The Idler.*

Vol. III. *The Adventurer. Lives of the Poets* (to Fenton).

Vol. IV. *Lives of the Poets* concluded. *Lives of Eminent Persons.*

Vol. V. *Philological Tracts, &c. Political Tracts. Miscellaneous Tracts. Dedications, &c. Reviews and Criticisms.*

Vol. VI. *Journey to the Western Islands of Scotland* (the date August 13 has been erroneously altered to August 28; that of September 20 has been retained, but the error about the Macleods has been corrected). *Rasselas. Tales of Imagination. Poems*, including *Irene. Letters. Prayers and Meditations. Sermons.* Index.

* The Works of Samuel Johnson, LL.D. With an Essay on his Life and Genius, by Arthur Murphy, Esq. In two

volumes complete. London: Published by Jones & Company. 1825. 8°.

Vol. I. *Rambler*, pp. viii, 1–351. *Idler*, pp. xii, 1–111. *Lives of the Poets*, pp. iv, 1–363 (three divisions, separate paginations). Vol. II. Murphy's Essay, pp. xl. Johnson's other works, pp. 1–687. Contents, p. 688.

* The Works of Samuel Johnson, L.L.D. (*sic*). A new edition, in six volumes. With an Essay *etc.* Philadelphia: H. C. Carey & I. Lea, Tower & Hogan, R. H. Small, *etc.* 1825. 8°.

The Works of Samuel Johnson, LL.D. A new edition, with an Essay *etc.* London: Henry G. Bohn. 1850. 2 vols. 8°.

Vol. I. Essay, pp. i–xl. *Rambler*, pp. 1–351. *Idler*, pp. 1–111. *Lives of the Poets*, pp. 1–363 (four divisions, separate paginations). Vol. II. Contents, pp. iii, iv; Johnson's other works, pp. 1–687.

The Works of Samuel Johnson, LL.D. Literary Club edition. Pafracts Book Company, Troy, New York [1903]. 16 volumes. 8°.

Johnson's Letters.

1788 Letters to and from the late Samuel Johnson, LL.D. To which are added Some Poems never before printed. Published from the original MSS. in her possession, By Hester Lynch Piozzi. In two volumes. Vol. I (II). London: Printed for A. Strahan; and T. Cadell, in the Strand. MDCCLXXXVIII. 8°.

[An edition was published at Dublin in the same year, 'Printed for Messrs. R. Moncrieffe, L. White, P. Byrne, P. Wogan, *etc.*' 2 vols. 8°. Ed.]

The poems are contained in vol. ii, p. 413 to end. They consist of Latin verses to Dr. Lawrence, translation of them by Mrs. Piozzi, and translations from *Boethius de consolatione philosophiae*, mainly by Johnson but with some lines by Mrs. Piozzi. George Daniel's copy, with a manuscript note by him, dated 'Canonbury, April 1857', is in the British Museum. In it are many notes by Baretti, containing severe reflections on the Thrales. Some letters of Dr. Johnson to Mrs. Thrale are printed in *Love Letters of Famous Men and Women*, ed. J. T. Merydew (1888), i. 254–64.

The letter from Johnson to Mr. William Drummond (August 13, 1766) is printed in [Christopher Anderson's] *Brief Sketch of attempts to diffuse a knowledge of the Holy Scriptures through . . . the Irish Language* (1818), App. K. It is given in *Boswell*, vol. ii, pp. 27–9.

1817 * Original Letters, from Richard Baxter, Matthew Prior, ... Dr. Samuel Johnson, *etc.* With Biographical Illustrations. Edited by Rebecca Warner, Of Beech Cottage, near Bath. Printed by Richard Cruttwell . . . Bath; and sold by Longman . . . London. 1817.

Three letters are here printed for the first time, pp. 205–10.

1822 Letters of Dr. Samuel Johnson, with explanatory Notes. To which are added Miscellaneous Essays by him. Edinburgh, 1822. 12°.

No copy in the British Museum.

1860–1 Original Letters of Dr. Johnson [to the Rev. Dr. Taylor]. Edited by Sir John Simeon. Miscellanies of the Philobiblon Society, vol. vi (1860–1), pp. 43.

1892 Letters of Samuel Johnson, LL.D. Collected and edited by George Birkbeck Hill, D.C.L. Oxford: At the Clarendon Press. MDCCCXCII. 2 vols. 8°.

The letters in Boswell are not reproduced by Hill. Each of them is indicated at the proper chronological date by 'the briefest notice of the person to whom it was addressed, the date at which it was written, and the volume and page where it will be found'. Hill's volumes were the subject of an article (pp. 142–90) in *Studies in some famous Letters*, by J. C. Bailey, 1899.

*Johnsonian Miscellanies. Arranged and edited by George Birkbeck Hill, D.C.L., LL.D. Vol. II. Oxford: At the Clarendon Press. MDCCCXCVII.

This volume contains, on pp. 435–56, twenty-three additional letters not printed in Hill's *Letters of Samuel Johnson.* Most of them were then printed for the first time.

Other letters to and from Johnson are contained in *Letters of Literary Men*, ed. F. A. Mumby (1906), vol. i, pp. 211–27.

Sermons.

1788 A Sermon, written by the late Samuel Johnson, LL.D. for the Funeral of his Wife. Published by the Rev. Samuel Hayes, A.M. Usher of Westminster-School. London: Printed for T. Cadell, in the Strand. MDCCLXXXVIII. 8°.

Title, etc., pp. 6; Sermon, pp. 1–18.

[The prefatory note, which is dated March 18, 1788, says that 'the following Sermon (the authenticity of which cannot be doubted) came, with many others, into the Hands of the Editor by the Death of Dr. Taylor, late Prebendary of Westminster, etc.'

The notice of it in the *Monthly Review* of October 1788, p. 384, is confined to the comment—'Worthy, in every respect worthy, the head, and heart, and pen of Samuel Johnson.' Ed.]

1788–9 Sermons on different subjects, left for publication by John Taylor, LL.D. Late Prebendary of Westminster, Rector of Bosworth, Leicestershire, and Minister of St. Margaret's, Westminster. Published by the Rev. Samuel Hayes, A.M. Usher of Westminster School. London: Printed for T. Cadell, in the Strand. MDCCLXXXVIII. —— Volume the second. Published by the Rev. Samuel Hayes, A.M., late Senior Usher of Westminster School. To which is added, A Sermon written by Samuel Johnson, LL.D., for the Funeral of his Wife [pp. 221–39]. London: Printed for T. Cadell in the Strand. MDCCLXXXIX. 8°.

It is believed that many of these sermons were composed by Johnson. [See *Boswell*, iii. 181, 182. In the notice of the first volume in the *Monthly Review*, December 1788, p. 528, it is said that 'the general opinion concerning them is that they are, in reality, the productions of the late Dr. Samuel Johnson'. Cf. the notice of the second volume, *id.* March 1790, p. 351. Ed.]

Sermons on different subjects, *etc.* Published by the Rev. Samuel Hayes, A.M., Usher of Westminster School. Vol. I. The second edition. London: MDCCXC. 8°.

The volume catalogued at the British Museum as the second of this edition is dated MDCCXCII.

Sermons on different subjects, *etc.* Published by the Rev. Samuel Hayes, A.M., Usher of Westminster School.

To which is added, A Sermon written by Samuel Johnson, LL.D., for the funeral of his wife. Dublin: Printed by P. Byrne, Grafton-street. MDCCXCIII. 8°.

Title 1 leaf, dedication, &c., pp. i–viii; then pp. 462.

Sermons on different subjects, *etc.* The fourth edition. London: Printed for T. Cadell, Jun. and W. Davies, in the Strand. 1800. 2 vols. 8°.

Sermons on different subjects, *etc.* Walpole, N. H. Printed for Thomas and Thomas, by G. W. Nichols, 1806. 8°. pp. viii, 9–256.

Sermons attributed to Samuel Johnson, LL.D., and left for publication by John Taylor, LL.D., late Prebendary of Westminster. The fifth edition. London: Printed for John Ebers, New Bond Street, *etc.* 1812. 8°. pp. xvi and 1–410.

British Prose Writers. Vol. XV. in 2 vols. Dr. Johnson's Sermons. London: Published by John Sharpe, Piccadilly, 1819[–21]. 2 vols. 12°.

Sermons left for publication by John Taylor. Ripon, 1835.

Taylor was the author of '*A Letter to Samuel Johnson, LL.D., on the subject of a Future State*, by John Taylor, LL.D., Prebendary of Westminster, Rector of Bosworth, Leicestershire, and Minister of St. Margaret's, Westminster. London: Printed for T. Cadell in the Strand. 1787.' 4°. 1*s.* No copy of this very rare work is in the library of the British Museum, but it is reproduced *in extenso*, in the '*Life of John Taylor* . . . by Thomas Taylor' [1911], pp. 27-45.

Much of Percy Fitzgerald's 'Rambles in Johnson Land', *Gent. Mag.*, vol. cclxxv (1893), pp. 145–57, related to Taylor and Birkbeck Hill.

Letter to Chesterfield.

The Celebrated Letter from Samuel Johnson, LL.D. to Philip Dormer Stanhope, Earl of Chesterfield; now first published, with notes, By James Boswell, Esq. London: Printed by Henry Baldwin; For Charles Dilly, in the Poultry. MDCCXC. [Price Half a Guinea.] 4°. pp. 4. **1790**

The manuscript copy of the letter given by Johnson to Bennet

Langton, and corrected by Johnson, was presented to the British Museum in June 1797, in pursuance of Boswell's intention (Add. MS. 5713).

Conversation with George III.

A Conversation between His Most Sacred Majesty George III and Samuel Johnson, LL.D. illustrated with observations, By James Boswell, Esq. London: Printed by Henry Baldwin; For Charles Dilly, in the Poultry. MDCCXC. [Price Half a Guinea.] 4°. pp. 8.

Boswell's Life.

1791 The Life of Samuel Johnson, LL.D. comprehending an account of his studies and numerous works, in chronological order, *etc.* By James Boswell, Esq. London, 1791. 2 vols. 4°.

Boswell's *Life* contains, in addition to many of Johnson's letters, the following arguments which had been dictated to him by Johnson:

(1) 1772. Argument in defence of a schoolmaster; for the House of Lords. i. 375-7.

(2) 1772. Argument in support of the Law of *Vicious Intromission*; for the Court of Session in Scotland. i. 382-6.

(3) 1773. Argument in Favour of the Rights of Lay Patrons; for the General Assembly of the Church of Scotland. i. 410-13.

(4) 1775. Argument on the Case of Dr. Memis; for the Court of Session of Scotland. i. 491-2.

(5) 1775. Argument to prove that the Corporation of Stirling was corrupt; for the House of Lords. i. 492-93.

(6) 1776. Argument in support of the right of immediate and personal reprehension from the pulpit. ii. 75-8.

(7) 1781. Argument on the importance of the registration of Deeds; for an Election Committee of the House of Commons. ii. 372-3.

(8) 1781. On the distinction between Tory and Whig. ii. 399-400.

(9) 1781. On vicarious punishments and the great propitiation for the sins of the world by Jesus Christ. ii. 403-4.

(10) 1781. Defence of Mr. Robertson, printer of the *Caledonian Mercury*, against the Society of Procurators of Edinburgh, for having inserted in his paper a ludicrous paragraph against them; demonstrating that it was not an injurious libel. ii. 407-8.

Johnson also dictated to Boswell (ed. Hill, iii. 202–3) an argument for the freedom of Joseph Knight, an African Negro. This was printed in the second edition (1793), Additions, pp. *xiv–*xvi in vol. i.

Mrs. Piozzi's 'British Synonymy'.

British Synonymy; or, an attempt at regulating the choice of words in familiar conversation . . . By Hester Lynch Piozzi. MDCCXCIV. 2 vols. 8°. **1794**

Contains (i. 359–60) Johnson's verses on 'A young heir's [Sir John Lade's] coming of age'. They were incorporated by Boswell in the subsequent edition of the *Life* (1799). I may perhaps be allowed to refer for Lade to my article on him in *Temple Bar*, February, 1902, pp. 199–215.

Johnson's 'Annals'.

An Account of the Life of DR. SAMUEL JOHNSON, from his birth to his eleventh year, written by himself. To which are added, Original Letters, to Dr. Samuel Johnson, by Miss Hill Boothby: From the MSS. preserved by the Doctor; and now in Possession of Richard Wright, Surgeon; Proprietor of the Museum of Antiquities, Natural and Artificial Curiosities, &c. Lichfield. London: Printed for Richard Phillips, No. 6, Bridge-Street, Blackfriars; by Nichols and Son, Red Lion Passage, Fleet Street. 1805. 8°. **1805**

Collation:—Title; Preface, pp. iii–viii; Annals, pp. 9–32; letters, *etc.*, pp. 33–144.

The Preface, dated Lichfield, March 2, 1805, explains that this fragment of Johnson's autobiography was taken by Francis Barber, his black servant, from the mass of papers which Johnson ordered to be burned a few days before his death.

This is contained in Henry Morley's edition of Boswell, *The Sir Joshua Reynolds Edition* (1885, 5 vols.), vol. i, pp. lv–lxii, and in the reissue, *The Library Edition* (1891, 5 vols.), vol. i, pp. lv–lxii.

The 'Account of the life' was reproduced in Croker and Wright's edition of Boswell (1835), vol. i, pp. 316–25, and in G. B. Hill's *Johnsonian Miscellanies* (1897), i. 125–40. The letters, with additions from other sources, are included in Mrs. Napier's

Johnsoniana (1884), pp. 129–67. They were inserted by Croker in his edition of 1831, vol. iv, pp. 524–59.

Journey in North Wales.

1816 A Diary of a Journey into North Wales, in the year 1774; By Samuel Johnson, LL.D. Edited, with illustrative notes, By R. Duppa, LL.B., barrister at law. London: Printed for Robert Jennings, 2, Poultry. M.DCCC.XVI.

Collation:—Half-title; Facsimile of Dr. Johnson's handwriting facing title (or after contents); title, p. [iii]; dedication to Edward Swinburne, dated from Lincoln's Inn, Sept. 18, 1816, pp. v–vi; preface, pp. vii–xi; contents, pp. xiii–xvi; second facsimile of handwriting; the diary, pp. 1–226; errata on slip at end.

It is stated in the *European Mag.*, vol. lxix (1816), p. 5, that this diary was nearly ready for the press and that it was under the editorial care of the Rev. Henry Gostling White. It had been delayed 'by the expectation of obtaining several additional *Original Letters*'.

This diary has been incorporated in the more elaborate editions of Boswell. It is included in the Rt. Hon. J. W. Croker's edition (1831), iii. 123-59; in the revised editions of Croker and John Wright, 1835 and 1859 (Bohn's Shilling Series), v. 194–216; in Croker's editions (1848, 1859 (dated 1860), and 1876), pp. 415–25; Alexander Napier's edition, iv (1884), pp. 387–410, and in the cheaper issue, v, pp. iv, 373–97; in Birkbeck Hill's edition (1887), v. 427–60.

Some information on the journey is given in Abraham Hayward's *Autobiography of Mrs. Piozzi*, 1861, vol. i, pp. 73–8; 2nd ed., 1861, vol. i, pp. 82–9; and in L. B. Seeley's *Memoir of Mrs. Thrale*, 1891, pp. 67–74. It is the subject of two articles (I) 'Dr. Johnson in Wales', in *The Red Dragon* (Cardiff), vol. vii (1885), pp. 51–60, and (II) 'Dr. Johnson's Tour in North Wales' in *Gallant little Wales*, by Jeannette Marks, 1912, pp. 59–85.

Two chapters (iv and v) entitled 'Mrs. Thrale's unpublished journal of her tour in Wales with Dr. Johnson, July–September 1774', and 'Dr. Johnson's diary during the Welsh tour of 1774' are in *Doctor Johnson and Mrs. Thrale*, by A. M. Bradley, MCMX, pp. 155–219 and 220–52. They contain a plan of the itinerary and many illustrations.

INDEX